Apologetic for *Filioque* in Medieval Theology

by Dennis Ngien

WIPF & STOCK · Eugene, Oregon

Wipf and Stock Publishers
199 W 8th Ave, Suite 3
Eugene, OR 97401

Apologetic for Filique in Medieval Theology
By Ngien, Dennis
Copyright©2005 Paternoster
ISBN 13: 978-1-62564-344-5
Publication date 9/16/2013
Previously published by Paternoster, 2005

This book is dedicated to my son,
Hansel-Timon,
with the hope that he will manifest
the fruit of the Holy Spirit

Contents

Preface		vii
Introduction		ix
Chapter 1	The *Filioque* Question: Theological Roots of Western Pneumatological Tradition	1
Chapter 2	The Necessary Reasons for *Filioque* in Anselm	23
Chapter 3	The Spirit as Co-Beloved (*Condilectus*) in Richard of St. Victor	51
Chapter 4	*Filioque*, Solitary Love and Mutual Love in Thomas Aquinas	76
Chapter 5	Fecundity, Mutual Love and *Filioque* in Bonaventure	115
Notes		144
Bibliography		181

Preface

This project, *Apologetic for Filioque in Medieval Theology*, was undertaken during the period of my appointment as visiting professor (2002-2004) at the Pontifical Institute of Medieval Studies, University of St. Michael's College within the University of Toronto, Canada. It is the library staff at this institute to whom my first debt of gratitude is due. I am also indebted to the cheering library team at Tyndale University College and Seminary, especially Emmie Leung, for acquiring sources through interlibrary loans; Ted Beverley, my research assistant, for collecting relevant materials; Ivy Milanowski, the administrative assistant of my *Centre for Mentorship and Theological Reflection*, for assisting initially in formatting; Robin Parry, the Commissioning Editor at Paternoster, for his work on the manuscript; and many mentorees and friends for encouraging me to write and publish. A special thank is due to my colleagues at Tyndale Seminary for their augmentation of my work in scholarship through the *Faculty Scholarship Award 2004*, one which I received wholeheartedly but with fear and trembling. Much appreciation is extended to several perceptive readers: Professors Clark Pinnock, formerly of McMaster Divinity College, Gerald Bray of Samford University, Mark Elliot of St Andrew's University, and Ralph Del Colle of Marquette University, all of whom in some measures helped crystallize my thinking.

With minor variations, the chapter on Anselm appears, as two parts, in *Churchman* 118 (2004); the chapter on Richard of St. Victor appears in *European Journal of Theology* 12 (2003). I am grateful to both journals for granting me the permission to include them in this monograph. It is the author's hope that the readers will appreciate the apologetic thrusts of the medieval minds, that the *filioque* doctrine as defended by them need not be offensive or divisive, that both East and West could find a kindred spirit in the medieval formulations.

Last but not least, this book would not have been completed without the perseverance and understanding of my life-companion, Ceceilia.

To God be the Glory!

Dennis Ngien (PhD)
Research Professor of Theology
Tyndale University College and Seminary
Toronto, CANADA
May 30, 2004

Introduction

The objective of this book is to examine the manner in which the *filioque* doctrine acquires its apologetic defence in the great minds of medieval theology. To understand the rational defence of the *filioque*, it seems necessary to provide a survey of its roots, i.e., the theological roots of Western pneumatological tradition. Rather than offering a comprehensive review of this, I have selected representative theological perspectives from four key Latin fathers Tertullian, Hilary, Ambrose and Augustine. Specifically, the corresponding relation between the temporal mission in time and the procession in eternity, between the economic and the immanent Trinity, a recurring theme in these fathers, contributes considerably to the Western formulation of the *filioque* doctrine. This formulation of the divine mystery, that the Holy Spirit proceeds from the Father 'and the Son', receives its dogmatic form and dynamic force in none other than Augustine. Yet Augustine himself does not claim originality for this, for there is continuity between what he holds to be true and what the antecedents have taught him about the dogma. Nevertheless Augustine's theology of the Trinity, especially the *filioque* doctrine, provides the theoretical foundation for Western tradition of conceiving the doctrine of the double procession of the Holy Spirit. Hence the historical background helps establish the context for a proper understanding of the *filioque* doctrine as apologetically defended in subsequent medieval theology.

The causal connection between the Latin tradition and the medieval scholastics is apparent. Specifically, traces of Augustine could be discernible throughout the writings of the medieval period. Augustine's vision of the Trinity, especially his unique formulation of the *filioque* doctrine, constitutes the foundation and shape of the later Latin theological tradition from Anselm, Aquinas and on to the Franciscan school and many of the late Protestant reformers. His doctrine of the Holy Spirit as love continues to dominate all great Western thinkers of the Middle Ages and beyond.[1] He opens two avenues of development, each with individual differences.[2] The first picks up his essentialist strands – his analysis of the activities of the spirit, understanding, and love, and is followed primarily by Anselm (d. 1109) and Aquinas (d. 1274); the second adopts his personalist strands – his theme of God-charity, and the Spirit as the mutual love, and is followed primarily by Richard of St. Victor (d. 1172), and Bonaventure (d. 1274). The focal point of this piece is to appreciate the apologetical defence of the *filioque* doctrine as formulated in the aforesaid theologians. Each chapter, standing on its own, will culminate in some critical reflections, delineating the problems and prospects of each theological perspective.

Augustine's profound insights on the doctrine of *filioque* re-emerge as an elaborated defence in St. Anselm's theological reflections in the Middle Ages. In fact, Anselm is the first Western theologian since Charlemagne to develop a rigorous apologetic for the Latin, Augustinian tradition. Like his predecessor, Anselm's starting point is the divine essence, rather than the persons. In repudiating the doctrine of *per filium* and monopatrism, Anselm furnishes two major arguments to substantiate *filioque*: first by way of necessary reasons, second by way of exegetical foundation. He assumes Augustine's analysis of the activities of the spirit, understanding and love, but gives it a scholastic spin. His axiom, '*in Deo omnia sunt unum, ubi non obviat relationis oppositio*', enables him to establish the ontological distinction of persons within the unity of God. The Spirit, then, proceeds from the Son as he does from the Father, but as from the same principle. What is crucial for Anselm is this: the origin of the Holy Spirit is not rooted in the mutual love between the Father and the Son as in Augustine, but in love as the eternal essence shared by both – viz., their one Godness of love. This is in line with his emphasis, not on the differentiation of persons but on the principle of unity, his dogmatic departure point. Anselm's is a thorough-going essentialist approach to the divine mystery of the Trinity.

Richard of St. Victor picks up the personalist strands in Augustine, and on that basis he proceeds to a consideration of the immanent Trinity on the basis of love. Whereas love requires a plurality of persons as its condition, perfected love demands a Trinity of persons. Since God is supremely loving, and only God is deserving of supreme love, the infinite love which is God presupposes an infinite object, even when there are no creatures. Love consists of three levels, moving from self-love (Father) to charity, in which a second is loved (Son), to complete charity, in which a third is mutually loved by the pair (Spirit). 'The perfection of the divine love is revealed by the fact that it is neither self-love nor the merely reciprocal love of two for each other, but a love intrinsically oriented to community'.[3] The love expressed by the Spirit is not of two turned towards each other as in Augustine, but rather of two turned to a third. A rational analysis of the nature of love, unaided by revelation, leads to the conclusion that the fulfillment of love demands a Trinity of persons. Contrary to Augustine, Richard's trinitarian language is love (Father), beloved (Son) and co-beloved (Spirit). This trinitarian configuration allows the distinctiveness of the third person to come through far more clearly and strongly than Augustine's mutual-love theory. Richard's is the personalist approach to the divine mystery of the Trinity, which is the very opposite of Anselm's.

Aquinas, of the Dominican order, teaches the doctrine of relations, that which is already found in Augustine and Anselm, and develops what he calls 'subsistent relations'. To him, relations are ontologically predicated of the One God, existing in themselves and are not mere 'accidents' attached to an already constituted reality. The necessary event-like attributes or notions of the Son's generation and the Spirit's spiration in the intra-triune life, which Aquinas explains by his language of subsistent relations, do not divide an existing substance or produce a new divine reality as occurs in the temporal order. Divine persons differ through the relations of origin to each other, and their unity is grounded in the One essence which the Son and the Spirit receive from the Father. God is substantively One without distinction, but relationally three with distinction. By identifying relation with God's essence, God is constituted as tripersonal. Although Aquinas is at odds with Richard's particular trinitarian model of love, which moves from human love to an ontological reflection on God's tripersonal life, he, like other medieval scholastics, endorses the radical *circumincessio* or *perichoresis* of love as ontologically reflective of God's innermost life. God exists not as a solitary monad, but as an infinitely intimate relationship with each other in an utter communion of love. On the one hand, Aquinas is with Anselm in giving priority to the solitary love as the formal reason of spiration; on the other hand, he does not distance himself from Augustine in affirming the Spirit as the fruit of the mutual love of Father and the Son for each other, and by way of John Damascene, he accentuates the personalist approach to the divine mystery.[4] His success lies in his ability to steer in between the extremely essentialist approach as in Anselm and an extremely personalist approach as in Richard of St. Victor. Aquinas holds the two in a synthetical balance, affirming not only the Spirit as proceeding from the love of the Infinite Being for itself, but also as the mutual love of the Father and the Son for each other. Whilst remaining tightly in his own Western tradition, Aquinas' double-prong may possibly prove fruitful in ecumenical discussions by paving the way for the East to agree with the West that the Spirit proceeds from both the Father and Son.

Last but not least, Bonaventure, of the Franciscan tradition, also stays within the Latin tradition, but moves beyond it to develop his doctrine of the Trinity more in line with the Eastern tradition. His view of *filioque* cannot be understood apart from the synthesis which he has with the thoughts of two major thinkers, Pseudo-Dionysius and Richard of Saint Victor. Derived from them are two great values, that the supreme good is diffusive of itself, and the highest good is love. Like Richard, Bonaventure applies the idea of love to the intra-divine life, describing the Trinity as perfect love. Supreme or perfect love cannot be self-enclosed, but tends towards the other. Perfect love directs lovers away from each other so as to share their love with the third. Richard's themes of *dilectus condign* and *condilectus*, the distinction between gratuitous love, received love, and the mixture of the two, enable Bonaventure, by way of his doctrine of emanation by mode of nature and by mode of will, to account for the necessary existence of the Holy Spirit. In speaking of the trinitarian dynamism of love, he expands the meaning of love in three ways: the essential predication, that love is predicated essentially of God, thus of all three persons; the notional predication, that the mutual love of the Father and Son conjoined in spiration; personal predication, love as the personal name of the Spirit. It is in the second sense that *filioque* is affirmed, that the Spirit is the mutual love of the first two persons, yet not that of the first two turned towards each other as in Augustine, but of the first two turned towards the third as in Richard – the third is the 'love' (the proper name of the Spirit) loved by the first two in harmony.[5] The love of the Father and the Son is of such great intimacy that the Spirit is spirated from them, but as from one principle. Bonaventure's inclusion of relationality as part of his definition of a divine person, and Damascene's idea of circumincession which he adopts, bring him closer to the Eastern tradition.

Chapter One

The *Filioque* Question

Theological Roots of Western Pneumatological Tradition

'Whether we like or not', Vladimir Lossky writes, 'the question of the procession of the Holy Spirit has been the sole dogmatic ground for the separation of East and West ... All the other divergences which, historically, accompanied or followed the first dogmatic controversy about the *filioque*, in the measure in which they too had some dogmatic importance, are more or less dependent upon that original issue.'[1] The unsettled question of the relation between the Son and the Spirit in the fourth-century debates is addressed in Western theology from an early stage in its history through what comes to be called the *filioque* doctrine. This chapter does not deal with the entire history of the *filioque* controversy; rather it focuses on the theological roots of the Western pneumatological tradition.[2] To this end, we shall concentrate our theological discussions on four key church fathers Tertullian, Hilary, Ambrose and Augustine, all of whom in some measures contributed, to the Western pneumatological defence of the *filioque* doctrine.[3] This doctrine, which has never been embraced by the East, reaches its height in the formulations of the Latin fathers, specifically in Augustine, whose pneumatological position comes to fruition in subsequent medieval theological reflections.

Tertullian (d. 220)

Considering his approach to the doctrine of God, Tertullian, similar to Irenaeus, has as his starting point God as he reveals himself in the process of creation and redemption.[4] He begins with the economic actions of the Triune God, not with God as he exists in his immanent being. His *Adversus Praxean*, in Margerie's assessment, marks a significant stage moving from 'a certain "cosmological" outlook on the Trinity toward a consideration of its inner life, by way of the doctrine of the missions of the Word and of the Spirit.'[5] Tertullian, the second-century African theologian, writes his *Adversus Praxean* as a theological response to the modalistic thinking rampant in Rome and the West. There he tries to defend the hypostatic individuality of the persons in terms of the *order* in which each communicates the divine substance to the others, the 'dispensation' (*oikonomia*) in human historical experience of Jesus and Holy Spirit.[6] The term 'economy', which he borrows from Ireaneus, illumines analogously that which occurs within God's inner life.[7] Along with his contemporaries, Tertullian adopts the analogy of an imperial king, whose sovereign '*monarchia*' remains undivided, even when the same sovereignty were shared with his coordinates.[8] The undivided sovereignty analogously reflects an undivided source, that which is rooted in the divine Godhead. Just as a king can share his own power with his son without disturbing his own monarchy, so, he writes, 'the Son is not prejudicial to the monarchy, although today [i.e., in this age, after the enthronement of the risen Christ] it is in the Son's hands, because it is both in its own quality [*statu*] in the Son's hands, and retaining its own quality will be restored to the Father by the Son.'[9] The same is true of sharing in the divine reality, in virtue of which the distinctiveness and divine status of the Spirit are maintained within the same undivided divine monarchy. How, then, could God be conceived to undergo division or partition in the Son and the Spirit, who are sequentially put in the 'second' and 'third' place, and are '*tam consortes substantiae patris*'? Tertullian writes of the sequential communication of the indivisible substance, as in undivided power, of the three persons in the same undivided Godhead:

> (T)hey are of the one, namely by unity of substance, while nonetheless is guarded the mystery of that economy which disposes the unity into trinity, setting forth Father and Son and Spirit as three, three however not in quality but in sequence, not in substance but in aspect, not in power but in manifestation, yet of one substance and one quality and one power, seeing it is one God...[10]

Tertullian's thought remains influential in the West, because he is the first to forge a distinctive Latin vocabulary by which divine unity and plurality can be thought together. He coins the formula, 'one substance, three persons' (*una substantia, tres personae*). By substance, he means that basic ontological-beingness which constitutes a thing as it is; by person he means that unique identity of action which manifests distinctiveness. Underlying his formulation is the basic idea of 'distinction without division.' He wants his audience to understand the idea of one substance, three persons as the one God performing three distinct yet related roles in the great drama of salvation. He is able to balance God's essential unity with the mystery of the economy. The inner trinitarian order must not be understood in an ontologically differentiated way so as to apply to the Being or Deity which each person singly and all triply have in common; rather it applies only to the mysterious 'economy, that the one only God has also a Son, His Word, Who has issued out of Himself ... which Son then sent, according to His promise, the Holy Spirit, the Paraclete, out of the Father.'[11] The economy of salvation is grounded in an ontological economy in which Unity is distributed into a Trinity of persons, displaying its susceptibility of being numbered but not divided or separated. All three are distinguished by sequence, yet are fully and perfectly equal by virtue of unity of substance. In chapter 26 of his *Adversus Praxean*, he stresses that the trinitarian distinctions of persons is at the heart of their indivisible unity of substance.

> This is my faith: the Father, the Son and the Spirit are inseparable one from the other. One is Father, another the Son, another the Spirit ... While they (the modalist Monarchians) affirm the identity of the Father, the Son and the Spirit and thus favour the monarchy over the economy, urged by necessity I say that the Son is another than the Father, not by diversity but their distribution; another not because

they are divided but because they are distinct, because the Father and the Son are not identical but numerically different one from the other. ...The Father is another than the Son since he is greater than the Son: for he who generates is one, he who is generated is another; he who sends is one, he who is sent is another; he who acts is one, he by whom he acts is another ... with regard to the person of Paraclete, ... the Lord affirms that the Paraclete is another than himself, just as we affirm that the Son is another than the Father, and he does this to signify that the Paraclete holds the third place, just as we have shown that the Son holds the second, with regard to the economy of the Trinity.[12]

Speaking of the 'third place', Tertullian reckons 'the Spirit (to proceed) from nowhere else than from the Father through the Son. Be careful not to destroy the monarchy', which is intrinsic of the substance of the Father within which the Son and Spirit subsist.[13] There is a trinitarian indwelling in the one essence from which the phrase 'from the father through the Son' receives its fundamental meaning. The Spirit proceeds principally *(principaliter)*[14] from the Father, the whole substance *(tota substantia)* without distinction, but through the Son because the Son dwells within that same ontologically undifferentiated Deity. The divine substance is communicated from the Father to the Son, then through the Son to the Spirit; all three are God, yet one God. What is affirmed in Tertullian is that the Son is already subsistent in God, and therefore is a necessary collaborator in the production of the Spirit. The Spirit receives his essence from the Son. It is in the mediation of the Son, the 'second place', where the full deity of the Spirit, who is counted 'third', is ascertained. This he explains by means of creaturely examples, which he also uses to demolish the depersonalizing Modalism of Praxeas:

> But if what proceeds from another is necessarily second with respect to the one from which it proceeds, it is not, for all that, separated from it. Where there is a second, they are inevitably two *(secundus ubi est, duo sunt)*, and where there is a third, they are necessarily three. But the Spirit is the third after God and the Son, just as the fruit produced by the stalk but which comes from the root is the third; third as the rivulet that derives from the river but comes from the source; third as the tip of the ray relative to the ray

and to the Sun. Nevertheless, none of these would be alien to the original matrix from which each receives its properties.

So the Trinity, which derives from the Father in strictly arranged degrees, does not in any way contradict the monarchy and protect the nature of the economy.[15]

At this stage, the more technical issue of the origin of the Spirit as a person, and the precise relation of the Spirit to the Father and Son, have not yet surfaced in Latin writers before Augustine. Historically the foundation of the Western doctrine laid by Tertullian early in the third century, finally, after an interval of two centuries, finds its completion in Augustine, and coincidently both belong to the same Church, that of North Africa.[16] Already latent in Tertullian is this: The 'trinity of one divinity' is an economic Trinity as well as an immanent Trinity.[17] This theme will recur subsequently, anticipating the later synthesis between two inseparate poles, the economic and the immanent, of the divine mystery. This represents the enduring worth of Tertullian's mind.

Hilary (d. 367)

Hilary of Poitiers writes his *On the Trinity* during the years of exile in Constantinople (356-359), when he incurs the Emperor's disapproval for his attack on the Homoean Arianism in Gaul. Like Tertullian, he does explore the relation of Spirit to Father and Son. Tertullian's view of the Spirit *a Patre per Filium* is also found in Hilary. Thus Hilary's most distinctive position, according to Congar and Swete, is that of the Eastern view, as is evident in his concluding prayer to God:

> But, for my part, ... I must also deny that this name of 'creature' belongs to the Holy Spirit, seeing that He proceeds from Thee and is sent through Him... so I hold fast in my consciousness the truth that thy Holy Spirit is from Thee and through Him, although I cannot by my intellect comprehend it ... Keep, I pray Thee, this my pious faith undefiled, and even until my spirit departs, grant that this may be the utterance of my convictions ... Let me, in short, adore Thee our

Father, and Thy Son together with Thee; let me win the favour of Thy Holy Spirit, who is from Thee, through thy Only-Begotten.[18]

Notwithstanding this, he is more than ready to 'confess him as having the Father and the Son as his source' (*qui patre et Filio auctoribus confitendus est*).[19] Later in the same work, he affirms a singularity of meaning between the *de meo accipiet* of John 16:14 and the *a Patre procedere* of John 15:26, thereby espousing a view similar to the Western doctrine of the *Filioque*:

> Accordingly he "receives" from the Son, (this Spirit) who is both sent by him and proceeds from the Father (an illusion to John 15:26 and 16:14-15). Now I ask whether to receive from the Son is the same thing as to proceed from the Father. But if one believes that there is a difference between receiving from the Son and proceeding from the Father, surely to receive from the Son and to receive from the Father will be regarded as one and the same thing... Such a unity admits no difference, nor does it make any difference from whom that is received, which, given by the Father, is described as given by the Son.[20]

This passage, Daley argues, pertains not to the primordial relationships that define their hypostatic identities, but primarily to the temporal sharing of the same divine attributes and activities as we experience them in the economy of salvation. Congar concurs with Daley's assessment, yet does not reject the congruence of temporal 'receiving' and eternal 'proceeding.'[21] Fairly speaking, Hilary does not explicitly state that the Spirit receives the divine nature from the Father and the Son, but, as Fortman points out, this is already contained when he says that the Spirit 'did not receive anything from creatures' but 'from those things which are proper to God.'[22] To him, 'to receive' is equivalent to 'to proceed, therefore both the Father and the Son are sources of the Spirit's immanent being, not only of his economic mission as the Paraclete. Not only temporally, but also eternally the Spirit receives from the Son, because all that the Father has are communicated to the Son. As regards source, he is sent by the Son and proceeds from the Father. Not only does he admit no difference between receiving from the Son and proceeding from the Father, but also no difference between receiving from the Father and receiving from the Son. This latter is indicative of the biblical language, that the Spirit is received from both the Father and the Son.[23] So the earlier passage, speaking of the Spirit as '*qui (a) Patre et Filio auctoribus, confitendus est*', probably does carry the meaning rendered by one translator E.W. Watson: 'We are bound to confess Him (the Spirit), proceeding, as he does, from Father and Son.'[24]

The importance of Hilary for Augustine is certain in that he is the only church father quoted by name in Augustine's *On the Trinity*, and esteemed as 'a man of no mediocre authority in treating the Scriptures and in asserting the faith.'[25] This suggests that Augustine might have Hilary's book before him when he writes his own. Hilary's teachings have implications for later development, especially in Augustine and later Anselm, both of whom assert that Jesus' 'breathing on the disciples' in John 20:22 implies the procession of the Spirit *a Filio*.[26] Furthermore as regards where to locate the unity of the Godhead, Hilary seems to ground it not in the differentiations of persons (as in the person of Father), but in the One being of God. As proof of this, he, commenting on John 14:6-11 at the end of Book VII, understands the unity not as a 'transfusion of the one into the other' but as 'a unity of the same nature in both through generation and birth.'[27] Consequently, the origin of the Spirit lies in the Divinity commonly shared by the Father and the Son. Thus the ontological priority of divine unity and the reciprocity of relations within that unity would have led him to conclude that the Spirit proceeds from the Father and the Son. Another facet of Hilary's teaching, which also draws the attention of Augustine, is the term 'Gift' – a technical title for the Spirit, which he interprets both economically and immanently. He summarizes as his confessional stance, '(Jesus) commanded them to baptize in the name of the Father, the Son, and the Holy Spirit, that is, in the confession of the Origin, the Only-Begotten, and the Gift ...We are bound to confess (that the Spirit) does exist, inasmuch as He is given, received, retained.'[28] There is a concord between giver and given. The Spirit, who receives/proceeds from the Father and the Son, is their mutual Gift. Hence the correspondence between the economic and immanent Trinity in Hilary, a theme which receives much attention in the later period, would also lead him to the conclusion that the economic Gift of the Spirit proceeds immanently *ex patre Filioque*.

Ambrose (d. 397)

Three decades after Hilary comes Ambrose, who is spoken of as 'the most brilliant man of his time.'[29] His brilliance lies not only in his appreciation of the achievements of the Greek theologians, but also in his ability to mediate them to the Latin Church, yet in his distinctively Western way.[30] Ambrose is apparently the first Western theologian devoted exclusively to the subject, and to make explicit use of the phrase *Spiritus procedit a Patre et Filio* – 'the Spirit proceeds from the Father and the Son.' He writes his treatise *On the Holy Spirit*, probably around 381, the year of the First Council of Constantinople, at the Emperor Gratian's command, but not without the doctrinal inspiration of the Greek fathers, especially Athanasius, Basil of Caesarea and Didymus of Alexandria.[31] There Ambrose asserts the Divinity of the Spirit, since the Spirit shares the 'evident glory of the Godhead', which is characterized by four chief 'marks': God is 'without sin', 'forgives sin', 'is not a creature but the Creator', and 'does not give but receives worship.'[32] For instance, commenting on Job 33:4, '*The Spirit of God has made me*', Ambrose attributes the work of creation to the Spirit, affirming therefore the Spirit as God. 'Let them', he writes, 'therefore, either say what it is which has been created without the Father, Son, and Holy Spirit, or let them confess that the Spirit also is of one Godhead with the Father and the Son.'[33] Where one person is named, the other two are included - this takes place not locally but eternally in the radically single being of God. Though three persons are named, the Divine Name is one (cf. Matt. 28:19). This Ambrose affirms in his *On the Christian Faith*: 'God is One, neither dividing His Son from Him, as do the heathen, nor denying, with the Jews (and Arius), that He was begotten of the Father before all worlds.'[34] He also warns his audience against Sabellius' collapse of the personal distinctions within God's one nature, and so maintain that 'the Father and the Son are one and the same Person.'[35] Throughout the treatise, he continues to speak of the Spirit interchangeably as the Spirit of grace or love (*caritas*), as the Spirit of truth who reveals to us the Father and the Son, as the Spirit who anoints Christ to his earthly office.[36] The Spirit's 'sending' of the Son (cf. Isa. 48:16), in this context, is not a reference to the origin of the eternal Son, but a reference to the earthly mission for which the incarnate Son is

Spirit-anointed. The work of the Spirit here has to do with the incarnate mode of the Son's existence, that the Son, in his union with our humanity, is sent by the Spirit, who anoints him to his office, rests upon him and leads him in his mission.[37] But as regards origin, the Son sends the Spirit, thus is the source of the Spirit; both are given by the Father.[38] Yet for Ambrose, both the Father and the Spirit give the Son, since they mutually coinhere in act.[39] Interestingly, Paul's preposition 'through' Ambrose does not use exclusively of the Son; he also uses it as a reference to the Father; and in some contexts, the prepositions 'through' and 'in' are interchangeably one.[40]

With rigor, Ambrose reflects on the import of the biblical language of the Spirit as being 'sent' by the Father or the Son. He apparently makes no distinction between procession and mission, although his emphasis throughout the treatise is on the activity or mission of the Spirit in the divine economy of salvation. He does not attempt to develop a theology of the immanental relationships of Father, Son and Spirit. However this does not mean that he says nothing of the immanent Trinity at all. This 'sent', he avers, is not to be understood in a local sense, implying a transposition from place to place or a partition of the Spirit from the Father or the Son from whom he comes. Rather it is an image for an essential and personal relationship to the divine reality in itself. Just as the Son's 'sending' in the incarnation does not entail his separation from the Father,

> the Holy Spirit, too, when he comes forth (*procedit a*) the Father and Son, is not separated from the Father, is not separated from the Son. For how can he be separated from the Father, who is "the breath of his mouth" (Ps. 33.6)? This, surely, is both an indication of eternity and an expression of unity.[41]

The statement, '*procedit a Patre et Filio*', the Benedictine editor refers to the temporal mission of the Spirit.[42] Nevertheless Ambrose understands the *de meo accipiet of* John 16:14 to include the essential communication of the divine life itself.[43] The relation between the eternal procession on the one hand and the temporal mission on the other, of the Spirit is brought into view. So it must not be taken to mean that the eternal procession is completely left out of account in Ambrose's thinking. It is certainly implied: 'For if the Spirit proceeds from the Son (*ex Filio*) in any other sense than that of motion from place to place, it can only be by some essential derivation from Him; and an essential relaton within the Godhead must be timeless, without beginning or end.'[44] Just as the Son is begotten of and is sent by the Father, yet remains in the same Godhead with the Father, the Spirit proceeds from the Father and is sent by the Son, yet does not depart from the same Godhead, and is one God with both. For the Spirit to 'breathe forth' upon the prophets, on Jesus and his Church is to be referred to his origin, the instrument of divine power. Hence for the Spirit to be 'breathed forth' is to be referred to his double procession. To further substantiate his claim, Ambrose writes,

> Observe now that just as the Father is the Fountain of Life, so, too, many have declared that the Son also is signified as the Fountain of Life, because, He says, with You, Almighty God, your Son is the Fountain of Life, that is, the Fountain of that Holy Spirit, since the Spirit is the Life ...Yet many wish that the Father alone be indicated in this passage by Fountain, although they see what Scripture has said. It says:"With thee is the Fountain of life," that is, with Father is the Son, for the Word is with God....[45]

Eternally, just as the Spirit proceeds from the Father, since the Father is the fountain of the Spirit, the Spirit thus 'proceeds forth from the Son', since the Son is 'the fountain of the Holy Spirit.'[46] Ambrose's view, Swete notes, has its root in S. Basil's teaching: *'ex uno Spiritu per unum Filium in unum Patrem cognitio nostra procedit; et ex uno Patre per unum Filium in unum Spiritum Sanctum bonitas es sanctificatio et imperiale jus erternae traditur potestatis.'*[47] In God's divine life the Divine essence flows from the Father through the Son into the Spirit, and thus is received by the Spirit from the Son. Analogous to the Spirit's procession from the Father is his receiving from the Son:*'Secundum divinitatem non super Christum est Spiritus sed in Christo ... manet enim in Deo qui ex Deo est ... et manet in Christo qui a Christo accipit.'*[48] The Spirit receives from the Son his very essence: *'Quod ex aliquo est aut ex substantia est aut ex potestate ejus. Ex substantia... sicut Spiritus qui a Patre procedit, de quo dicit Filius, "ille me clarificabit quia de meo accipiet.'*[49] All three persons are never separated in being and act, since the entire Trinity is indivisibly and intrinsically One. The entire Godhead has only one operation and will. The Son receives from the Father, and the Spirit receives from the Son, by virtue of unity of essence. All his gifts pass from the Father through the Son. The Spirit is of the Father, since he proceeds from him; the Spirit is also of the Son, since he too proceeds from the Son. Prior to the Father's sending of the Son in his incarnation, the Son is of the Father ontologically; likewise, prior to the Spirit's mission in time, the Spirit is of the Father ontologically, thus also of the Son ontologically. Unlike the apparent reserve of his Eastern contemporaries, Ambrose is not reticent in speaking of the Spirit as proceeding from the Son, despite the event that the Council of Constantinople adheres to the language of Scripture: the Spirit proceeds from the Father.

Augustine (d. 430)

However, the Latin West is never satisfied with the scriptural formulation of the East. It is Augustine who, more than any other thinkers, furnishes the theoretical foundation for the Western understanding of the procession. It is from him that the *filioque* doctrine receives both form and force. Thus he occupies a central place in the history of the doctrine of the double procession of the Spirit. The Alexandrian perspective, driven by its soteriological reason, frequently puts the emphasis on the economic actions of the Spirit in the life of the Church, and the role of the Logos. Cyril of Alexandria himself would acknowledge that the Spirit is 'the proper Spirit of the Son', that 'He arises from the Son', 'from the Father and the Son', or 'proceeds substantially from the Two, that is, from the Father through the Son', that 'the Spirit derives, that is from the Father, as from a Source, but He is sent to the creature by the Son.' However these statements Cyril never intends to correspond to the *filioque* doctrine, although by them he could be easily interpreted as the Greek patristic authority in support of the double procession of the Spirit.[50] The ambiguity behind them is then cleared up by Theodoret of Cyrus:

> If Cyril says that the Spirit is proper to the Son, in the sense that He is consubstantial to Him and proceeds from the Father, then we agree with him and view his expression as being in conformity with piety.

But if, on the contrary, it is in the sense that Spirit draws His substance from the Son or through the Son, then we repudiate this expression as blasphemous and impious. For we believe the Lord who has said: 'the Spirit of Truth who proceeds from the Father.'[51]

'According to him (Cyril)', concludes Theodoret, 'the Holy Spirit does not have His subsistence from the Son or through the Son, but proceeds from the Father, and is called the *proprium* of the Son, because of His consubstantiality.'[52] Theodoret's explanation finds its approval in Cyril's triadological interpretation: 'The Spirit was and is the Son's as He was and is the Father's; for though He proceeds from the Father, yet He is not alien from the Son; for the Son has all things in common with the Father as the Lord has Himself taught us.'[53] Like Cyril, Augustine comes from an Anti-Arian perspective. His notably work *De Trinitate*, written probably over a period from 400 to 416, lays the foundation for subsequent development of Western trinitarian theology. Unlike Cyril, Augustine develops a theology of the Spirit that entirely corresponds to the doctrine of the double procession: 'The Holy Spirit is communicated by the Father and the Son. He is their mutual Gift.'[54]

Biblically, the word most commonly linked to the Spirit is 'gift' (cf. Acts 2.38; 8.20; 10.45; 11.17; cf. Luke 11.13). The Spirit is Gift, for it comes to the Son from the Father and to the Father from the Son. It is also gift because it is given to us, the recipients of the benefits of the cross, as a gift from both. Along with Hilary, Augustine does not confine the meaning of gift to the temporal realm, as a gift bestowed only in time. There is a congruence of the economic and immanent rendering of gift so that the Spirit may be called Gift (*donum*) eternally prior to his being given (*Donatum*) in history. He writes:

> A further question has been raised; whether, just as the Son derives from his begetting not merely his sonship but his actual existence, so also the Holy Spirit derives from his being given, not only his character as a gift, but his actual existence; whether he existed before he was given, but was not yet a gift, or whether he was a gift even before he was given, in that God was to give him. But if he does not proceed except when he is given, he clearly could not proceed until there was someone to whom he might be given ... Does the Holy

Spirit always proceed, not in time only, but from eternity? But because he proceeded in order to be potentially a gift, he was already a gift before there was any recipient. ... For a gift can exist before it is given ... The Spirit is eternally a gift, but the gift is bestowed in time.'[55]

The question of the relation of the *opera ad extra Trinitatis* to the *opera ad intra Trinitatis* is resolved in Augustine by reasoning *a posteriori* from a mission in time to an affirmation of a procession in eternity. The Spirit is beforehand in eternity as the one that he reveals himself to be, namely Gift. Immanently, not just economically, the Spirit is to be referred to both the Father and the Son. The Spirit is the common gift of the Father and the Son in the immanent Trinity. The reciprocity of gift exchange, which is the Holy Spirit, is to be understood as 'a certain unutterable communion of the Father and the Son. ... (B)oth the Father is a spirit and the son a spirit, both the Father is holy, and the Son holy. In order, therefore, that the communion of both may be signified from a name which is suitable to both, the Holy Spirit is called the gift of both.'[56] Yet this inexpressible communion is best described as 'love': 'Therefore, the Holy Spirit, whatever it is, is something common both to the Father and the Son. But that communion itself is consubstantial and coeternal; and if it may fitly be called friendship, let it be so called; but it is more aptly called love.'[57] As regards this point, Augustine begins with our experience of the Spirit in the economy of salvation, as the love of God poured out in our hearts (Rom. 5:5), to conceive love as the most appropriate term for the Spirit as a divine person. He is aware that the Scripture does not explicitly say that the Holy Spirit is love. However he argues that if God's being is defined in I John 4:8 as love, and the Spirit is God, it follows naturally that the Holy Spirit is love. He speaks of the Spirit as proceeding from the mutual love of the first two persons for each other. The love, which God is, is bestowed first on the Son, who in turn returns the received love to the Father, with the Spirit binding them as mutual love. The love which proceeds from the Father and the Son is the fruit of and reality of their mutual love. 'The divine act of love', O'Collins explains, 'gives rise to its eternal, immanent fruit (*impressio amati in amato*), the Holy Spirit.'[58] The Spirit, the gift of both the Father and the Son, is love, and thus he reveals to us the 'common love' by which the first two persons mutually love each other. Toward the end of his *De Trinitate*, Augustine argues from the mutual love to the ontological communion between the first two persons, showing that both ideas are practically interchangeable: 'And if the love by which the Father loves the Son and the Son loves the Father ineffably demonstrates the communion of both, what is more suitable than that He should properly be called love who is Spirit, common to both.'[59]

In *The City of God*, Augustine's remark, that 'God is everything that he has except for the relations through which each person is referred to each other',[60] accentuates the principle (or claim) that persons are distinguished from one another not in terms of substance which each individually or all three together have in common, but in terms of unchangeable relations to one another in their *intra* life: paternity, filiation and gift. It also anticipates the subsequent development of the doctrine of divine persons as reciprocal relations, especially as found in Anselm and Aquinas. Speaking of God with respect to relation (*ad aliquid*), for example of the Father to the Son and the Son to the Father, Augustine dispels a late Arian argument against Nicea, '(t)his is no accident because the one is always the Father and the other always the Son.'[61] The plural relations predicated of the one God are ontological, not accidental because the Father is always the Father of the Son; the Son is always the Son of the Father; thus the Spirit is the Spirit of both, binding them together in a essential 'bond of love' (*vinculum caritatis*). In the traditional 'order' in which persons in God are logically, not chronologically, arranged, the Father is placed 'first' as the original source of the Spirit; the Son's role, which he derives from the Father, is in the 'second' place; the Spirit is in the third, coming forth from the first two. And yet this order has nothing to do with the ranking of being, but rather with the order of nature. No temporal or privileged priority is implied in the divine order of procession, and with this, Augustine removes all subordinationisms.

Building upon Hilary and Ambrose, according to whom temporal mission corresponds to eternal procession, the former reveals a divine person in his eternal origin, Augustine argues that the Spirit has to be thought of as proceeding from the Son. One of his main proof texts is John 20.22, wherein the risen Christ is reportedly 'breathing upon his disciples', and saying, 'Receive the

Holy Spirit.' Augustine understands this to correspond to the eternal procession of the Spirit from the Son.

> For as to be born, in respect to the Son, means to be from the Father; so to be sent, in respect to the Son, means to be known to be from the Father. And as to be the gift of God in respect to the Holy Spirit, means to proceed from the Father; so to be sent, is to be known to proceed from the Father. Neither can we say that the Holy Spirit does not also proceed from the Son, for the same Spirit is not without reason said to be the Spirit both of the Father and of the Son. Nor do I see what else He intended to signify, when He breathed on the face of the disciples, and said, 'receive ye the Holy Spirit.' For that bodily breathing, proceeding from the body with the feeling of bodily touching, was not the substance of the Holy Spirit, but a declaration by a fitting sign, that the Holy Spirit proceeds not only from the Father, but also from the Son.[62]

Subsequently, Augustine writes of the manner in which the Son is the principle of the Spirit. The Father endows the Son with the capacity to spirate the Spirit. It is in a 'primordial' sense (*principaliter*) that the Spirit proceeds from the Father (*de Patre principaliter*), but only in 'derivative' sense that he proceeds from the Son.[63] Augustine draws on Tertullian's term '*principaliter*' to defend the distinctive role of the Father within the Godhead. Commenting on John 15:26, where the Lord says, "whom (Holy Spirit) I send unto you from the Father", he writes: 'The original source (*principium*) of the entire divinity (*divinitatis*) – or to put it better, of the being of God (*deitatis*) – is the Father.'[64]

> ... God the Father *alone* is He from whom the Word is born, and from whom the Holy Spirit principally proceeds. And therefore I have added the word *principally* (corresponds to the Greek saying, 'by way of the first principle'), because we find that the Holy Spirit proceeds from the Son also. But the Father gave him this too, not as to one already existing, and not yet having it; but whatever he gave to the only-begotten Word, he gave by begetting him. Therefore he so begat him as that the *common Gift* should proceed from him also, and the Holy Spirit should be the Spirit of both.[65]

For Augustine, any rejection of the Spirit's spiration from the Father and the Son, 'as from one principle' (*tanquam ab uno principio*), is tantamount to dividing the divine unity.[66] He is keenly cognizant of the unity issue posed by the Greeks. In his view, the *per filium* is to be understood in the sense that the Son, being equal with the Father, is the agent of the Father in this spiration. Unlike the Greeks, he admits the distinctive role of the Son in the production of the Spirit. What the Son does here is not independently but 'by the Father's gift and without interval of time', just as his divinity is received from the Father within the same Godhead.[67] The Spirit is breathed out equally and simultaneously from the Father and the Son. The Son, who receives all things from the Father via the eternal act of generation, also receives from him the very role of being an origin for the Spirit's procession. The Son thus owes all that he has (attributes) or is (essence) to the Father, including his power to produce the Spirit. This enables Augustine to carefully deal with the all-important matter for the Greeks, that there is one *proprium*, not two primordial springs of the deity. The Greek theologians regard as axiomatic, that the Father *alone* is the ultimate source or fountainhead of deity, that the Son cannot be the causal participant in the hypostatic origin of the Spirit. Contrarily, Augustine asserts the idea of the Son constituting with the Father a single co-principle for the procession of the Spirit. The Son's co-equality with the Father in the production of the Spirit is crucial in view of confronting the Arian challenges to the Son's true and equal divinity. The Son's spirating act in a derivative way does not infringe his divine unity with the Father, for the Son is of one being with the Father. Both Father and Son, together as One God, in one spiration, communicate their own being and divinity to the Spirit. The action of the Father and Son in causing the *processio* of the Spirit is indivisibly one, as is the common action of all three persons in creation. The procession of the Spirit constitutes one eternal act of the one ontologically undifferentiated Divinity commonly shared by the Father and the Son. This reveals Augustine's essentialist position, that the origin of the procession belongs to the divine essence, although the Father is the unitary source of the entire Divinity. The *filioque*, therefore, safeguards the fundamental unity, attributing not two separate sources but one to the Spirit.[68]

That being said, what are we to do with statements in Augustine that seem to locate the unity of the Godhead in the Father, not in the divine essence? In his *On Faith and the Creed* (393), the earliest dogmatic work, he writes as a young priest: 'They (early fathers) affirm that He (Holy Spirit) is the Gift of God, in such sense that God's Gift is to be believed not inferior to God Himself. They add, however, this reservation, that though the Spirit is not said to be generated, as the Son is, from the Father... His being is not underived, but He owes it to the Father from whom are all things. This is stated in order to guard against the presumption that there are two first principles (*principia sine principio*) - a most false and absurd notion which is not part of the Catholic Faith, but belongs to the erroneous systems of certain heretics.'[69] However this is written, after recognizing that the fathers have not discussed fully the role of the Son in the origin and communication of the Holy Spirit. Three years later, Augustine, now a Bishop, writes *On Christian Teaching* (396), where he states explicitly, 'In the Father there is unity…And the three are all one because of the Father, all equal because of the Son, and all in harmony because of the Holy Spirit.'[70] From this, Olson and Hall suggest, 'Perhaps surprisingly, in light of the current debate, Augustine proceeds to locate the unity of the persons, not in the divine essence, but in the Father.'[71] But they propose this tentatively, and claim that the resolution of the debate will hinge upon a thorough grounding in Augustine's trinitarian thought, amply laid out in his *De Trinitate* and other writings.[72] To do justice, one must observe the progressive development of Augustine's thinking so that the earlier texts cited do not represent the position of Augustine in its entirety. Between the aforementioned passage and the 15th chapter of his *De Trinitate* is his *Tractatus in S. Joannem*, his sermons on John's Gospel (eg. Jn. vii.16; xvi.13; xx.22), preached probably around 416. For instance, in *Sermon* 71, he already claims that both the Father and the Son, as One principle, cause the spiration of the Holy Spirit:

> The Catholic Church holds and preaches that God the Holy Spirit is not the Spirit of the Father only or of the Son only, but of the Father and the Son…He is Their common life (*communitas*). It was therefore Their will to give us communion with one another and with Themselves through that which is common to Them Both; to

gather us together in one by this Gift which Both have in common, namely, by the Holy Spirit, who is God and the Gift of God.[73]

In the same work, he affirms *filioque* openly, 'Why should we not believe that the Holy Spirit proceeds also from the Son, since he is the Spirit of the Son also?'[74] Christ would not have breathed the Holy Spirit on his disciples, he argues, if the Spirit does not proceed from him: 'What else did that breathing signify except that the Holy Spirit proceeds also from him?'[75] As regards the question why the Son claims 'the Spirit proceeds from the Father', Augustine answers by appealing to Christ's humility, since Christ always refers everything that he has to the Father. Christ's statement, 'My doctrine is not Mine, but His that sent me' (Jn. 5:16), Augustine takes with literal seriousness:

> If, then, it is here understood to be his doctrine, regardless of the fact that he said it is not his, but the Father's – how much more must we then understand the Holy Spirit to proceed from him also, where, speaking of the Spirit 'proceeding from the Father,' he is careful not to say 'he does not proceed from me?'[76]

Thus he opts for the simultaneous procession of the Spirit from the Father and the Son: 'The Holy Spirit does not proceed from the Father into the Son, and from the Son to the creatures ... but he proceeds at once from both.'[77]

Augustine's essentialist position, shared by many Augustine scholars,[78] appears in his later and most matured dogmatic work, *De Trinitate* (400-16), which he belabours over a period of 16 years. There he claims explicitly *filioque* as his definitive position:

> As the Father has in Himself that the Holy Spirit should proceed from Him so has He given to the Son that the same Holy Spirit should proceed from Him, and be both apart from the Father as that it be understood that His proceeding also from the Son, is a property derived by the Son from the Father.[79]

The difference between the Cappadocians and Augustine becomes all the more obvious when they try to determine the eternal relations of the three persons. Underlying the position of the Greek

East and the Latin West on the procession of the Spirit were two different approaches: 'whereas the Capaddocians knew God as three persons before they knew Him as one God, Augustine knows Him as one God before he knows Him as three persons.'[80] For the Greeks, the idea of a real distinction of persons constituted by their relatedness is at the fore; for Augustine, the idea of the entire simplicity and non-differentiation of divine essence supporting the hypostatic identities is at the fore. Moving from the One essence to the Three, Augustine proceeds to clarify the relations of the trinitarian persons within the One divine essence. This he does by way of the pyschological analogies, which mirror the threefold being of God. Along the same path, he brings out the basic trinitarian structures in humans, namely the three activities of the human spirit: the mind itself, knowledge and love. Interestingly, what he intends in these categories, which are drawn from the inner mental world, to be illustrative in character becomes a criterion for systematic characterization of later theological thought, as in Anselm and Thomism.[81] What he does here is more than merely constructing illustrative analogies, but is in fact, by this analysis, constructing an essentialist approach to his doctrine of God. Thus the ontological foundations of the doctrine of the Trinity are to be founded not so much in the economy of salvation as in his idea of a threefold mind. Quoting Augustine:

> (T)his triad of memory, understanding and will are not three lives, but one; nor three minds, but one. It follows that they are not three substances, but one substance ... But they are three inasmuch as they are related to one another (*ad se invicem referuntur*) ... And these three constitute one thing, one life, one mind, one essence. We might now attempt to raise our thoughts ... towards the supreme and most exalted essence of which the human mind is an image – inadequate indeed, but still an image.[82]

The relations between memory, understanding and will correspond in some measure to the relations between the Divine Persons in God's Being. Augustine continues his explanation, seeking to conceive how the doctrine of the Spirit enters to complete the trinitarian circle in the same Godhead. This he summarizes in Book XIV of his *De Trinitate* his earlier argument:

> (W)e developed an account of the mental trinity, in which memory supplied the source from which the thinker's view received its form, the confrontation itself being a kind of image imprinted by the memory, and the agency by which the two are conjoined being love or will. Thus when the mind regards itself in the act of thought, it understands and takes knowledge of itself: we may say that it begets this understanding and self-knowledge ... But this begetting by the mind of self-knowledge ... does not imply that it was previously unknown to itself ... And to these two, the begetter and the begotten, we have to add the love which joins them together, and is simply the will, pursuing or embracing an object of enjoyment.[83]

For him, love follows knowledge; God is his own Memory, that he knows himself, and is his own love. By the principle of divine 'appropriations', the cognitive function is primarily proper to the Word or Son; the titles of love or will are most proper to the Spirit, as he says, 'For what else is will but love' – 'the strongest kind of will.'[84] The Trinity reflected in human nature consists of the mind which loves, the knowledge without which there is no love, and the love which abides in knowledge. Put it differently, I love myself, I am loved by myself, and in between is the third, i.e., the love by which I love, and am loved. "Therefore there are not more than three, one who loves Him who is from Himself, and One who loves Him from whom He is, and love (*dilectio*) itself.'[85] His *filioque* doctrine is manifested in his popular analogy of the Lover (Father), the Beloved (Son) and the Love (Spirit), according to which he writes: 'He who is the Holy Spirit, ... is neither of the Father alone, nor of the Son alone, but of both, therefore intimates to us the mutual love by which the Father and the Son love one another.'[86] The Spirit is the principle of the differentiated unity within God's life, therefore is 'not one of the two' but a third 'through whom both are joined, through whom the Begotten is loved by the Begetter and loves Him that begot Him.'[87] The love expressed by the Spirit is of the mutual love of the first two persons, of the first two lovers turned towards each other. This, to a certain extent, brings out the relational dynamism of the triune God, in which the Father is identified as the pole of bestowing, the Son as the pole of receptivity, and the Spirit as the pole of reciprocity – all three are ontologically constitutive of the One Being of God. Augustine's concept of the Spirit as the reciprocal bond of love has the immediate significance for the Western theological tradition. Badcock comments:

> This is closely related to the idea that the trinitarian persons are constituted by relationships. The relationship of the Spirit to Father and Son is constituted by the procession of the Spirit, so that the two, relation and procession, are identical. The Spirit, then, having a relation to the Son, being therefore proceed from the Son as well as from the Father, whose love for the Son the Spirit is also. The Spirit therefore necessarily proceeds from both.[88]

Augustine's position in the North African church at the time when he produces his *On The Trinity* is well-known, and unassailable. It must be borne in mind that he claims no ultimate authority for his views. What he does is merely presenting them for consideration by the wider church. The subsequent Western pneumatological tradition, however, promulgates his views, although without intending to move beyond the universal faith of the 4th century. Beginning in Spain and Southern Gaul, and at least by the Third Synod of Toledo in 587, the *filioque* doctrine is raised to dogmatic status through its insertion into the Constantinopolitan Creed. However it is not a conscious intent on the part of the Western Church to insert *filioque* into the Latin version, and in so doing, alter unilaterally what is ecumenically canonized. The *Filioque* theology is useful as a weapon which the Spanish theologians of the Council of Toledo employ to protect and defend the divine consubstantiality of the Son with the Father against the heresies of Arianism associated with Macedonius, and Priscillianism associated with Sabellius. The discovery of Richard Haugh still rings true:

> It is strikingly clear that the Council of Toledo did not consciously alter the Ecumenical Creed. They obviously believed that the *Filioque* was included in the original Nicene-Constantinopolitan Creed. The *Filioque*, both as a doctrine and as found in various creedal statements and professions of faith, had so firmly rooted itself in the Latin West after Augustine that its authenticity and authority were simply taken for granted.[89]

Historically the Latin version of the Creed, containing the word *filioque*, may have been brought by Alcuin of York to the Court of Charlemagne. Charlemagne, in turn, promotes the addition of *filioque* through the Synods of Frankfurt (794) and Friuli (796). He even makes an attempt to persuade Pope Leo III to implement the practice as a norm in Rome (809), but fails. Pope Leo is more theologically inclined toward the Western formulation, although he insists on using the original formula, that the Spirit proceeds from the Father, simply for no other reason than the fact that he does not want to risk tampering with a conciliar text. The so-called Athanasian Creed (*Quicunque*), dated early sixth century, does not use the technical term *filioque*, yet the substances of which are incorporated in it.[90] Even though the doctrine is defended, the next five hundred years witness a sporadic use of the *filioque* in the liturgy. By 1014, however, this clause is included on papal authority as constitutive of the Western version of the Nicene Creed. So it is probably around this time, a few decades before the final schism between Latin West and Greek East, that the chanting of the Creed with the *Filioque* becomes a regular practice in Rome. The medieval Catholic Church's defence of *Filioque* as officially formulated at two Councils, Lateran IV (1215) and Florence (1438-1445), is traceable to Augustine, the greatest of the Latin fathers. Similar to Lateran IV, the Council of Florence professes that

> the Holy Spirit is eternally from the Father and the Son, and has His essence and his subsistent being from the Father and Son simultaneously, and proceeds from both eternally as from one principle and one spiration; we declare that what the holy Doctors and Fathers say, namely, that the Holy Spirit proceeds from the Father through the Son, tends to this meaning, that by this is signified that the Son is also according to the Greeks the cause, and according to the Latins the principle of the subsistence of the Holy Spirit, as is the Father also. And since all things which are the Father's, the Father has given to the Son in generating Him – except to be Father – so the Son has eternally from the Father that the Holy Spirit should proceed from the Son... In addition we define that the explication of those words *Filioque* has been lawfully and reasonably added to the Creed for the sake of declaring the truth and because of imminent necessity.[91]

Chapter Two

The necessary reasons for *Filioque*
Anselm of Canterbury

Anselm of Canterbury (1093), often ranked as the father of scholasticism, seeks to explore the logical status of Christian dogmas such as the Trinity and incarnation. Anselm adopts Augustine's first principle: to understand, by the use of reason, what he believes. Elsewhere he declares: 'I thank you (God), because what I already believed by your grace I now understand by your illumination, to the point that if I refused to believe it, my understanding would force me to recognize it.'[1] He is affirmative about the ability of the human mind to demonstrate the rationality and thus the logical necessity of all Christian doctrines, believing that reason and revelation are both gifts of God. He is best known for his 'ontological argument' for the existence of God in his *Proslogion*. He is also remembered for his formulations of a 'proof' of the dogma of two-nature Christology in his *Cur Deus Homo?*, resulting in what comes to be known as the 'Satisfaction theory' of the atonement. Not only God's existence, argues Anselm, but also God's nature as triune can be proven. The *Monologion* represents the extended attempt to find such arguments for it. This is not to say that he tries to prove philosophically that God's being is constituted as triune; rather he attempts to show, in his *De incarnatione Verbi* and *De processione Sancti Spiritus*, that the doctrine of God's triunity, an article of faith, is at least rationally grounded and logically consistent.[2]

Augustine's profound approach and insights into the doctrine of the Trinity, especially the *filioque*, constitutes the foundation and shape of the later Latin theological tradition beginning with Anselm, Aquinas right through to the Franciscan school and many of the late Protestant reformers.[3] The doctrine of *filioque*, which originates with the Latin tradition, re-emerges in Anselm's theological reflection, but as an elaborated defense. The Father, who is without beginning, is the principle of the Son and the Spirit. The Son comes from a principle – the Father, but is himself, together with the Father, the principle of the Holy Spirit. The Holy Spirit is not the principle of another. To avoid collapsing the personal distinctions in the Trinity with the essence common to all three, Anselm turns to the definition of the persons by relationships – an understanding which is already in Augustine and the Greeks. This chapter seeks to provide an exposition of Anselm's *filioque*, showing that he belongs essentially to the Western tradition.

Una substantia, tres personae

Influenced by Platonic philosophy, Augustine has as his point of departure the unity of the Godhead. Unlike the Cappadocians whose starting-point is persons (*hypostases*), Augustine gives primacy to the one indivisible divine substance (*substantia*). This he states very clearly at the outset of his *De Trinitate*. 'We shall undertake,' he writes, 'to the best of our ability ... to account for the one and only and true God being a Trinity, and for the rightness of saying, believing, understanding that the Father and the Son and the Holy Spirit are of one and the same substance or essence.'[4] He affirms the teaching of the Catholic tradition, according to which 'Father and Son and Holy Spirit in the inseparable equality of one substance present a divine unity; and there are not three gods but one God.'[5] God is substantively one, but is relationally distinct. Father, Son and Spirit exist in a differentiated unity of the one indivisible essence, thereby forming a con-substantial triad.

Anselm does not deviate from Augustine's description of God as one substance, and three persons *(una substantia, tres personae)*. In his letter to John the Monk concerning his opponent, Roscelin, he argues potently that three persons do not mean three gods, a position which he ascribes to Roscelin.[6] He takes great pains to point out that the divine substance cannot lose its simplicity; it cannot be divided into parts. In God, one is three; three is one. However he oscillates in the usage of these terms, substance and persons, because of the uneasiness these terms convey. In his *Monologion* preface, he attributes to the Greeks the concept of God existing as three substances in one person.[7] In the last chapters of the same, he goes so far as to identify *substantia* with *personae*, seemingly willing to describe God as either three persons or three substances. For the early Scholastics, the term substance is ordinarily applied to individual beings, which especially are subject to accidents.[8] Anselm sees in this an inadequacy to express the notion of the unity of a thing as it undergoes change. But the Supreme Being, to which the idea of accidents is inadmissible, cannot be called, Anselm explains, a substance, except as the word *substance* is used in the same sense with the word *Essence* or *being*.[9] Hence on the ground of this 'rational necessity, the Supreme Trinity which is one, or Supreme Unity, which is trine, can irreproachably be called one being and three persons or three substances.'[10] So having spoken of the unity of the essence, it is necessary to speak about an essence and about three persons or three substances. Also the term person fails to represent the notion of plurality in the Trinity, for this term usually refers to individuals existing separately from each other. In the Trinity, the three distinct persons do not exist as three independent individuals. Compelled by the lack of an appropriate term, Anselm uses person but with reservation. Augustine, having recognized the ineffability of the tripersonal God, and the limitation of human language, writes, 'But the formula "three persons" has been coined, not in order to give a complete explanation by means of it, but in order that we might not be obliged to remain silent.'[11] Likewise Anselm affirms: there is 'a unity because of the unity of essence; a trinity, because of the three I know not what (*trinitatem propter tres nescio quid*).'[12] Truly, therefore, God remains ineffably One and Three. In spite of his oscillation, Anselm in the body of his *Monologion*, rejects the Greek rendering of God as existing as one person in favour of God as existing as one essence or nature. His definitive position, reminiscent of the language of his *Monologion* preface, is clearly stated in *De Incarnatione Verbi*, where he writes: 'The Latins call these three persons, the Greeks (three) substances. For just as we say that in God there is one substance and three persons, so they say one person and three substances. But they mean by "substance" what we means by "person", so that in faith they do not differ from us in any respect.'[13]

Although the persons in the Trinity are distinguished, they are not separate, because each is essentially God. If Roscelin is saying that there are three Gods, then God is more than one substance. This would disrupt the simplicity of the divine essence, thereby violating the Boethian idea, that what is simple is greater than what is composite. One cannot conceive of, Anselm argues, anything greater than God, and likewise cannot conceive of plurality of substance, essence or nature in the highest Good. God has no parts; there is no partition in God's essence; the divine essence is indivisibly one. The highest Good must necessarily be wholly one, not many. Father, Son and Holy Spirit do not differ as God, for they are co-eternal, co-equal, and co-exist in a con-substantial triad. They differ in the way each person is God in relation to the others. Augustine's remark, 'God is everything that he has except for the relations through which each person is referred to the other', is picked up by Anselm.[14] In his *De Incarnatione Verbi*, Anselm takes issue with Roscelin's miscontrual of the three persons in God. Roscelin asserts that the three persons are only one 'thing' (*res*), not three things, regarding which Anselm accuses him of Sabellianism – a position which abolishes the personal distinctions in the Trinity. Roscelin's position is this: God is but one person who assumes three different modes of being; there are not three persons in God, for they have the same substance; they have the same characteristics of relation, in virtue of which Father and Spirit are said to be incarnate with the Son. If the three persons are one thing, not three separate things, like three angels, and if they share a commonality of power and will, says Roscelin, then the Father and the Holy Spirit must be incarnate with the Son. This, argues Anselm, constitutes a repudiation of the Christian faith, which affirms that Father, Son and Holy Spirit are numerically one with respect to his essence, but numerically three with respect to his persons. This relational dynamism in the same Godhead allows the incarnation of the Son, the assumption of humanity 'not into a unity of nature but into a unity of person', yet without necessitates the incarnation of all three. In Anselm's words:

> For my opponent (Roscelin) does not deny that there are several persons, since he admits that they are distinct from one another. If they were not different from one another, they would not be several. ...The Father and the Son, therefore, are not several or different from each

other with respect to substance – for they are not two substances. The Father is not one substance and the Son another; rather, the Father and the Son are the one and the same substance. However, with respect to person, they were several and different from each other – for the Father and the Son are not one and the same person, but two persons who are different from each other. My opponent says: "If the Son was incarnate, and is not a different thing from the Father, but is numerically one and the same thing as the Father, then the Father also must have been incarnate. For it is impossible for a thing which is numerically one and the same both to be and not to be at the same time incarnate in the same man." To this I reply that if the Son is incarnate, and if the Son is not numerically one and the same person as the Father, but another person, then it is not necessary for the Father also to be incarnate. For it is possible for one person to be incarnate in one man and for another person not to be incarnate in this same man together with Him. ... For whoever accepts His incarnation rightly, believes that he assumed manhood not into a unity of nature but into a unity of person.[15]

There abides in Anselm a sharp distinction between substantival unity of deity and personal unity of humanity. The incarnation pertains to the personal unity, that the Son of God assumes humanity into his person, not his nature. The plurality of persons makes it impossible for the Father to be incarnate together with the Son.

Furthermore Roscelin's error lies in his blurring Augustine's distinction between those attributes – his omnipotence, benevolence, eternity – which are proper to God's unity and those attributes – Fatherhood, Sonship, and so on – which are proper to individual persons.[16] Anselm writes: 'Those things which are common to them – like omnipotence, eternity – are understood to belong only to their unity, and those things which are proper to them individually – like "begetter" or "begetting" to the Father or "word" and "begotten" to the Son – are signified by these two names, that is, those of Father and Son.'[17] The context here has to do with the relationship of signification which obtains between *res* and *verbum*. When the words 'Father' or 'Son' are mentioned, we understand the *res* unique to each, for instance, 'begetter' or 'the one who is begotten.' When the word 'God' is used, we understand it to signify that which is common to all the persons as God. So when we say the two persons are two 'things', avers Anselm, we are predicating a relation in respect to that which is peculiar to each, but not that of one being to another, in which case it entails two substances or beings – a position he ascribes to Roscelin. That the *res* itself is, paradoxically, both one and three, is a deep mystery but Anselm sees no mystery over its specific application.

Anselm's treatment of the procession of the Holy Spirit falls into two parts: first, by way of logical argument; second, by working out the implications of the Scriptural texts.

Filioque: A Rational Argument

Filioque is required in order to establish a proper distinction between the Son and the Spirit. Anselm, following Augustine, contends that, necessarily, the divine persons are distinguished by relations of origin. Without this relation between the Son and the Spirit, they cannot be said in any sense to be distinct from each other. Although the Franciscan theologian Duns Scotus agrees with Augustine and Anselm that persons are distinguished by their relations of origin, he rejects the necessity of such a relation to obtain a distinction between the Son and the Spirit.[18] With the Greeks, Scotus asserts: that which distinguishes the Son from the Spirit is his peculiar property of begottenness; conversely, the peculiar property of Spirit as proceeding distinguishes him from the Son. The distinction between divine persons is adequately explained by virtue of the unique properties each possesses. What distinguishes the persons, therefore, was not so much their opposing relations of origin as their different ways in which the Son and Spirit proceed from the Father. The difference between these two modes of origin constitutes the basis for distinguishing between the Son and the Spirit. Contrarily, Anselm sees the distinction as deriving from relationships of origin. The persons are distinguished because they are related to one another as source and derivation from source, and yet one source.[19] The Spirit's distinction from the Son is obtainable only if the one is the source of the other. In his work against the Greeks, Anselm stresses the equality of the Father and the Son as source, the former being the principal source and the latter being a derivative source. For Augustine, the Spirit proceeds in a 'principal' sense from the

Father (*de Patre principaliter*), but also in a 'derivative' sense from the Son. This shows the *filioque* is defensible, in that the procession of the Spirit from the Father is inseparable from the relation between the Father and the Son. Anselm argues that *filioque* is not only defensible, but also necessary. He does not repudiate Augustine's *principaliter a patre*, but places it within the framework, in which the Son's begetting and the Spirit's procession are understood against an identity of essence and an equality of divinity, both of which are intrinsic to the divinity.[20] The Father communicates his spirative power to the Son so that the Son is also the ontological cause of the Spirit. Governed by *una substantia* as his prolegomena, and alike Augustine, Anselm affirms that the Spirit proceeds from the Father and the Son, as from one principle, *a Patre Filioque tanquam ad uno principio*. The Spirit exists not from two sources but from one source, i.e. he exists from the one Godness of the Father and of the Son. There is a fatherly cause as well as a sonly cause, yet one cause due to one essence common to both. The Son, who receives his being from the Father, participates as the Father's agent in the causal derivation of the Spirit. Therefore being and acting in this derivative manner does not entail a rejection of an equality of divinity in the production of the Spirit. Anselm writes of this:

> The Holy Spirit comes from that in which the Father and the Son are one, that is, from God, not from that in which they differ from each other.... and because the Father is neither before nor after the Son, neither greater nor lesser, and because the one is neither more nor less God than the other, the Holy Spirit is not from the Father before (being from) the Son. If, then, it is said that the Holy Spirit comes from the Father as the principle, nothing more than this is meant: the Son himself, from whom the Spirit comes, has it from the Father that the Spirit comes from him.[21]

The Son forms with the Father a single co-principle in the spiration of the Spirit — an understanding exactly opposite to the monopatrism of the Eastern Church, which affirms the monarchy of the Father. Seemingly unaware of the importance the Eastern fathers give to the formula *a Patre per filium*, from the Father through the Son, Anselm writes:

> As the Father and the Son do not differ in the unity of the deity and as the Holy Spirit only proceeds from the Father as the deity, if that deity is similarly in the Son, it is not possible to see how the Spirit would proceed from the deity of the Father through the deity of the Son and not (immediately) from that same deity of the Father, but from his fatherhood, and that he proceeds through the sonship of the Son and not through his deity – but that idea is clearly stupid.[22]

Anselm looks for analogies from the created order which will illuminate the mystery of triunity. One of these is the 'Nile image', in which the Persons of the Trinity are likened to the spring, flowing through the river into a lake.[23] The spring is not the river nor is the lake; the lake is not the spring nor is the river. Yet the spring is the Nile; the river is the Nile; and the lake is the Nile. Collectively the three are called Nile, for the three is predicated of one complete whole. Yet there are not three Niles, but only one. The Nile is one nature, one watercourse predicated of all three. The spring, the river, and the lake are three distinct things, which are not predicated of one another. However, the spring does not exist from the river or from the lake; the river exists only from the spring, not from the lake; the lake exists from both the spring and the river. In other words, the whole river exists from the whole spring; the whole lake exists from the whole river and the whole spring. Transposed this image trinitarianly, it means the Son exists from the Father; the Holy Spirit exists from the Father and the Son in another way, so that the Holy Spirit is not the Son, but one who proceeds. The Holy Spirit does not come from nobody, *nullo*; He is from the Father and the Son, not as Father and Son, but as God. The Holy Spirit is not the Father nor is the Son; yet he is what the Father and the Son are – viz., God. Abiding here is a unity without distinction in respect to the divine essence, and also a unity with distinction in respect to the persons; the former is logically prior to the latter. The divine essence, not the Father, is the ultimate source of the other persons.

This image is also found in the Greek fathers, who use it to express their idea of the Spirit (lake) proceeding through the Son (river), not from the Father (spring) and Son (river) conjointly. Gregory of Nyssa, for example, admits that the Son could be the cause of the Spirit not in the same absolute sense as the Father is, but only in a secondary sense, that the Spirit is said to proceed from the Father 'through' the Son.²⁴ The Greeks reason that although the lake comes from the river, it does not proceed from the river; rather it accumulates from the river. So even if the Holy Spirit exists from the Son, he cannot be properly said to proceed from the Son; rather he is properly understood to proceed from the Father, as from his source of origin. This reasoning, says Anselm, is valid only insofar as the Son, in being begotten from the Father proceeds 'outside' the Father, and if there exists a 'spatial interval' between the Holy Spirit existing from the Father 'before' existing from the Son. 'For the river flowing from the spring proceeds outside the spring and after an interval accumulates into a lake.' An interval occurs between the lake existing from the spring 'before' existing from the river. So the lake exists from the spring through the river, not from the spring and river as from one source. Anselm's reply is this: the image, in the created order, may not convey the latter idea; but in the uncreated order, the word *principaliter* takes on a different meaning within the deity. There is no lesser or later, before or after, no intervals, no grades or degrees in God. Things must be different in God, for one cannot separate the Son from the Father because the Son is in the Father, and is in no way different from him in essence. Just as the lake does not exist from that by reason of which the spring and the river differ from each other but exists from the water in virtue of which they are the same, so the Holy Spirit does not exist from that by reason of which the Father and the Son differ from each other, but from the divine substance in which they are one. The origin is neither person taken by himself, but the divine essence which both persons possess – the Father has it in himself, the Son has it from the Father. He continues his argument in the line of Augustine: 'But in being begotten from the Father, the Son does not pass outside the Father but remains within Him and does not differ from the Father spatially or temporally or essentially; moreover, that from which the Holy Spirit proceeds is one and the same for the Father and the Son.'²⁵ Since God exists from 'within' God, not 'outside' God, all three persons retain in their deity a singularity. Heron clarifies: 'The origin of the Spirit lies in the divinity shared by the Father and the Son, not in their relationship: he cannot therefore proceed in one way from the Father and in another way through the Son, for this would make the differentiation between the Father and the Son ontologically prior to his own being.'²⁶ Thus the *filioque*, far from dividing the Godhead into two separate sources, safeguards its fundamental unity. Even though the Spirit does not proceed from the Son in the same way as from the Father, it is vitally necessary that we name the Father and the Son together in affirming his procession; otherwise we might exclude the Spirit from the ontologically fundamental unity. In chapter one of his *De Processione Spiritus Sancti*, Anselm firmly counters Greek theologians in defence of the *filioque*. He draws two basic expressions: (A) 'God from whom God exists' and (B) 'God from God.'[27] In Anselm's words:

> God the Father is *A* because the Son is begotten from Him and because the Holy Spirit proceeds from Him; He is not *B*, since He neither proceeds nor is begotten. God the Son is *B* since He is begotten; and He is *A* since the Holy Spirit proceeds also from Him. God the Holy Spirit is *B* since He proceeds from the Father and the Son; but He is not *A*, since neither the Father nor the Son proceeds from Him or is begotten from Him.[28]

In the second chapter of the same, Anselm, following Augustine, makes a distinction between the Holy Spirit as immanently 'proceeding' and as economically 'sent' or 'given.' Here the relation between the immanent Trinity and the economic Trinity is brought into view, the former being the presupposition of the latter. A correspondence, not a difference, occurs between the immanent proceeding and economic giving or sending. For the Son to be sent is to be referred to his origin from the Father; likewise for the Holy Spirit to be sent or given is to be referred to his procession from the Father and the Son. Anselm relates the eternal generation of the Son and eternal procession of the Spirit on the one hand to the temporal missions of the Son and the Spirit in the world on the other. The Holy Spirit exists by proceeding from the Father eternally, as having his being from him. But he is given or sent by the Son to the creatures. This giving or sending is also eternal in relation to the Holy Spirit, although this giving or sending happens in time. If the Holy Spirit proceeds only by existing from the Father, he argues, he must also exist by proceeding from the Son, because he is God from God, and the Son is God. The Holy Spirit proceeds from the Father, and since the Father is God, the Eastern Creed sufficiently declares that the Holy Spirit proceeds from God. In similar fashion, Anselm intimates: 'when the Creed says that the Holy Spirit proceeds from God, then since the Son is God, the Creed indicates plainly that the Holy Spirit proceeds from the Son.' What the Spirit receives from the Father is his being God, which is precisely what the Father and the Son have in common – the Father and the Son are one God. 'Therefore, if the Holy Spirit exists from the Father because He exists from God, who is Father, then since He exists from God, who is Son, He cannot be denied to exist also from the Son.'[29] Along the line of Augustine, Anselm affirms: just as the Son is begotten of the Father, yet does not depart but remains in the same Godhead with the Father, and is one God with him, so also the Holy Spirit proceeds from the Father and is sent by the Son, yet does not depart but remains with the Father and the Son in the same Godhead, and is one God with both.

To reconcile unity and plurality in God, Anselm coins the famous phrase which the Council of Florence later elevates to dogmatic status: 'unity does not lose its consequence unless some opposition of relation stands in the way' (*ubi non obviat aliqua relationis oppositio*).[30] With Augustine, Anselm affirms: 'everything in God is identical except where there are opposed relations of origin (as there are in Father, Son and Holy Spirit).'[31] The relations of the Father, the Son and the Spirit expressed distinctively in their names constitute their particular identities. Persons are three distinct ways of being one God. The relations, which denote their distinctive modes of origin, are irreversible. The only thing, he argues, that makes the Son not the Father is that he is begotten by him; the only thing that makes the Holy Spirit not the Father or the Son is that he proceeds from both. Thus the Son cannot be the Father, because he exists from the Father; the Holy Spirit cannot be the Father because he proceeds from the Father. But how are the Son and the Spirit really distinct? Only if the one proceeds from the other. Anselm resorts to the later medieval principle of the wholes and parts to explain the way in which 'God exists from God.' Either the whole exists from the whole or the part exists from the part; or else the whole exists from the part or a part exists from a whole. But God has no parts. The only adequate explanation for God to exist from God is the whole from whole. But if we argue that the Son exists from the whole of God, we must also concede that he exists from both the Father and the Holy Spirit; likewise the Holy Spirit, if he exists from the whole of

God, must exist from both the Father and the Son. The conclusion, that both the Son exists from the Holy Spirit and the Holy Spirit exists from the Son, is impossible because of the opposition of relations: The Son's (A) origin from the Spirit (B) precludes the Spirit's (B) origin from the Son (A). Here a set of anomalies would emerge in the 'existing from' as operating between the Son and the Holy Spirit. Anselm resolves it by speaking of two different ways of being 'God from God.' If the Holy Spirit is 'begotten' of the Son, he argues, then the Holy Spirit would be the Son's son as the Son is the Father's. Thus the Spirit exists from the Son as he exists from the Father by 'procession', not by generation. Now either the Holy Spirit exists from the Son or the Son exists from the Holy Spirit. Anselm argues for the former, contending that the Son is not begotten of the Holy Spirit, because if he were, the Holy Spirit would be his father. But the Holy Spirit is not the Father. The Son does not proceed from the Holy Spirit, because if he were, he would be the son of the Holy Spirit. Therefore by 'unassailable reason', the Holy Spirit must proceed from the Son as He is from the Father.[32] Just as the Son cannot be really distinct from the Father unless he exists (proceeds) from the Father by begetting, so the Holy Spirit cannot be really distinct from the Son unless he exists from the Son by proceeding.[33] The relation of the Father (the begetter) and the Son (the begotten) is such that if the Holy Spirit exists by proceeding from the Father, he too exists by proceeding from the Son. The principle of the ontological unity of the Godhead is to be maintained insofar as it does not infringe the distinct characteristics of the individual persons. So there can be no Father except the Father of the Son, no Son except the Son of the Father, and no Holy Spirit other than the Spirit of the Father and the Son. Evans summarizes Anselm's unity-trinity dialectic:

> His (Anselm's) argument turns on symmetry. Only if the Spirit proceeds from the Father and the Son do we have a situation in which each person of the Trinity is peculiar to himself and each has an attribute which he shares with the other two. Only the Son has a Father; only the Father has a Son; only the Spirit does not have a Spirit proceeding from himself. But both the Father and the Spirit do not have a Father; both the Spirit and the Son do not have a Son; and both the Father and the Son have a Spirit proceeding from themselves.[34]

Anselm uses Augustine's 'psychological' model of the trinity – memory, intelligence, and love – to furnish a logical explanation of how the distinction of persons accords with the unity of essence in God.[35] Augustine sees in the human image merely a reflection of the divine. However Anselm goes beyond Augustine, providing instead a metaphysical account of what transpires within a 'Supreme Spirit' (Father). The Supreme Spirit knows itself; the resultant self-knowledge is the Son; it also, in the dyadic form of the Father and the Son, loves itself, and the resultant self-love is the Holy Spirit. Anselm observes a parallelism between the effect of the Supreme Spirit's self-knowledge and the effect of its self-love. The Supreme Spirit loves itself, regarding which he writes, 'But, lo, as I contemplate with delight the distinguishing properties of the Father and the Son, together with what they have in common, I find in the Father and the Son nothing more delightful reflection upon than the affection of mutual love.'[36] Just as God may be thought to remember and understand himself, he is also thought to love himself, so that 'if the Father is referred to as the memory of the Supreme Spirit, and if the Son ... as the understanding of the Supreme Spirit, then it is obvious that the love of the Supreme Spirit proceeds equally from the Father and the Son.'[37] The Father and the Son love themselves, and each other with an equal love. This Love is as great as the Supreme Spirit, and hence it is the Supreme Spirit (or Being). To quote Anselm:

> But what can be equal to the Supreme Spirit except the Supreme Spirit? Hence, this Love is the Supreme Spirit. In fact, if there never had been a creature – i.e., if nothing had ever existed other than the Supreme Spirit, who is Father and Son – nonetheless, the Father and the Son would still have loved themselves and each other. Hence, it follows that this Love is identical with what the Father and the Son are, viz., the Supreme Being. Now, since there cannot be many supreme beings, what is more necessary than that the Father, the Son, and their Love be one Supreme Being? Therefore, this Love is the Supreme Wisdom, the Supreme Truth, the Supreme Good, and whatever else can be predicated of the substance of the Supreme Spirit.[38]

Likewise the love of the Supreme Spirit proceeds from the Father and the Son, not as two loves, but as one and the same whole. Just as the Supreme Spirit generates the Son by an act of self-knowledge, so too does the Supreme Spirit, now existing as dyad – as Father (or memory) and Son (or intelligence), produces the Holy Spirit (love) by an act of self-love. The Son as the Father's eternal self-expression is not identical with the Father because he is begotten as thought is begotten by intellect. The Father and the Son are mutually related as mind and thought are. Strictly speaking, they are one as to essence or being, but distinct as to modality or relation. 'Two such relations within one essential, intellectual being must have a third as the love that binds them together and that is the Holy Spirit – the third relation within the divine essence that proceeds eternally from both the Father (lover) and the Son (beloved).'[39] The Divinity's love of itself, a parallel to the divinity's knowledge of itself, produces the third person. 'Since all things in God are perfect and simple, the love "breathed forth" as Spirit by Father and Son, Mind and Word', Daley explains, 'is co-extensive with them both; love, according to I John 4, is what God is, so that the Holy Spirit, as love, is precisely the "supreme essence" as shared by the Father and the Son, given not in virtue of the personal qualities of either of them, but "in virtue of their being".'[40] What is crucial for Anselm is this: the origin of the Holy Spirit is not rooted in the mutual love between the Father and the Son, but in love as the divine essence shared by both – viz., their one Godness of love. 'For the Father and the Son equally send forth such a great good not from their relations, which are plural (the one relation is that of Father, the other that of Son), but from their essence, which does not admit of plurality.'[41] This is in keeping with Anselm's dominant emphasis on the principle of unity – the 'one nature, highest of all the things that are, alone sufficient unto itself in its eternal beatitude.'[42]

Filioque: An Exegetical Foundation

Augustine does not seek to substantiate his *filioque* from Scripture, although one could find in him scriptural foundation for it.[43] Anselm goes further than Augustine, seeking to justify his *filioque* exegetically. The New Testament, he argues, witnesses to the Spirit as being the Spirit of both of the Father and the Son. His argument for the *filioque* is based primarily on a number of texts which the polemicists tend to ignore.[44] He attacks the Eastern exegesis for isolating John 15:26 from the wider context of texts. He argues that John 14:26, 'whom the Father will send in my name', must be taken together with John 15:26, 'whom I will send to you from the Father.'[45] Whereas the Eastern Church focuses on the part of John 15:26 – 'who goes out from the Father' – to argue for a single procession of the Spirit, Anselm insists that the two verses, when read together, reveal that each person sends the Spirit on behalf of the other. The Father sends the Spirit in the name of the Son; the Son also sends the Spirit in the name of the Father. The Spirit is sent, therefore, from the (single) name of both Father and Son. The Son with the Father constitutes the co-principle and co-sender of the Holy Spirit. In Anselm's words:

> So what does 'whom the Father will send in my name' mean except that whom the Father will send the Son also will send? – just as when the Son says 'whom I shall send from the Father,' nothing else is meant except 'I and the Father shall send.' For 'Son' is the name of Him who said 'the Father will send in my name.' Therefore, 'the Father will send in my name' means only 'the Father will send in the name of the Son.' Hence, what does 'the Father will send in the name of the Son' mean except that the Father will send as if the Son were sending, so that when the Father sends, the Son is understood to send. But how are the Son's words 'whom I shall send from the Father' to be interpreted? Assuredly, the Holy Spirit is sent from Him from whom the Son sends Him. Now, the Son sends Him from the Father. Therefore, the Holy Spirit is sent from the Father. But the one from whom the Holy Spirit is sent sends (the Holy Spirit). Hence, when the Son says, 'I shall send from the Father,' the Father is understood to send. So what does 'I shall send from the Father' mean except 'I shall send as if the Father were sending, so that my sending and the Father's sending are one and the same'?[46]

The economical sending of the Spirit, in Anselm, is rooted in the immanental relationships of the Trinity. The Son sends the Spirit from the Father. The Spirit who is 'sent' from the Father also 'proceeds' from the Father. Thus being sent and proceeding belong to the same order of reality, according to which the sending of the Spirit by the Father mirrors the procession from the Father, and in like manner, the sending of the Spirit by the Son also mirrors the procession from the Son. Anselm clarifies, 'Now, if "proceeding" meant being given or sent, then it would be as true that the Holy Spirit proceeds from the Son as that he proceeds from the Father, since He is likewise given and sent by the Son.'[47] This means that the economic relations of the Trinity corresponds to the ontological relations of the Godhead, therefore accentuating the knowledge of God as he is in himself.

Anselm also deduces the *filioque* doctrine from Matt. 11:27, 'No one knows the Son except the Father, nor does anyone know the Father except the Son and anyone to whom the Son chooses to reveal him.'[48] John 10:30 ('I and the Father are one') affirms the identity of essence between the Father and the Son, which is the ground of their mutual knowledge. The Son says about the Holy Spirit in John 16:13: 'He will not speak on His own authority, but whatsoever He will hear that will He speak.' This means that the Holy Spirit must have received knowledge of the Father and the Son about which He will speak. But how does he receive the things of God other than 'his essence' which is one with the Father and the Son? 'He exists (*habet essentiam*) from the one (the Son) from whom He hears what He speaks and teaches'?[49] This assertion is reinforced by John 16:14, where the Son says, 'He (the Holy Spirit) will glorify me because He will receive from me and will declare unto you.' This shows clearly that the Son himself is the one from whom the Holy Spirit receives his knowledge and his essence, otherwise he would be less than the Son (and the Father), and therefore not God. Anselm elaborates: 'He (the Son) shows plainly that the Holy Spirit exists (*essentiam habere*) and proceeds from Himself (i.e., from his own essence). For what is not divine essence is inferior to the Holy Spirit; and the Holy Spirit does not receive something from that which is inferior to Himself. Therefore, when the Son says, "He will receive from me," He signifies here nothing of His own except His own essence.'[50]

The New Testament indisputably associates the Spirit closely with Christ. John 15:26 must not be understood in isolation but in relation to John 20:22-23, where the Risen Christ 'breathes' upon the disciples and says, 'Receive the Holy Spirit.'[51] Here Anselm's interpretation is dependent on Augustine's distinction between the sign and the thing signified, which mirrors the biblical truth that

God accommodates himself to meet us in visible signs.[52] Scripture signifies a hidden thing by means of the 'likeness', not 'identity', to perceptible things; that which signifies and that which is signified are not 'alike in all respects.' Anselm has the Risen Christ say: 'Just as you see this breath – through which I signify to you the Holy Spirit (imperceptible things being able to be signified by perceptible things) – proceeds from the depths of my body and from my person, so know that the Holy Spirit whom I signify to you through this breath, proceeds from the hiddenness of my deity and from the person.'[53] And yet the person of the Word and of the man is one, in whom are two natures, viz. a divine and human nature. The Holy Spirit is revealed to and recognized by us in this peculiar form of the 'breath.' Based on these texts, Ps. 32:6; 33:6; Isa. 11:4; Ezek. 36:26-27; and II Thess. 2:8, he draws the conclusion that the Holy Spirit is signified by these phrases: 'the breath of the Lord's mouth (Father's)', by whose words the heavens are established; 'the breath of the Lord Jesus' mouth', by whose words the wicked are killed; and 'the breath of Jesus' lips', by which he converts the wicked. The efficacy does not lie in audible words and perceptible breath, but in the thing they signify, i.e., the Holy Spirit, by whom God speaks and acts. God employs the selected elements of his created order (e.g. breath) as his instrument of power to effect his saving will. If we maintain with the Greeks to understand 'Father's mouth' as the Father's 'essence', out of which proceeds his word and his breath, he argues, 'what is clearer than that just as the breath of the Father's mouth exists and proceeds from the Father's essence, so the breath of the Son's mouth and lips exists and proceeds from the Son's essence?'[54] Therefore one must concede that the Holy Spirit proceeds equally from Him (Son) of whose mouth and lips He is called the breath.

The New Testament puts the Holy Spirit in close proximity with Christ in such a way that the Person and work of the Spirit are to be understood via the Person and work of Christ. However could one reverse the order, defining the Person and the work of Christ in terms of the Spirit? Didn't Luke 4:18ff speak of Christ as the designated Son of God by the descent of the Spirit on him at his Baptism? Christ himself claims that 'the Spirit of the Lord is upon me.' In addition, both Matt. 1:20 and Luke 1:35 ascribe his virgin birth to the work of the Holy Spirit, implying that Christ is 'of the Spirit' just as much as the Spirit is 'of Christ.' All these verses, he argues, point to the operation of the Spirit in virtue of Christ's humanity, not his divinity. The Spirit's descent on him at Baptism is his commissioning to achieve the work of redemption via the concrete unity of his two natures, but with an emphasis on his humanity. The Spirit's work in his birth is to prepare the humanity for its union with the Word, endowing it with his presence in that union. What is ascribed to the Holy Spirit in the virgin birth is the assumption of humanity into unity with God in the Logos' mode of existence. Furthermore the Son himself speaks through the prophet: 'And now the Lord God and His Spirit have sent me' (Isa. 48:16) – this, for the Greeks, clearly means that the Holy Spirit also sends the Son, concluding that the Son exists from the Spirit. To this objection, Anselm replies that this verse applies also to 'the human nature assumed by the Son, who by the common will and ordinance of the Father and the Spirit' appears in order to achieve the work of redemption.[55] It pleases the Father, the Son and the Spirit that the Son alone be the one to assume our flesh, subsequently to be anointed with the Spirit in his concrete salvation history of obedience. Jesus' anointing with the Spirit is an implication of the hypostatic union. *Filioque* doctrine thus requires that the hypostatic union is the presupposition, not the consequence of Jesus' anointing with the Spirit. Whereas the activity of the Word is primary in the Incarnation, the activity of the Spirit is posterior to it, and is logically, if not chronologically, dependent on it.

In order to affirm the Son's participation with the Father in the causal procession of the Holy Spirit, the Greeks maintain that the Holy Spirit proceeds from the Father 'through' the Son (*per filium*) instead of 'from' the Son (*a Filio*).[56] Their key text, which Anselm wonders speculatively, is Roman 11:36, where Apostle Paul says, 'All things are from Him and through Him and in Him.' Beyond dispute is the Credal assertion that 'all things' means 'all divinely created beings', which exist 'through the Son.' What is created by the Father through the Son may also be said to have been created by the Son, for the Scripture teaches, 'Whatever the Father does, this the Son does likewise' (Jn. 5:19). From this instance, he sees no conceptual difference between the two expressions, *a filio* and *per filium*, which are interchangeably one. Consequently if the Holy Spirit proceeds from the deity of the Father 'through' the deity of the Son, then since the Father and the Son have the same essence, he can also proceed 'from' the deity of the Son. However deeper problems arise when the Greeks include in the designation 'all things' the Holy Spirit to justify his origin *per filium*. This interpretation, he argues, collapses the distinction between the created beings and the uncreated being. Anselm writes: "Whatever is created is not identical with God, but different from Him.'[57] The Holy Spirit is not different from God, but is one and the same God as the Father and the Son, therefore cannot be identified with or reduced to any divinely created beings. Furthermore he rejects Greek exegesis on this verse, contending that if the Holy Spirit is included among 'all things' which Paul states to exist through the Son, so too are the Father and the Son. For to include any one person of the three among all things and to exclude the other two is inconceivable.[58] In short, Anselm concludes, the Eastern Church has no basis in Scripture for denying the *filioque*.

Concluding Remarks

The aforementioned shows that Anselm opts for the Western procession model of *filioque*, denying the Eastern procession model of *per filium* and monopatrism. Augustine's *De Trinitate* is the major influence of Anselm's *filioque*. In his *Prologus* to *Monologion*, Anselm admits his indebtedness to Augustine:

> As often I examined this work, I could find nothing in it which was not in harmony with the writings of the Catholic fathers and especially St. Augustine. For this reason, if it seems to anyone that I have proposed anything in this small work which is either new or dissents from the truth, I ask that he not immediately denounce me as a rash innovator or a vile prevaricator, but that he first attentively check the books of the aforementioned teacher Augustine, *De Trinitate*, and then judge my little work by them.[59]

However the *filioque* model is not without criticisms. Augustine interpreters, Marsh and Gunton, contend that Augustine errs in grounding his thought on the Trinity in the unity of divine substance. Marsh charges that Augustine has abandoned the earlier Latin tradition's 'strong sense of divine monarchy – the one God is first and foremost the Father' for the 'one God to mean the divine substance or nature which then is verified in Father, Son and Holy Spirit.'[60] By separating the substance from the persons, and in giving primacy to the former, Augustine ends up discarding 'the concept of *taxis* or order from its central place in the traditional understanding of the Triad', thereby introducing 'an impersonal concept of God.'[61] This shift of emphasis also confronts him with the problem of how to conceive distinctions in God without implying modalism.[62] Gunton's criticism of Augustine springs mainly from his deep appreciation of the Cappadocians, who in his view, have wisely perceived God's being as ontologically relational, in virtue of which there is no divine substance or essence behind, supporting the hypostatic relations. 'For them, the three persons are what they are in their relations, and therefore the relations qualify them ontologically, in terms of what they are.'[63] By viewing 'relation as a logical rather than an ontological predicate', Augustine is 'precluded from being able to make claims about the being of the particular persons, who, because they lack distinguishable identity tend to disappear into the all-embracing oneness of God.'[64] In Gunton's estimation, Augustine 'either did not understand the trinitarian theology of his predecessors, both East and West, or looked at their works with spectacles so strongly tinted with neo-platonic assumptions that they have distorted his work.'[65]

At basic level, the same criticisms levelled against Augustine may also be levelled against Anselm. That is, Anselm also fails to see the relations between Father, Son, and Spirit as grounded in the ontology of God. Instead of conceiving God's being as constituted by their relatedness, Anselm puts the emphasis on the view of divine substance preceding or supporting the person, making it ontologically primary as Augustine does. By overstressing the ontological unity of God's being, Anselm may be criticized as tending towards modalism, absorbing the distinguishing identity of each individual person into the oneness of God's being. Anselm, undoubtedly, is keenly aware of this danger, and has tried as Augustine does before him, to move away from the limitations of analogy of memory, understanding and will. Such analogy sounds as though the one 'Supreme Spirit' is simply active in three modes, just as the one human mind is active in three modes without being truly three in itself. Although Anselm does not use the term *circumincession* (or *perichoresis*), the substances of the concept are found in him.[66] The patristic idea of *circumincession* grounds the persons' unity of essence so that each exists fully in the others, yet without exceeding the others. The Father is in the Son and in the Spirit common to him and the Son; the Son is in the Father and in this same Spirit; this common Spirit is in the Father and in the Son. By *perichoresis*, Anselm argues that each person of the Trinity possesses equally all the intellectual perfections; otherwise each person would not be fully God, in which case the unity of essence would be destroyed. The Father, for example, does not need the Son to understand. He states, 'We must not suppose that the Father can only remember through himself, while being able to understand only through the Son and to love only through His and the Son's Spirit … For each of these three singly is the Supreme Being … so perfectly that this Being … remembers, understands, and loves through itself.' For each person, by himself, is 'essentially memory, understanding, love, and whatever must be present in the Supreme Being.'[67] If each person is memory, understanding, and love, one may ask, does that not collapse the trinitarian distinctions in God? The significance of the Augustinian analogy, Levering writes, lies in the fact that it helps us see the intra-divine processions, *ad intra* life of God.[68] Thus when the Father is referred to as memory, this is not done in order to exclude the essential properties of understanding and loving from him; rather it is solely to specify the Father's unique place in the intra-divine processions that distinguish the persons. Speaking of the Father, for example, Anselm states, 'whatever he is, is only the begetter and the one from whom another proceeds.'[69] To avoid modalism, Anselm makes a helpful distinction between (A) begetting and proceeding which distinguish the persons; and (B) the three persons who exist in a perichoretic unity of essence so that these essential properties – remembering, understanding and loving – mutually coinhere, and are equally predicated of each of the persons. All three persons mutually share in the life of the others so that none is isolated or detached from the actions of the others. This is far from Modalism.

Despite the aforementioned criticisms, Anselm's *filioque* doctrine is worthy of assertion. First, in respect to the life of faith, it ties the Spirit closely to Christ. The work of the Holy Spirit is to communicate to us the gospel, that in Christ's cross and resurrection divine mercy has conquered divine wrath. The work of redemption is completed, and the benefits which Christ has acquired and won for us by his sufferings, death, and resurrection belong to us in faith. But this work remains hidden and is of no use to us unless God causes us to perceive and receive it. Not until the Holy Spirit comes to offer and apply to us this treasure of salvation, the work of Christ would have been all in vain. Thus he who spurns knowing the Father in the Son loses all knowledge of God. It is by the Holy Spirit that we are led to see God in the flesh, in whom the Father is mirrored. The God who came to us in Christ is indeed the same God who comes as the Holy Spirit. Redemption is accomplished by Christ, but the Holy Spirit carries his work incessantly until the last day. When considering the work of inculcating the benefits of Christ's cross and sufferings for our salvation, which is precisely the Spirit's, we must think of *filioque* in which the work of Son and the work of the Spirit are closely related. The foundation of their reality consists in the single essence (love) which all three share in a differentiated unity verified distinguishably as relations. In saying this, the Holy Spirit participates fully and equally in the mutual love between the Father and the Son, which he also conveys to the believer. God has revealed himself and opened to us the profundity of his sheer, boundless love. Moreover, none could come to recognize the Father's love were it not for the Lord Christ, who is the mirror of God's fatherly heart. But neither could we know of Christ's heart had it not been revealed by the Holy Spirit. The love that flows between the Father and the Son is the love of the atoning sacrifice of Calvary. In it God's forgiveness and God's self-offering coincide. Thus a denial of the *filioque*, says Bray, implies a denial of the Son's atoning love in the life of the believer, although Anselm does not explicitly draw such conclusion.[70]

Second, the *filioque* doctrine possesses its force in enabling contemporary theology to take seriously the divine life proper, that which transpires within God's interior life. Anselm does not develop his pneumatology within the framework of the history of salvation; he moves too quickly from the economic action to the eternal procession.[71] By the principle, that the temporal missions of the Trinity reflect the eternal relations of the Godhead, Anselm concludes that the New Testament witnesses to the Spirit as being the Spirit of both the Father and the Son. The relation between the Son and the Holy Spirit is not restricted to the temporal trinitarian relations within the economy of salvation, but belongs ontologically to the primal trinitarian relations; conversely, there already is an inner-trinitarian basis for the temporal sending of the Spirit through Jesus Christ, the Son of God. Moltmann, in his discussion of the *filioque* problem, recognizes how important this principle is for contemporary theological reflection which, if it is accepted, would lead to Anselm's position (although Moltmann himself proposes the opposite, that the Spirit proceeds 'from the Father of the Son' eternally). Moltmann makes a distinction between 'existence' and 'form': 'The Holy Spirit who proceeds from the Father of the Son and receives his "form" from the Father and the Son.'[72] This is a modified but acutely speculative version of the *filioque*, suggesting that the being (divinity) of the Spirit comes from the Father alone, but his person is from the relational form between the Father and the Son. Moltmann's view, Thompsom criticizes,

> ... is dubious theologically and unlikely to gain much acceptance since it introduces a further speculative suggestion as a possible solution. The distinction between existence and form is difficult to maintain. Moltmann's view must be argued on better exegesis of the text and a more adequate Christology. This will not in the end deny mutuality but lead to a more limited application within the parameters of the nature of revelation. ... The result of the more speculative views of Moltmann leads to a plethora of possibilities which the limitations of revelation forbid.[73]

More sympathetic to the *filioque* is Barth, who accentuates the Anselmian principle, seeing the whole pattern of relationship linking the three persons in the work of Revelation and Redemption as the basis for our understanding of God's inner-trinitarian life.[74] Although Barth and Moltmann differ on the issue of the *filioque*, they concur with each other insofar as they do not posit a difference between the temporal missions of the Spirit and the intra-relations of the Trinity, but affirm their intrinsic connection. They maintain with Anselm the principle of correspondence, one of the most basic principles of divine self-revelation. We know of the inner economy of the Trinity only by way of Revelation. We formulate the doctrine of the Trinity on the basis of historical Revelation in Christ and the Church's experience of the Spirit.

Without *filioque*, we have only knowledge of the economic relationship between the Son and the Spirit, and we have no knowledge of God's actual being, of the immanental relationships between the Son and the Spirit within God's triune life. Anselm's *filioque* doctrine underscores the principle that God remains true to himself, that God is indeed in his own being what he reveals himself to be, the immanent Trinity is known by the economic Trinity. Thus we can speak only of one Trinity, and of its economy of salvation, otherwise we are introducing a contradiction in God's being (cf. II Tim. 2:13).

Third, directly related to the principle of correspondence between the economic Trinity and the immanent Trinity is the question of how Anselm conceives of the cross of Jesus Christ. Is the suffering of Jesus Christ merely an outward event, belonging only to the economic Trinity? Or is it an intra-trinitarian event in which God as God identifies himself with the crucified Jesus? If 'God is love', which Anselm affirms, then the logical conclusion is that God and suffering coincide in Christ and his cross. Since the Spirit proceeds as a *hypostasis* from the Father and the Son, he must be in his person the communion of love that exists between them. The Spirit is both the principle of unity and relationship in God's immanental life. Peters expands on the theological import that *filioque* has on what is called the divine life proper, deducing that the Spirit maintains 'unity in difference.'[75] The Spirit is the principle of the differentiated unity within God's life, in virtue of which the Father is the Father in relation to the Son, and conversely, the Son is who he is due to a corresponding relationship, and the Spirit is the reciprocity of love between them. If this were true of Anselm, it means there already is a mutuality of self-giving love in the immanent Trinity, awaiting its concretization in history: in love the Father surrenders the Son, and in love the Son surrenders himself, and the Spirit of love is between them. God, in unity with the crucified Jesus, suffers as God the Son being forsaken by God the Father, and he is God the Spirit, who lets the Father and the Son be one in the death of Jesus. Father, Son and Holy Spirit are distinguished, but united as one God in this cross event that assumes suffering and death into his own life. Trinity is the conceptuality of the cross: the Son relates to the Father in obedient suffering and love, and the Father suffers the loss of his Son, with the Spirit binding them, even in the loss. Since the Father and the Son are one in essence and act, as Anselm affirms, then the Father is said to suffer through a perichoretic unity with the Son, except that it is the Son who suffers dying on the cross. A modalistic doctrine endangers the trinitarian distinctions of persons; a perichoretic doctrine would have enabled Anselm to see the differentiated ways in which God suffers uniquely as Father and as Son. Since God is wholly one, and has no parts, the separation that occurs between the Father and the Son cannot be ontological, but relational. This relational break defines the Father as Father, the one who gives his Son up to death in love, and the Son as Son, the one who gives himself up in love, but is healed by the Spirit, the unitive principle of love. He is God the Spirit who unites the Father and the Son in love in the cross event of God-forsakenness. The passion and death of Jesus Christ is thus the revelation of the immanent Trinity. The perception of the suffering Christ as the lowly servant is thus carried into the inner life of God, allowing a predication of Christ's suffering not only of the economic Trinity, but also of the immanent Trinity, the former being the self-manifestation of the latter. The God of Jesus and therefore of Christians is a passible God, not the passionless, immutable and impassible deity of the Greek. That being said, it is my contention that Anselm as a medieval scholastic does not, and in fact, cannot draw the conclusion which modern theologians – Barth, Moltmann and Jüngel – have made, because his thinking is still under the grip of Aristotelian philosophy, especially its idea of divine *apatheia*.[76] Suffering, which is predicated only of Christ's humanity, cannot be predicated of Christ's divinity, which he has with the Father and the Spirit. There is a forever untouched hinterland in God's being. Anselm denies God any real feelings of love and compassion, insisting that although we experience God as compassionate, there is really no compassion in God himself. We may experience the effects of God's love, yet God's being is not affected by our experiences. Anselm's solution to the paradox of a compassionate and an impassible God is to assert that

> ...thou art compassionate in terms of our experience, but not compassionate in terms of thy being.

> ...Truly, thou art so in terms of our experience, but thou art not in terms of thine own. For when thou beholdest us in our

wretchedness, we experience the feeling of compassion, but thou does not experience the feeling. Therefore, thou art both compassionate, because thou dost save the wretched, and spare those who sin against thee; and not compassionate, because thou art affected by no sympathy for wretchedness.[77]

Finally, there is a sense in which *filioque* enables Anselm to speak of the Spirit as ontologically and logically, if not chronologically, dependent upon the two persons within the divine life. The unitive principle of relationship depends upon the twoness in order to relate. The language of dependency does not imply an inferiority of the Spirit, relegating him to something secondary. This dependency is not a temporal priority, as in a modalistic presentation of the divine successively; rather it is an ontological and logical priority, for the Spirit, who is 'God from God', never exists 'outside' the Godhead, but is eternal with the Father and the Son. In Peters' words, 'The Spirit is the condition whereby the generation of the Son is made possible, yet without the Son to whom the Father relates there would be no divine Spirit.'[78] In relation to the Spirit, an ontological and logical priority is due to the Son; and correspondingly the Spirit is an ontological and logical posteriority to the Son, but is equal to the Son who is of one essence with the Father. In the eternal begetting of the Son, the Father manifests himself as the Father, and the Son manifests himself as the Son; in the eternal procession of the Spirit from the Father and the Son, the Spirit is ontologically and logically posterior to the Father and the Son. This evinces a certain priority of the Father-Son relation; and the Spirit, strictly speaking, is essentially this relation within God's *intra* life.[79] So constitutionally, there is an economic subordination of the Spirit without jeopardizing his con-substantiality with and equality to the Father and the Son. Anselm elaborates:

> Perhaps someone will marvel and ask: "How can it be comprehended that one thing exists from another without the other from which it exists somehow existing more principally and more valuably, and without the thing which exists from this other somehow existing inferiorly and as something secondary? ... To this query we must reply: Just as the existence of God is vastly different and diverse from created existence, so when we say that God exists

from God by being begotten and by proceeding, this begottenness and this procession must be understood in a far different way from when, in other cases, we say that something proceeds or is begotten. For in the case of God neither naturally nor temporally nor in any respect is anything earlier or later, more or less, or at all in need of anything. Rather, the whole of what God is is not so much equal to and similar to and coeternal with itself as it is identical with itself and altogether sufficient unto itself through itself; in the case of God nothing proceeds or is begotten in the sense of passing from not-being to being. ... Now (in God) that which is begotten or that which proceeds is no other than that from which it proceeds or is begotten, viz., the one and only God. Consequently, just as God is not greater or lesser than Himself; so in the case of the three (persons) there is not anything greater or lesser; and no one of them is what He is any more or less than is another of them, even though it is true that God exists from God by proceeding and by being begotten.[80]

Forsyth's phrase, 'subordination is not inferiority', echoes Anselm's view.[81] Divine self-subordination, in Anselm's account, lies at the heart of God's nature. It is precisely God-like to possess the glory of divine self-subordination on an infinite scale in the Godhead. The subordination is not enforced; rather it is that which is rendered by God to himself as is proper to the relation of the Spirit to the Son – the Spirit takes what is the Son's and reveals it to us; likewise, the obedience within God is that which is rendered by God to himself as is proper to the relation of the Son to the Father – the Son became 'obedient unto death' on the cross. This means there is already in God a divine self-subordination, which forms the basis of the economic subordination of the Spirit to the Son. And yet this godlike glory of self-subordination does not compromise the unity and equality of a being like God. Just as it is the nature of the Son to be obedient to the Father who sends him, so it is the nature of the Spirit to be subordinate to both the Father and the Son, who as one principle send the Spirit. This is the order in the Godhead, and he keeps it in its proper place without attributing diminutive inferiority or slavish obedience to a being as God. For the order has nothing to do with the order of importance or value, but has to do with relationship within God's immanental life. Self-subordination is thereby ontologized, belonging to God's eternal essence, which is commonly shared by all three persons existing in a perichoretic unity. This is also an implication of Anselm's *filioque*, the justification of which must be sought in the ontologically fundamental unity of the Father with the Son rather than their differentiation.

Chapter Three

The Spirit as Co-Beloved (*Condilectus*)
Richard of St. Victor

Well-known as the greatest theoretical teacher of mysticism in the Middle Ages, Richard has also been prized as 'a theologian of the spiritual life.'[1] With Hugh's scholastic knife, he carves out a highly articulated and complete system of contemplation, representing a landmark in the growth of Western mysticism. His two famous treatises on mystical theology are *The Twelve Patriarchs* and *The Mystical Ark,* often referred to as *Benjamin Major* and *Benjamin Minor*.[2] Although he does not compose a doctrinal *summa*, his treatise on his richly speculative and affective *De Trinitate* is a major development of insights from Augustine and Dinoysius.[3]

Augustine's doctrine of the Spirit as love continues to dominate all great western thinkers of the Middle Ages and beyond.[4] His theme of God-charity and the Spirit as the mutual love between the Father and the Son is followed primarily by Richard of Victor (d. 1172).[5] Richard makes full and systematic elaboration of Augustine's treatment of the lover, the beloved and love, and develops what Ewert Cousins calls appropriately, 'A Theology of Interpersonal Relations.'[6] The Trinity is the ideal of perfect interpersonal relations because in Divine existence there is an infinite self-giving and receiving of love, without entailing a loss of one's identity or a rejection by the other. Human interpersonal relations, are only images of God's divine life. Richard's theology of Supreme charity, and concept of Spirit as co-beloved, *condilectus*, will form the main substance of this chapter. We shall see how a rational analysis of love constitutes not only his famous proof of the Trinity, but also the basis of the Spirit as the 'co-beloved' of the Father and the Son.

Richard begins with the human persons, with the personal love of one for another, and moves to an unselfish love of friendship, wherein one gives himself wholly to another. In this he catches a glimpse of a divine love of friendship. However, human love is lacking for it excludes a third from sharing this love. In God there must be charity in its most perfect form. Perfect charity is all that God is and possesses. This means that there abides in God one supreme love, and three perfect lovers, in such a fashion that one (i.e., the Father) is the source of a condign beloved (i.e., the Son), and these two lovers (Father and the Son), united by 'the flame of love', constitute the single cause of an equal co-beloved, namely the Holy Spirit.[7] The Trinity, thus, is understood as ontological love, which is self-diffusive and self-differentiating.

Richard's Theological Method: Faith and Reason

Augustine addresses the question of human reason at some length in his *De Trinitate*. His basic argument is that if God is to be discerned within the creation, we should be able to find God at the height of that creation. There are some link-ups between the Creator God and his own creations. The height of God's creation, for Augustine, is human nature. On the basis of neo-Platonic metaphysics which he inherits from his cultural milieu, he argues that the height of human nature is the capacity to reason. Therefore, he concludes that one could find traces of God, or more appropriately, the 'vestiges of the Trinity' in the process of human reasoning.

Like Augustine and Anselm, Richard believes that it is possible to find the 'necessary reasons' for the Trinity in a reflection made in faith. To clarify, the phrase 'necessary reasons' does not carry the modern sense of a hard-line rationalistic attempt to prove the existence of mysteries, totally independently of faith. Instead the 'necessary reasons' are the resultant fruit of human understanding transformed by contemplation, or more precisely by love. Reason itself cannot comprehend the interior depths of divine mysteries, the truth of which is confirmed in experience: 'But if experience teaches you that something in human nature is beyond understanding, should it not by that very fact have taught you that there is something in the divine nature that is above your understanding.'[8] Speaking of the Trinity, he admits: 'Which of these propositions can be better grasped, which better comprehended: that one substance is these three realities or that three persons are one substance? Each is beyond comprehension, but neither is beyond belief.'[9] So there is a realm of knowledge into which we enter only by faith. In his prologue to *De Trinitate*, he takes faith as his point of departure, but adds that he would strive 'as much as this is right or possible, to comprehend by reason what we hold by faith.'[10] Faith and reason constitutes an organic unity within faith. They do not operate in airtight compartments, with no interactions between them. Although faith precedes reason, he adds, once we enter into faith, we should not stop there but enter into faith-seeking-understanding of those interior things which we hold by faith. When inquiring such a sublime subject as the Trinity, Richard, like Augustine, cautions that we must apply greater care in pursuing more ardently the divine things from the testimony of reason.

> In connection with the proposal of my investigation, let him who wishes, laugh; let him who wishes mock – and rightly so. For, if I speak truth here, it is not so much knowledge that lifts me up, but rather the ardour of a burning soul that urges me to try this. …What if I falter in running the course? Well, I will rejoice that I totally ran, laboured and sweated to the extent of my powers in seeking the face of my Lord.[11]

The surest access to the theology of the Trinity is through the monastic contemplation on the dynamic of human love.[12] The 'image-likeness' thought common in monasticism forms the anthropological basis of Richard's contemplative discipline. In developing his approach to trinitarian speculation, Richard begins from what is visible in the created order:

> Thus, reasoning from the visible makes us conclude to the invisible, from the transitory to the eternal, from the earthly to the above-earthly, from the human to the divine. Because, "That which is invisible of God, from the creation of the world, is revealed by the spirit through that which has been made" (Rom. 1:20).[13]

The creaturely world, which bears the image and likeness of God, reveals God. The human spirit contains within itself the postulates of divine mystery. Therefore human experience of self and creation are ladders through which one ascends to know God in unity and Trinity. Yet this knowing God presupposes the spiritual experience of the contemplative who has ascended the mount of Transfiguration, and who now, with the help of the Spirit, ascends to the third heaven in intimate knowledge of the Trinity. 'It is toward this heaven that we are carried by the Spirit who elevates us, each time that the grace of contemplation makes us reach to the understanding of the eternal.'[14] Richard writes also in his *The Twelve Patriarchs*, 'Ascend to this mountain (transfiguration), learn to know yourself.'[15] From the human experience of self-knowledge, he contends, knowledge which transcends experience itself could be deduced.

Book III of his *De Trinitate* represents Richard's rational attempt to arrive at the necessary reason for the Trinity. The effulgence of the divine is reflected in the creaturely phenomenon of loving. Interpersonal love is an analog of the Trinity. Instead of looking at the inner soul for his clues to the nature of God, Richard looks at human persons in relation. To penetrate into the inner life of the Trinity, he moves through human love to divine love, uniting these two poles, seeing in this union interpenetration in experience. For in the perfection of human love, where one person transcends himself in the love of another, Richard sees a reflection of the infinite self-transcending love of the Trinitarian existence. He expressly states his vision as follows:

> ... in that supreme and altogether perfect good there is fullness and perfection of all goodness. However, where there is fullness of all goodness, true and supreme charity cannot be lacking. For nothing is better than charity; nothing is more perfect than charity. However, no one is properly said to have charity on the basis of his own private love of himself. And so it is necessary for love to be directed toward another for it to be charity. Therefore, where a plurality of persons is lacking, charity cannot exist.[16]

Charity: Love for another person (*Dilectus*)

Drawing on experience, Richard deduces that nothing is better than charity. If God is not only greater but also better, then God must be love. God must possess charity in the highest degree. The sovereign charity cannot be self-love, but is self-transcending love for the other, yet of the same or equal dignity, which no creature shares or attains. Charity, which is all that God possesses, is personal. Therefore, in God's divine being, there must be a self-transcending love of one divine person for another divine person. He justifies his stance by means of three propositions:

A. 'For nothing is better than charity; nothing is more perfect than charity.'[17] He sees no need of providing proof of this proposition, but merely asks that we accept it as an ontological given, rooted in human experience. 'Let each person examine his consciousness; without doubt and without contradiction he will discover that just as nothing is better than charity, so nothing is more pleasing than charity. Nature herself teaches us this; many experiences do the very same.'[18] What Richard sees is a reflection of the absolute good in the human experience of charity; more than that, he grasps the highest reflection, as his first proposition confirms this, that 'nothing is better than charity; nothing is more perfect than charity.' The reflection of the absolute good in human experience is not to be grasped by deductive proofs, but by internal analysis of self-consciousness, which is luminary of the eternal dimension of experience.

B. 'But fullness of goodness could not exist without fullness of charity.'[19] Charity is a perfection, which only God possesses to the fullest, and in the highest degree. He argues, 'in that supreme and altogether perfect good there is fullness and perfection of all goodness.'[20] In speaking of the fullness of all goodness, he borrows from Dionysius's postulate *bonum est diffusivum sui*, goodness is self-diffusive. He affirms that God's existence is constituted as *summum bonum*, the highest goodness which he identifies as love.[21] In LaCugna's words, 'God as the supreme good is supremely self-communicating and is the finality of all beings.'[22] Perfect goodness is not static but dynamic; it is not self-contained but self-communicative. It necessarily goes out to another and returns, and therefore it is charity. '*Oportet itaque ut amor in alterum tendat, ut caritas esse queat.*'[23] Thus where perfect goodness exists, perfect charity cannot be absent.

C. 'However, no one is properly said to have charity on the basis of his own private love of himself. And so it is necessary for love to be directed toward another for it to be charity.'[24] The third proposition is revelatory of charity in its truest and highest form. Richard draws a succinct distinction between charity and self-love, the former being superior to the latter. Richard's thought corresponds to Gregory the Great, who asserts: '...there cannot be charity among less than two. For no one is said, strictly speaking, to have charity toward himself, but love is directed to another in order for it to be charity.'[25] If God is by nature love, his 'private love' of himself would be a lesser form of love than other-love. Charity is not self-love; it is self-transcending love for another. Charity is superior to self-love precisely because it is reciprocal. Perfect love wishes, in the act of ex-centricity (out of self), to flow beyond oneself so as to embrace the one who is personally over and against it. A love that is curved in upon itself is no true love. Charity, the supreme excellence, transcends itself in openness to a new reality. The perfection of self-transcending love becomes, for Richard, the necessary reason why plurality of persons must not be lacking in true Divinity.

After establishing self-transcending love as the supreme perfection of God, Richard anticipates an objection: Could God's self-transcending love be accounted by means of God's relation to his creation, without the need of another divine person? Could God's self-transcending love be explained merely in view of God-world relation, without ever introducing divine self-relatedness? 'But you might say, "Even if there were only one person in that true Divinity, nevertheless He could still have charity toward His creation – indeed He would have it".'[26] He answers this objection by invoking the concept of 'ordered love' (*caritas ordinata*), that the supreme charity cannot be addressed to a limited creature and lack a divine consort. '*Oportuit divinam aliquam personam persone condigne, et eo ipse divine, consortio non carere.*'[27] The fullness of charity demands nothing less than 'a person of equal dignity and therefore a divine person.' He further explains:

> But certainly He could not have supreme charity toward a created person. For charity would be disordered if He loved supremely someone who should not be supremely loved. But in that supremely wise goodness it is impossible for charity to be disordered. Therefore a divine person could not have supreme charity toward a person who was not worthy of supreme love.[28]

God's infinite love demands that the other be infinite. The creaturely other, the object of God's infinite love, is incapable of receiving or responding to such love in an infinite mode. 'Thus God cannot love his creature *objectively* as much as he loves himself – that is, whereas he wills to himself an infinite good, he wills to the creature only its particular finite goodness – and accordingly such love falls short of unconditioned perfection.'[29] Perfect love demands a return of the love offered. The supreme lover must be loved as much as he loves, but no creature can return to God an infinite love. Since God alone must be loved supremely, a divine person could not express supreme love to a person who lacks divinity. For to love with the highest love that which does not deserve such a love, in Richard's rendering, is a 'disordered love', which God cannot exhibit. The object of his love cannot be human beings. God's love, like *Eros*, is guided by the worth of the object. Only God, the Supreme Good, is worthy of absolute love, and therefore the infinite love which is God must always have had an infinite object even when creatures are absent. A second person is needed within the Divinity as an object on which the Divine love bestows without limit. Thus the one to whom supreme charity is expressed fully, and without disorderly waste, has to be divine as well.

Furthermore he approaches the objection from another perspective, that of Anselm's point of departure – *id quo nihil maius cogitari potest*, 'that than which it is not possible to conceive anything greater.' But Richard's is '*id quo nihil est maius, quo nihil est melius*, 'a being, greater or better than whom there is nothing.'[30] In God charity is the greatest perfection, and hence it must be so great that than which no greater could ever be conceived. If God were to immerse totally in his 'private love' of himself, he would never reach the highest degree of charity because his self-love would always be greater than his charity. Richard obviously follows Anselm's designation of God in his ontological argument to flesh out his answer:

However, in order that charity be supreme and supremely perfect, it is necessary that it be so great that nothing greater can exist and that it be of such a kind that nothing better can exist. However, as long as anyone loves no one else as much as he loves himself, that private love which he has for himself shows clearly that he has not reached the surpeme level of charity. But a divine person certainly would not have anyone to love as worthily as Himself if He did not have a person of equal worth. However a person who is not God would not be equal in worth to a divine person. Therefore, so that fullness of charity might have a place in that true Divinity, it is necessary that a divine person not lack a relationship with an equally worthy person, who is, for this reason, divine.[31]

Human Experiences: Happiness and Generosity

The aforementioned answer reinforces his proposition that charity is more perfect than self-love. Richard continues to explore human experience of happiness and generosity, both of which, in his view, confirm his teaching on charity 'with such transparent reasoning' that anyone who fails to see it clearly suffers from the disease of folly, and is therefore weak in mind.[32] If one is to be supremely happy, he must have charity, which presupposes an otherness for an appropriate giving and receiving of love. "There, in supreme happiness it is necessary that charity not be lacking. However, so that charity may be in the supreme good, it is impossible that there be lacking either one who can show charity or one to whom charity can be shown.'[33] Happiness requires a reciprocity of relationship in which there is mutual giving and receiving, yet without destroying oneself nor the other. Happiness demands a return of love. He elaborates:

> However it is a characteristic of love, and one without which it cannot possibly exist, to wish to be loved much by the one whom you love much. Therefore, love cannot be pleasing if it is not mutual. Therefore, in that true and supreme happiness, just as pleasing love cannot be lacking, so mutual love cannot be lacking. However, in

mutual love it is absolutely necessary that there be both one who gives love and one who returns love. Therefore one will be the offerer of love and the other the returner of love. Now, where the one and the other are clearly shown to exist, true plurality is discovered. In that fullness of true happiness, a plurality of persons cannot be lacking. However it is agreed that supreme happiness is nothing other than Divinity itself. Therefore, the showing of love freely given and the repayment of love that is due prove without any doubt that in true Divinity a plurality of persons cannot be lacking.[34]

This also casts light on Richard's doctrine of God, that God does not exist in an immortal solitariness. His God is not a solitary monad, who sits alone on his throne of majesty. Divine existence is not a pathetic one, in which it cannot enjoy pleasure sweeter and more pleasing than the delights of charity in eternity. For the divine person to be eternally deprived of this satisfying delights is to be eternally deprived of joy. Such a God would not only be unhappy but also would not share his infinite abundance of his fullness.

> Certainly, if we say that in true Divinity there exists only one person, just as there is only one substance, then without doubt according to this He will not have anyone with whom He could share that infinite abundance of His fullness. But, how can this be, I ask? Would it be because even though He wished to, He could not have one who would share with Him? Or is it because He would not wish to, even if He could? But He who is undoubtedly omnipotent cannot be excused on the grounds of impossibility. But could not that which is not due to a defect of power be due to a defect of benevolence alone? But if He would not be absolutely unwilling to have one to share with Him when He really could if He wanted, then observe, I ask you, what a defect of benevolence this would be in a divine person and how great it would be.[35]

A solitary God is not worthy to be recognized, much less worshipped. What a great deficiency of benevolence that would be if God should want to reserve for himself in a miserly fashion the abundance of his fullness, which if he wishes, he could communicate to another and consequently enjoy such great satisfying pleasure!

And if such a great lack of benevolence were in God, he would be better off hiding from the gaze of all, including the angels in his heavenly existence. '(Q)uite rightly He should blush with shame to be seen or recognized.'[36] But this is improper for a being like God, who is far from being impassive and selfish. It is precisely God-like to give joyously. God is most glorious in communicating himself completely. '(W)hat is more glorious, what is truly more magnificent than to have nothing that one does not want to share? And so it is evident that in that unfailing good and supremely wise counsel there can be no miserly holding back just as there can be no inordinate squandering.'[37] God's omnipotent love seeks to give freely and fully, and this constitutes the fullness of God's glory. Yet only a divine person could love to the fullness of his power, without disorderly waste. God's self-transcending love does not imply an impairment of being, an imperfect being who necessarily seeks his perfection and tries to overcome his deficiency through actions.[38] C. S. Lewis's distinction between 'gift love' (*agape*) and 'need love' (*eros*) helps elucidate Richard's thought.[39] God does not act out of need love – a love dominated by self-seeking desires. Rather, God acts out of gift love – a free, self-giving love, sharing his boundless goodness, without a miserly holding back. God as love does not wish to exist without a loved one. The self-transcending love, thus, is the joyful sharing of that supra-abundance of his fullness, yet without implying a diminution of being or a deficiency of being. So nothing is more pleasing or sweeter than this, that the supreme charity, which God is, desires to communicate to another with perfect satisfying joy and pleasure. This truth is confirmed in the life of reason.[40]

Supreme Charity: Shared Love for a Third (*Condilectus*)

The divine being must be three incommunicable existents or persons, Richard argues, if God is love (I Jn. 4:8, 16). That is because perfect love is always other-directed, toward what is distinct from and in some sense outside the self. Self-love is a defect, which cannot be attributed to God. God's love must be perfect, and must not be contingent upon the creation. God's love must be other-directed within God himself. This explains why there must be at least two persons within God: the lover and the beloved. But why must it be more than two? Why not binity rather than Trinity? He argues that love between two is less perfect than among three. For selfishness or complacency may surface in the mutual love of only two persons, and only when a third is introduced into a circle of love is love perfected: 'in mutual love that is very fervent there is nothing rarer, nothing more excellent than that you wish another to be equally loved by him whom you love supremely and by whom you are supremely loved.'[41] Since we are dealing with God's supreme charity, it must be perfect in every way. It must possess supreme excellence, in that it must be 'so great that nothing greater can exist', and 'such that nothing better can exist.'[42] Not willing to share the love with which he is loved is a sign of immaturity and weakness. Accordingly, Richard lays down three stages of attitudes of mature and perfect charity: To be able to share love is a sign of perfection; to be willing to share with joy is better; and to search for it with longing is the best of all. 'The first is a great good; the second, a better one; but the third, the best. Therefore, let us offer to the supreme what is excellent; to the best, what is best.'[43] Hence the proof of perfected love lies in a willing sharing of the love that has been given to you. The most fervent kind of love presupposes another person who could be loved equally by the one whom you love supremely and by whom you are loved supremely. 'For the one loving supremely and longing to be loved supremely, surely the most excellent joy lies in the fulfillment of his own longing, namely in the attainment of longed-for love.'[44] Hence perfect love such as God is must not be short of a Trinity of persons. The term *condilectus* refers to the third person, who is the completion of the mutual love of the two. Richard elaborates on the meaning of this term:

> When one person gives love to another and he alone loves only the other, there certainly is love, but it is not shared love. When two love each other mutually and give to each other the affection of supreme longing; when the affection of the first goes out to the second and the affection of the second goes out to the first and tends as it were in diverse ways – in this case there certainly is love on both sides, but it is not shared love. Shared love is properly said to exist when a third

person is loved by two persons harmoniously and in community, and the affection of the two persons is fused into one affection by the flame of love for the third. From these things it is evident that shared love would have no place in Divinity itself if a third person were lacking ... Here we are not speaking of just any shared love but of supreme shared love – a shared love of a sort such that a creature would never merit from the Creator and for which it would never be found worthy.[45]

Richard moves from self-love (first stage) to other-love (second stage), from which he moves to the sharing of this mutual love with a third (third stage). If there were only duality, love will be self-enclosed. If the pair who loves does not move to the third stage, he argues, their love might fall back to the first stage. He asks, 'For if he does not will what perfect goodness demands, where will the fullness of goodness be? If he wills what cannot be done, where will fullness of power be?'[46] The perfection of charity demands love for another person, and the fulfillment of their mutual love demands shared love for the third. 'And in those who are mutually loved', he explains, 'the perfection of each, in order to be completed, requires with equal reason a sharer of the love that have been shown to them.'[47] The love of the two is not simply mutual love, but a common love for the third that establishes their union. What is required for perfect love is 'union with the third.'

But can there be a fourth person? No. Here Richard turns to the logic of divine processions. Within God, there exists only one person who is principle only, the one who is term only, and the one who is both term and principle. Only one person has the source from himself, the one is from the other, and one who is from both others; one who only gives, one who only receives, one who gives and receives.[48] In order to avoid an infinite processional series, logic demands that the third person be the completion of the Trinity.[49]

Like what he does in his treatment of the love of the pair, Richard seeks to confirm his position by turning again to human happiness and generosity. In happiness, he shows that if the two refuse to share their love with a third, they would have reason to grieve. Supposing that there exists in God only two lovers. Why would they not have someone to share their supreme joy? Perhaps both are unwilling to share, or one is willing while the other not, in which case there is a cause for grieving. Consequently the oneness of mind and intimate harmony which we find in perfect friends would be lacking.

> But if someone should say that neither is able to find repose in the sharing of love that has been shown to them, how, I ask, will that person be able to excuse them of the defect of love mentioned above? Now we know that nothing can be hidden from those who are supremely wise. And so if they love each other truly and supremely, how will one of them be able to see a defect in the other and not grieve? For if one of the two sees a defect in the other and does not grieve, where will fullness of love be? If He sees and grieves, where will fullness of happiness be?[50]

The same logic applies to the experience of generosity. If one refuses to share his joy, Richard argues, not only would the other grieve, but at the same time the first would be ashamed. 'For just as a true and intimate friend cannot see the defect of one who is loved intimately and not grieve, so surely in the presence of a friend he cannot fail to be ashamed over his own defect.'[51] But shame is inapplicable to a perfect being like God. 'But just as in supreme happiness there cannot be a cause of grieving, so in the fullness of supreme glory there cannot be matter for embarrassment.'[52] There should be no defect in that supreme charity. Fullness of goodness and fullness of happiness and glory in accord witness to the fullness of all perfection. In order for charity to be true, plurality of persons cannot be lacking; in order for charity to be perfected, a Trinity of persons is required.

> And so sharing of love cannot exist among any less than three persons. Now, as has been said, nothing is more glorious, nothing is more magnificent, than to share in common whatever you have that is useful and pleasant. But this cannot be hidden from supreme wisdom, nor can it fail to be pleasing to supreme benevolence. And as the happiness of the supremely powerful One and the power of supremely happy One cannot be lacking in what pleases Him, so in Divinity it is impossible for two persons not to be united to a third.[53]

Trinity: Persons and Processions

In his *De Trinitate*, Richard, unlike Augustine and Anselm, has as his starting point, not the unity of essence, but the persons of the Trinity. He demonstrates how the unity of essence is required by perfect love between persons. Boethius defines person as 'an individual substance of reasonable nature', emphasizing rationality as the chief characteristic of a person.[54] However Richard modifies Boethius' definition and introduces his own distinctive concept of person as 'an incommunicable existence of an intelligent nature.'[55] The divine persons are three incommunicable existents, each in his unique and incommunicable self ' exists in himself alone, according to a certain mode of reasonable existence.'[56] Each person is distinguishable by a property that belongs incommunicably to him. 'Reflect attentively and note well that the word substance signifies less someone than something; to the contrary, the word person designates less something than someone.'[57] To elaborate, he asserts that the person is not a *quid* (what), but a *quis* (who), thus putting the emphasis on relationality. *Quid* refers to substance, whereas *quis* refers to person. 'The word person always designates someone who is one and unique, distinguished from everyone else by a singular property.'[58] This way of thinking accentuates the dynamic of personal and individual action. To account for an ontological distinction of persons in the unity of the divine substance, Richard says, we must 'know both what the person is and from where this person gets his origin.'[59] Here he turns to the noun *exsistentia*, in virtue of which *sistence* is synonymous with essence, and *ex-sistentia* designates the way in which *sistence* manifests itself with a unique and peculiar property. The term *existentia* is a predicate of the person, expressing both the essence (*sistere*) and the origin (*ex*) of the person. 'The one verb *exisistere* or the one noun *exsistentia*, indicates both that which refers to the nature of the being and that which refers to its person.'[60] Richard introduces a conceptuality of personhood which is both ontological and relational. This relationality, in Torrance's words, is indeed 'an inherent and ontological determination of personal existence.'[61] Each person, within the community of one indivisible substance, has his own mode of subsistence. In God's own life, there are three persons who share the same essence, but each possesses a unique property by which he may be distinguished. The persons of the Godhead are one according to their mode of being, but three according to their mode of existing. Moltmann's explication of Richard's intra-trinitarian dynamic by way of the patristic idea of *perichoresis* is appropriately adequate:

> ... being a person does not merely mean subsisting; nor does it mean subsisting-in relation. It means existing. ... By the word 'existence' – *eksistentia* – he meant: existence, in light of another. It is true that in the first place he related this other to the divine nature. But it can be related to the other persons too. Then existence means a deepening of the concept of relation: every divine person exists in the light of the other and in the other. By virtue of the love they have for one another they ex-ist totally in the other: the Father, ex-ists by virtue of his love, as himself entirely in the Son; the Son, by virtue of his self-surrender, ex-ists as himself totally in the Father; and so on. Each Person finds his existence and his joy in the other. Each person receives the fullness of eternal life from the other.[62]

How does Richard explain the procession of persons, that which makes each person share uniquely in the divine essence? He again resorts to human experience as an indication of divine mystery: 'In the human world, we observe a person proceeding from another person, and this procession can evidently be realized from another person sometimes in a manner only immediate, sometimes in a manner only mediate, and sometimes in a manner both mediate and immediate.'[63] To illustrate this, Richard uses three Old Testament saints, Abraham, Isaac and Jacob, the latter two proceed from the former, but in different ways. Isaac proceeds immediately from Abraham; Jacob proceeds only mediately from Abraham through (*per*) Isaac, the intermediary.[64] Although human generation is not identical with divine generation, there is still a certain likeness in them because humans bear the likeness of God. 'It is necessary', Richard states, 'beginning with this (human) nature, to erect a mirror for contemplation and following the consideration indicated, search out with a very great effort that which is found in God and that which is not found in God, according to the relationship of likeness and unlikeness.'[65] The Father exists of himself alone, possessing an independently incommunicable existence which is rightly his. Because the Father's mode of existence is incommunicable, the Son and the Spirit must be seen as existing from another. The Son is the immediate procession in God. The Father requires another of equal dignity so that there will be fullness of charity. Since the Son possesses the same power as the Father, the Spirit does not proceed from the Father alone, but from both the Father and the Son. 'This is required by the perfection of love of the first two persons who require a third person to be loved by both the first and second persons. The *condilectus*, the third person, is the unity of the shared love of the two. Thus, the third person proceeds in a procession that is both immediate and mediate.'[66] No other person proceeds from the Holy Spirit. Why? Nico's explanation elucidates:

> If divine love is mutual love, the Son returns the Father's love and the Spirit returns the love of both the Father and the Son. Now, processions have only one direction. The Spirit, for instance, proceeds from the Father and the Son, but they in turn do not proceed from the Spirit. On account of Richard's own principle – that in God loving, as any quality, is the same as being – one should conclude that returning love would necessarily imply returning being: a procession in the other direction.[67]

There is a divine order of things, which enables Richard to account for the difference between the procession of the second and that of the third. Here we detect Richard's two distinct ways of producing (*modus procedendi*): the first one, generating, is willing a beloved (*dilectus*) responding love, while the second one, proceeding, is willing a companion in love (*condilectus*).

Through the Spirit, God as love is showered upon the believer. Hence the Spirit is appropriately called 'Gift': '...this gift is sent to us, this mission is given to us at the same time and in the same way by the Father and by the Son. It is, after all, from the one (Father) and from the other (Son) than the Spirit has everything that he possesses.'[68] And because the Spirit has his being, power and will from the Father and the Son, it is they who send and give him. The Spirit, being sent, receives from them the power and the will to indwell us. The Spirit, as pure receptivity, fills the human hearts with the love that he receives from the hearts of both the Father and the Son. Inflamed by the Spirit, the 'divine fire', says Richard, 'the human soul loses progressively all darkness, coldness and hardness:

the soul passes entirely into the likeness of him who enflames', and finally is configured to him. It is the property of the Spirit to constitute from 'a multitude of hearts' a community of 'one heart and one soul.'[69]

Love: Trinity of Persons

The concept of charity as self-transcending love is most original and contributive to his reflection and development of his Trinitarian theology. The love of human persons, which Richard uses as a point of departure, enables him to grasp analogously the love of the persons of the Trinity. Love consists of three levels, moving from self-love to charity, in which the second is loved, to complete charity, in which a third is mutually loved by the pair. In Richard's own terms the three levels are private love (*amor privatus*) whose object is one's self, mutual love (*amor mutuus* or *caritas*) whose object is a person of equal dignity, and consummated love (*caritas consummata*) whose object is a person mutually loved (*condilectus*).[70] Love overflows the lover, but also overflows the union of the pair. Drawn together by one affection, they do not allow their mutual love to remain in a selfish and static state. Because the union is dynamic, it overflows beyond itself into the third. The love of the pair converges in the single 'flame of love' they have for the third. Speaking of the inner relations of the Trinity, Richard speaks of 'the flood of divinity', in which there is 'the flowing abundance of supreme love.'[71] This indeed constitutes the core of Richard's interpersonal theology of the Trinity:

> For when two persons who mutually love embrace each other with supreme longing and take supreme delight in each other's love, then the supreme joy of the first is in intimate love of the second, and conversely the excellent joy of the second is in love of the first. As long as only the first is loved by the second, he alone seems to possess the delights of his excellent sweetness. Similarly, as long as the second does not have someone who shares in love for a third, he lacks the sharing of excellent joy. In order that both may be able to share delights of that kind, it is necessary for them to have someone who shares in love for a third.[72]

Trinitarianly, the love of Father and Son overflows and expresses itself in the Holy Spirit, who is pure charity. This divine overflowing is best expressed by the *filioque*. "If the two (the Father and the Son) possess the same power, it must be concluded that it is from both that the Third Person of the Trinity received his being and has his existence."[73] The third person proceeds both from the one who cannot be born (*innascibilis*), namely the Father, and the one who was born (*nascibilis*), namely the Son. There is an immediate procession of the Son from the Father; there is an immediate procession from the Father and mediate procession from the Son, namely the *Condilectus* or the Spirit.[74] Both the Father and the Son form a single principle of the Spirit. To account for an ontological distinction of persons, Richard does not make use of Anselm's principle of an opposition of relations. Instead he distinguishes between the persons through an analysis of love in its absolute perfection and the distinctions that are found in that perfect love. In God there is charity in the highest form. There must be in God one infinite love and three infinite lovers, in such a way that the one (the Father) is the causal principle of a condign beloved (the Son) and these two form the single causal principle of an equal co-beloved (the Spirit). Love begins by the Father gratuitously pouring unto another, namely the Son, who receives. This is reflective of the dyadic relationship between purely gratuitous (*gratuitus*) love (the Father) and received or indebted (*debitus*) love (the Son). However, this dyadic love shared by only two is lacking, and does not meet the status of supreme love. Perfect love desires to move beyond the intimacy of the two, embracing a third loved by both; it steers lovers away from each other so as to share their love with a third. This third is what Richard calls, the *condilectus*, a 'co-beloved' – that which is loved together with their reciprocal love. And this third is the Holy Spirit – the love that is purely received, purely indebted (*debitus*). 'That the divine Persons are three derives from the idea that, in the perfection of charity, the adequate beloved is *condilectus*, one willing to share the love received: *oportet ut pari voto condilectum requirat*.'[75] Not only does the perfection of love demand love for another person, but the consummation of mutual love demands shared love for a third. In Congar's words: 'The special way of existing which characterizes the divine Persons consists in a manner of living and realizing Love.' That Love is either pure grace, or it is received and giving, or it is purely received and due.'[76] In Richard's words:

> It is certain that true love can be either exclusively gracious or exclusively owed or uniting both, that is to say gracious on one hand and owed on the other hand. Love is gracious when one gives gratuitously to him from whom one has received nothing. Love is owed when to him from whom one has received gratuitously one renders in exchange only love. Love is mixed when, in a double attitude of love, gratuitously one receives and gratuitously one gives.[77]

Each person possesses love, which is God's essence. Each, based on the infinite giving and receiving of love, exists according to his distinct mode of origin: the Father is the fullness of giving love; the Son is the fullness of both giving and receiving love; the Spirit is the fullness of receiving love. The trinitarianly-shared love, where each person is totally different from the other two but totally equal with them, is the perfect love which befits God. The distinction of divine processions stems from Richard's unique conception of God's nature as love, which by its very constitution requires divine relationality and community in God's inner life.

Concluding Reflections

To be fair, it is Richard's appropriation of Augustine's ideas that helps establish his *De Trinitate* as the *locus classicus* of the interpersonal approach. Although the dominant image of Augustine's *De Trinitate* is a trinity of mind, knowledge and love, he does not reject completely inter-personal relations as the image or rather the vestige of the Trinity. He knows the limitation of the interpersonal analogy: 'If we recognize the image of the Trinity not in one but in three human beings, namely father, mother and son, it follows that man was not made in the image of God until he had a wife and begot a child – because till then there was no trinity.'[78] However in Treatise XIV of *Tractatus in Ioannem*, Augustine's comments on Acts 4:32, 'the multitude of believers had but one heart and one soul', lends support to inter-personal love as the appropriate image of the Trinity.

> If charity made so many souls into one soul, and so many hearts into one heart – how great is the charity between Father and Son? Certainly greater than uniting those men whose heart was one. If, therefore, through charity the heart of many brethren is one and through charity the soul of many brethren is one, God the Father and God the Son – are you going to say that they are two Gods? If they are two Gods, there is not supreme charity there in heaven. For if here on earth charity is so great as to make your friend's soul one with yours, is it possible that there in heaven God the Father and God the Son are not one God? True faith cannot admit the notion! The excellence of their (divine) charity may be gauged from this: the souls of many men are many; if they love one another, they are 'one soul', yet they can also be said to be 'many souls' – this is possible among men, because the union between them isnot so great'; but there in heaven, although you can say 'one God', you cannot say 'three Gods' or 'two Gods.' This shows the superlative excellence of their charity – so great that no greater is possible.[79]

In seeking an image for the Trinity in love of neighbor, McGinn writes, Richard doubtless owes something to Book 8 of Augustine's *De Trinitate*, that from which he develops his own distinctive theology of consummated charity (*amor consummatus*).[80] And the highest form of this demands the overflowing of the supreme and perfectly shared love found in the Trinity. In commending to our reason the revealed doctrine of the unity of the divine substance and the trinity of persons, Richard assumes and elaborates the meaning of charity given in Augustine. Why there must be three persons in one Divinity has been explained, to a certain extent, in Richard's theology of interpersonal relation, although his is not a scholastic proof of the kind we find in Anselm.

But has Richard answered the question: why only three? He is right to say that there is at least a third to open up the two, but why stop at three? The strength of Augustine's idea of the Spirit as the bond of love lies in the fact that it answers the question, 'why three?' For in God, there are two, and the reciprocity of the two. But this thinking seems to underplay the distinct identity of the Spirit, which Richard seeks to avoid. Augustine's mutual love theory has been criticized for depersonalizing the Holy Spirit. In an I-Thou relationship, the love that the Father and the Son bestow upon each other is not a distinct person; at least, it is not an activity that defines a person distinct from the 'I' and the 'Thou.' The Holy Spirit, for Augustine, is the Gift of mutual love between Father and Son. The Spirit has little function, if any except as a link between Father and Son. Richard develops this love analogy further, insisting that the Spirit is not the mutual love between Father and Son; rather it is the mutual love between Father and Son turned to the third. Mutual love, to be perfect, must be love shared with the third. 'In God we find not just an I-Thou relationship of reciprocal love', O'Collins writes, 'but also the Holy Spirit as the "Co-beloved" (*Condilectus*).'[81] There is a movement from self-love (Father) to mutual love (Father and Son) to trinitarianly-shared love (Father, Son, and Holy Spirit). The Spirit, thus, is the specific and incommunicable mode of existence of the divine substance constituted as love. In Gunton's words: 'The Holy Spirit is then indeed the dynamic of the divine love, but one that seeks to involve the other in the movement of giving and receiving that is the Trinity: that is, *to perfect the love of Father and Son by moving it beyond itself.*'[82] Richard's view of God as the perfect communion of love allows the distinctiveness of Holy Spirit to come through far more clearly and strongly than Augustine's mutual love-theory. In lieu of Augustinian language of lover, beloved and love, Richard's trinitarian language is lover, beloved and co-beloved. Person is understood as being in relation or communion. In other words, God's being is a relational unity. Thompson writes of the 'two main effects [of Richard's view]: it gives concrete particularity to the persons who interrelate and so constitute the deity, and at the same time it conceives of God's being in these distinctions as creative of or in fact existing as communion.'[83] This social view of the Trinity has profound implication for understanding humanity, in view of which human personhood is not to be understood in purely individualistic terms, but in concrete, communicatarian and relational terms. That which defines personhood is indeed its reciprocity and relationship. Divine existence, thus, is the ideal of personal existence.

Beyond dispute, Richard's thought differs with Augustine's. With Anselm, Richard affirms that the Spirit is not the mutual love of the Father and the Son. For Anselm, the source of the Spirit lies in the love the Father and the Son have for the divine essence, the divine goodness, rather than a mutual love between persons. For Richard, the love expressed by the Spirit is not of two lovers turned towards each other as in Augustine, but rather of two turned to a third. Richard's position, in that respect, distances itself more from Augustine's idea than Anselm's, since the Spirit's love for its divinity includes a love for the dyadic lovers (Father and the Son).[84] Badcock explains:

> In the trinitarian sense, furthermore, love is what God is; love is not to be appropriated technically to the Holy Spirit as the third person of the Trinity, as in Augustine, but is rather to be understood in terms of the divine being itself, so that it is from this that the distinctive logic of God as a Trinity of persons flows. Because God is love, and specifically the perfection of love, God is necessarily a community of love, Trinity.[85]

Although Richard stands within the Latin tradition, his view shows affinity with the Greek tradition, that which retains the identity of the Spirit as the one who opens up the relationship of the other two, even though it is not clear why must there be only three. Richard's *De Trinitate* has revived the social analogy, which is already there in the Cappadocian fathers, who draw on human social life as analogies for God's three-in-oneness. Gregory of Nyssa, for one, in his *Not Three Gods: To Ablabius*, uses the analogy of Jesus' three disciples, Peter, James and John. There he argues that just as they are three yet one according to their human nature, so the Godhead is three identities yet one as to their divine nature. However he stresses that the unity of the divine persons transcends the unity of any three humans.[86] The divine persons act in full unity with themselves in all things, whereas any three humans may act at times contrarily of each other. Gregory writes: 'In the case of the Divine nature we do not (as in the case of men) learn that the Father does anything by Himself in which the Son does not work conjointly, or again that the Son has any special operation apart from the Holy Spirit.'[87] It is an analogy, however imperfect, of God's triunity whose community makes up one eternal Godhead.

Richard's view is not without criticisms. Richard appears to say that the Father first loves himself, then extends his love to the Son, and finally together with the Son enters into a shared love for the Spirit. What is the origin of such plurality in God? His language of love – private love, mutual love and consummated love – in which the respective objects are the self, the equal other and their co-beloved, as Hill argues, may result in

> a certain inconsistency in Richard's thought, but it can also be somewhat misleading. His emphasis seems to fall, not upon love as a dynamism giving rise to the Word and the *Pneuma*, but upon the very nature of love as presupposing an inner relationality that is personal in kind. This is his primal and dominating principle to which the doctrine of the processions is subordinate. The universal tradition on the invariant order among the Persons demanded that he give consideration to the processions. But there his system reaches an impasse, because love may well require a plurality of persons as its condition, it does not explain the origin of such plurality. If the processions also constitute a structure indigenous to love, then it is difficult to explain that the Father is without origin, that the Son arises from the Father alone, and that the Spirit's origin is from Father and Son (this is the Western tradition which Richard represents). That is, it is difficult to maintain a distinct personal identity for each of the Three. One is inclined to think of one person who reproduces himself twice over.[88]

Hill's criticism is justified, however, only insofar as the only real relations are the processions, as in the Augustinian view. Hill fails to see Richard's affinity with the Eastern tradition in this aspect: persons are distinguished by origin, not by relation; the relations merely express personal distinction. Furthermore the basic presupposition at work in Richard's formulation is that trinitarian relations need not necessarily be relations of origin or processions. Hence the Son and Spirit can be eternally related, without having their eternal origin in one another. The possibility of genuinely interpersonal relations of love is dependent not upon origin, but on their individual personalities. Persons as persons, in Richard's view, are capable of being the subject of acts that relate each to the other; they are capable of loving relationships within the one substance of God who is love. As such Richard's view is an alternative in Western theology to the predominant Augustinian position.[89]

Pannenberg observes with approval how the antinomy between the personal character of the Three in God, on the one hand, and the unity of the divine essence, on the other, is resolved in Richard's intimation.[90] Personal autonomy is established precisely in the relation of origin through which the persons are bound together in the one indivisible essence. However, he sees in Richard the tendency of over-emphasizing the independence of persons at the expense of the divine unity. Richard is successful in deducing the immanent-Trinitarian dynamic from the essence of God's love, yet he fails to derive God's unity from the reciprocity of the persons. Furthermore Richard does not develop his theory from the perspective of the economy of salvation, and thus the immanental relations are really devoid of any definite content. How God might be in and for himself is Richard's preoccupation; how God might be for us is left unattended.

Augustine holds that love as 'ordered love' must take into consideration the worth of the object. This view is shared by Medieval theology, too: the greater the good, the greatest the love.[91] From this, Richard deduces that God as the highest good must love himself supremely. If God is love, the object on which God's love bestows must be infinite. To love supremely that which is not worthy of such infinite love would be to exhibit a 'disordered' love, which is inapplicable to a being like God. Nygren criticizes:

> The unquestioned premise of this argument is that God's love must not be an "unordered" love. It must not, as Agape does, leave the scale of values out of account, but like Eros it must be guided by the worth of the object. Richard of St. Victor has no room for the New Testament idea that the highest love is precisely that which loves those who are not worthy of it (Rom. v. 8). In other words, Richard will not allow God's love to be spontaneous and unmotivated, to be Agape. The result is that in the last resort it can only be conceived as Divine self-love, God's "*amor sui*".[92]

Nygren's criticism, that God's love need not have an object of infinite value to be the highest love, would undermine the entire argument of Richard if his criticism is allowed to do its work.[93] In my view, his criticism of Richard is wrong-headed. He does not observe the fundamental distinction between Supreme love and creaturely love. The basic point emphasized by Richard, which Bonaventure accepts, is that the finite cannot be the perfect self-communication of God, for then creation would, of necessity, be equal to God, in which case it would be divine like God is.[94] This is tantamount to collapsing the distinction between the uncreated order and created order. The maximum of self-diffusion can be realized only in the Trinity, not in creation, since creation itself cannot meet the demands of divine 'fecundity' (Bonaventure's term) or production. This brings out his vision of God, that God is the purest and perfect self-communicative love which is productive within the Godhead, prior to and independently of creation. This crucial point Nygren fails to see.

Richard's conception of the unity of the divine nature as a dynamic one grounded in the community of intrinsically-related persons is praiseworthy. It gives rise to a concept of what it is *to be*, i.e. God's being is constituted by the relationship of persons in a communion of love. Richard's view of God as a community of persons is also a contribution to the development of the twentieth century social doctrine of the Trinity.[95]

Chapter Four

Filioque, *Solitary love and mutual love*
Thomas Aquinas

Thomas Aquinas (1227–1274), born near Aquino, a town between Rome and Naples, has been called 'the clearest thinker and the boldest innovator' in medieval scholastic and speculative theology.[1] His works on the Trinity appear most thoroughly in his *Commentary on the Sentences*, the *Summa contra gentiles*, the *Summa Theologica* and the *Disputed Questions on the Power of God*.[2] The views expressed in his *Commentary on the Sentences* coincide substantially with those found in his *Summa Theologica* (or *Summa*). Thus there is no need to give them separate consideration. This study deals with the third article of faith, more concentratedly on the eternal procession of the Holy Spirit, showing that Aquinas too, like Anselm and Richard of Victor, adheres essentially to the *filioque* doctrine of Latin Tradition, that the Spirit proceeds from the Father 'and the Son.' However Aquinas is more open than Anselm to the doctrine of *per filium*, that the Spirit proceeds from the Father 'through the Son', but not without clarifications. In relation to himself God knows himself as the Word, and loves himself as Holy Spirit, so that the generation of the Son and the procession of the Spirit constitute the eternal distinctions in God, yet without compromising the simplicity of the One essence. Divine persons differ through relations of origin to each other, and their unity is grounded in the One essence which the Son and the Spirit receive from the Father. It will be made clear that on the one hand Aquinas is with Anselm in giving priority to the solitary love as the formal reason (*ratio formalis*) of spiration, while on the other hand he is with Augustine and Damascene in affirming the Spirit as the fruit of the love of two subjects, Father and Son. In other words, Aquinas has it both ways, that the Spirit proceeds by the love of the Infinite Being for itself, but also as the mutual love of the Father and the Son for each other. This is his ecumenical contribution, pointing the way for the East to agree with the West, while remaining faithful to his own language and tradition.

Natural Theology and Trinity as an Article of Faith

Aquinas is first and foremost a Christian, a medieval, and Western Catholic theologian, who rightly observes the distinction between theology and other spheres of knowledge. 'While its subject matter is revelation and grace in life, the first principles of theology are drawn from the Bible and from the creeds and teachings of the church. Revelation, faith, and theology cannot find expression apart from human culture, but the role of culture's expression is not to prove what is revealed but to explain it.'[3] He sees a close relation between faith and reason. To abandon faith in favour of reason or to give up reason for faith, in Aquinas' eyes, commits a 'treason against God, the living truth.'[4] Although he accentuates the positive role of natural theology, he acknowledges what it cannot establish. Rational arguments, as in his '*Five Proofs*', can establish the existence of a single Absolute, a God who is the source of everything that is. But 'as far as natural theology goes, the question whether many distinct Persons can be one and the same God is *demonstrably undecidable*, on Aquinas' view.'[5] Quoting Aquinas:

> It is impossible to come to the knowledge of the Trinity of divine persons through natural reason. For it has been shown already that through natural reason human beings can know God only from creatures; and they lead to the knowledge of God as effects do to their causes. Therefore by natural reason we can know of God only what characterizes him necessarily as the source of all beings... Now the creative power of God is shared by the whole Trinity; hence it goes with the unity of nature, not with distinction of persons. Therefore through natural reason we can know what has to do with the unity of nature, but not with the distinction of persons.[6]

Natural theology can establish what is true of being with respect to his being God, but cannot discern the essence of being itself, or God as he is in himself. This is where philosophy can take us so far and no further. There are theological truths which he takes to be beyond the power of reason (*supra rationem*) to demonstrate, and can only be known in revelation, by the gratuitous self-disclosure of God. Thus he warns against any rational incursion into the inner mystery of the Trinity, about which we simply have to be taught.

> Those who try to prove the Trinity of persons by natural powers of reason detract from faith in two ways. First on the point of its dignity, for the object of faith is those invisible realities which are beyond the reach of human reason ... Secondly, on the point of advantage in bringing others to faith. For when people want to support faith by unconvincing arguments, they become a laughing stock for the unbelievers, who think that we rely on such arguments and believe because of them.[7]

With Augustine, he writes: 'that God is triune is uniquely an object of belief, and one cannot prove it in any demonstrable way. Some reasons can be advanced but they are not necessitating, and they have probability only for the believer.'[8] Human reason can discern what belongs to 'the unity of essence', not what belongs to 'the distinction of persons.'[9] Thus the philosophers could know 'some of the essential attributes appropriated to the persons, as power to the Father, wisdom to the Son, goodness to the Holy Spirit', but cannot grasp the mystery of the Trinity of divine persons 'by its proper attributes, namely, paternity, filiation, and procession.'[10] Seemingly as a criticism of Augustinian analogy of the mind, he states, 'Nor is the divine image in the intellect an adequate proof about anything in God, since intellect is not in God and ourselves univocally.'[11] To further elucidate:

> For the human intellect is not able to reach a comprehension of the divine substance through its natural power. For, according to its manner of knowing in the present life, the intellect depends on the sense for the origin of knowledge; and so those things that do not fall under the senses cannot be grasped by the human intellect except in so far as the knowledge of them is gathered from sensible things. Now,

sensible things cannot lead the human intellect to the point of seeing in them the nature of divine substance; for sensible things are effects that fall short of the power of their cause.[12]

Aquinas' view is at odds with Alexander of Hales (1186-1245) who attributes the inefficacy of our mind 'in dealing with what most truly is' to original sin.[13] Reason by itself, regardless of original sin, in Aquinas' eyes, is intrinsically incapable of grasping the necessity, that God is a Trinity. He rejects Anselm's attempt in furnishing the 'necessary reasons' (*rationes necessariae*) for the necessity, that which faith believes to be necessarily true.[14] Likewise he objects to Richard of St. Victor's view that 'not only probable but even necessary arguments can be found for any explanation of the truth.'[15] Contrarily, for Aquinas, 'Arguments (at best) may be said to manifest (not to prove) the Trinity; that is to say, given the doctrine of the Trinity (an article of faith), we find arguments in harmony with it.' He acquiesces with Hilary and Ambrose that natural reason cannot obtain the sacred mystery of the trinity of divine persons, 'that for which no necessary arguments can be given.'[16] Quoting Ambrose: 'It is impossible to know the secret of generation. The mind fails, the voice is silent.'[17] '(T)he inner life of God, the personal structure of God's being that is the foundation for his gratuitous self-communication within created history', Daley writes of Aquinas, 'can only be known through that historical revelation: through the Scriptures, which speak to us of the incarnate Word and his Spirit, that leads us to the Father.'[18]

The Holy Spirit as a Subsistent Person in God

In part IV of his *Contra Gentiles* (1264), especially the concluding section, Aquinas offers a fuller reflection than his earlier works do on the procession of the Holy Spirit. He begins with exegesis of the relevant passages in Scripture as Matthew 28: 19, I John 5: 7, John 15: 26 etc. Chapter 17, entitled '*Quod Spiritus sanctus sit verus Deus*', is his combat with the teachings of Arius and Macedonius that the Holy Spirit belongs to the created order, that the Spirit is a creature. I Cor. 6. 19, which speaks of our bodies as 'the temple of the Holy Spirit', and I Cor. 6:15, which speaks of our bodies as 'members of

Christ', when taken together, point to the divinity of the Spirit. For 'since Christ is true God', argues Aquinas, 'it would be inappropriate that the members of Christ should be a temple of the Holy Spirit, unless the Holy Spirit were God.'[19] He points out that because the Holy Spirit performs various works which are exclusively Divine, he must share the Divine Nature. For instance, if sanctification is exclusively a divine work (cf. Lev. 22:9), and if it is the Holy Spirit who sanctifies (cf. I Cor. 6:11; 2 Thess. 2:13), then the Holy Spirit must be God. Creation is a work performed exclusively by God, and because Scripture attributes the operations of creation to the Spirit, then the Spirit's Godhead is affirmed (cf. Job 33:4). The Spirit cannot be a creature, for he searches the deep things of God (cf. I Cor. 2: 10-11), a work which is beyond human possibility, but solely Divine. Aquinas adopts a form of argument from human personality to divine personality. Analogously the Holy Spirit is to God just as the spirit of man is to man. 'But the spirit of man is essential (*intrinsecus*) to man and not of a nature strange to him, but it is actually part of him. Therefore the Holy Spirit is not of a nature strange to God.'[20] That the Spirit is the Revealer of the mysteries of God is another indication of his Deity. Furthermore, 'To adopt as sons of God cannot be the work of any other than God', he writes, 'The Holy Spirit is the Cause of adoption, so says the Apostle in Rom. 8. ...Therefore the Holy Spirit is not a creature, but God.'[21]

The aforementioned reasoning means Divine acts correspond to Divine nature. Taking his cue from Aristotle, according to whom 'for as everything is so does it operate', Aquinas affirms that God's being is his doing; the divine nature is divine agency.[22] The divine nature is located in the act which he performs so that the God-at-work is indeed the God-revealed. There is a unity of operation between the Father and the Son, hence there is a unity of nature between them. Likewise the unity of operation between the Son and the Spirit (Matt. 10: 20) means, 'therefore the nature of the Son and of the Holy Spirit is the same; and, consequently, the Nature of the Father, since it has been shown that the Father and the Son possess one Nature.'[23]

In chapter 18 of the same, Aquinas seeks to show that the Spirit is not an 'accident' in God, but is a 'subsistent person', numbered along with the Father and the Son. Against the Macedonians, Aquinas repudiates any thought of the Spirit as 'some accidental perfection of the mind' bestowed upon us by God, as, for example, wisdom or love. The Spirit is presented in Scripture as 'the Cause of all the perfections of the human mind (Rom. v. 5; I Cor. xii.. 8).'[24] Scripture, he adds, also makes it clear that the Spirit is not the 'Godhead Itself' (Essence) of the Father and the Son, in which case he could not be distinguished personally from them. 'For the Holy Spirit proceeds from the Father (John xv. 26), and receives from the Son (John xvi. 14), which are functions not of the Divine Essence, but of a subsistent person.' 'Since the Father and the Son are subsistent Persons, and of the Divine nature, the Holy Spirit would not be numbered with Them unless he were a Person subsisting in the Divine Nature; but He is numbered with Them (Matt. xxviii, 19; 2 Cor. xiii, 14; I John v, 7). From which it is clearly shown that not only is He a subsistent Person just as the Father and the Son, but also that He possesses a unity of Essence along with Them.'[25] The Spirit belongs essentially to the uncreated order, and cannot be numbered with any created accidents. Thus Aquinas holds this firmly concerning the Holy Spirit that He is true God, subsisting in the Divine Nature, and is personally distinct from the other two in the same Godhead. 'As the begetting of the Son is coeternal with the begetter (hence the Father does not exist before begetting the Son), so the procession of the Holy Spirit is coeternal with His principle. Hence, the Son was not begotten before the Holy Spirit proceeded; but each of the operations is eternal.'[26] In the procession order, neither the Son nor the Spirit is subsequent to the Father, even if they proceed from him.

The Divine Processions

The term 'procession' refers to origin in the general sense, applicable most suitably to a being like God. Aquinas writes, 'Since divinity is better designated by what is common than by what is special, in the origin of divine persons the verb *proceeding* is most suitable.'[27] In God there are two 'processions', which he explains by the structure of the 'spirit' itself, namely by thinking (knowing) and willing (loving) of itself. The spirit, in Congar's words, 'exists in its being as reality, in its thought as a known "object" and in its will as a loved "object".'[28] Thinking and willing, as functions of spiritual being, remain immanently in the subject as its life. Within the divine nature, in other words, there is knowing and willing.[29] Theologically, these processions can be understood as emanations of the nature of the spirit by mode of intellectual understanding and by mode of will, without intending an essential division as in creaturely and material individuation. Indebted to Augustine's psychological analogy, he defines the image of the Trinity primarily in terms of two processions of the Word and love.[30] He endorses a clear distinction between two divine processions, 'generation' and 'procession.'[31] The former is an intellectual act of conception which begets its likeness from its own substance, in which case the Father, through an exercise of the divine knowing, reproduces his own likeness in the Son; the latter he understands as an 'impulse' or 'movement' of the divine will, which produces that which is other than his own reproduction of itself.[32] Just as this dynamic movement is perfect, as it must be within the Godhead, the resulting product must also be fully God. Intellect and will, though distinct, are essentially one in God. Every act of the will has its origin from love. He clarifies, 'in every intellectual nature there is will, and that God, of course, is intelligent …, there must, then, be will in Him; the will of God, to be sure, is not something which accrues to His essence, just as His intellect is not, … but the will of God is His very substance. And since the intellect of God, as well, is His very substance, it follows that the one thing in God is intellect and will.'[33] The act of will proceeding by way of love is a distinction which is ontologically constitutive of God's Deity. Given that all that is in God is God, this love, as a proceeding in God, is also divine. Hence love, as being in God and as eternally oriented toward himself, is called Holy Spirit, whose procession from the divine will produces not a 'son', but a 'spirit.' The same contents emerge in his *Summa*:

> In God procession corresponds only to an action which remains within the agent himself, not to one bent on something external. In the spiritual world the only actions of this kind are those of the intellect and will. But the Word's procession corresponds to the action of the intellect. Now in us there is another spiritual process following the action of the will, namely the coming forth of love, whereby what is loved is in the lover, just as the thing expressed or actually understood in the conceiving of an idea is in the knower. For this reason besides the procession of the Word another procession is posited in God, namely the procession of love.[34]

The Spirit arises as a distinct 'inclination', characterized above all by 'affective' love, as in Daley's words, 'a force of attraction.'[35] Through 'natural inclination', the 'lover' embraces its term or object, its 'beloved' in himself so that 'the beloved is in the lover.' But will 'bears a certain order to the conception by which the intellect conceives a thing.' He, like Augustine, accentuates the priority of knowing over willing, that something must be 'known' before it would be 'loved.' From the processional model that the Holy Spirit proceeds by way of will and the Son by way of intellect, it follows that the Holy Spirit is from the Son. 'For love proceeds from a word: we are able to love nothing but that which a word of the heart conceives.'[36] The Word, begotten by the Father, is a Word from whom Love proceeds. He is '*Verbum non qualecumque, sed spirans amorem.*'[37] An inner word must be conceived within the mind before love proceeds as a response. Aquinas writes: 'Necessarily, therefore, does the love (fittingly, the Holy Spirit) by which God is in the divine will as a beloved in a lover proceed both from the Word of God and from the God whose Word He is.' Thus the Spirit's 'proceeding' is not that of 'generation.' The Spirit proceeds not as another word, but as 'somehow inwardly impelling the lover toward the very thing beloved.' Holy Spirit, who proceeds by way of love as 'a kind of existing spiration', does not proceed as 'begotten.'[38] Therefore he cannot be called the Son. The Son proceeds from the Father by way of knowledge with which God knows himself; the Holy Spirit proceeds from the Father and the Son by way of love with which God loves himself. The Son's procession as 'generation' clearly sets him apart from the Spirit's as 'spiration.' Here Aquinas finds no created analogy for the communication of essence in respect of the procession from the will resulting in a third, as distinct from the second.[39] The term 'spiration', used for the Spirit's procession, indicates its inner dynamic movement towards the production of 'spirit', which is distinct from the 'son.'[40] This Davies illumines: 'When P understands X there is a likeness between P and X. But not so when P loves X. The procession of love is therefore thought of in terms of motion towards. And "spirit" is a proper way of naming this motion since it bears the sense of living motion and impulse, as when one says that people are impelled by love to do something.'[41]

The term 'love', in Aquinas, can be used of the divinity both 'essentially' and 'personally.' Essentially, Augustine speaks of all three persons as love so that it cannot be exclusively used for the Spirit.

But when taken personally, Aquinas avers, love is a name proper to the Holy Spirit, for it signifies the relation between the lover and the beloved. In this sense, love indicates a going out, a *processio* in God. As regards the second Person, the term 'Word' is used to indicate what is going out in God, and the term 'to speak' is used to indicate the *relation* between the Word spoken and its origin. Likewise, as regards the third Person, Aquinas writes:

> For as far as we use the words *amor* and *dilectio* to express the relation of what comes forth by way of love to its origin and vice versa, by 'love' is understood the forthcoming love, and by 'to love' the breathing of forthcoming love. In this sense, 'love is the name for the Person and 'to love' (*amare, diligere*) the notional term, as 'to speak' and 'to beget.'[42]

For Augustine, love is predicated equally of all the three persons, which presents for him difficulties in distinguishing the procession of the Spirit.[43] Contrarily, Aquinas says that the Spirit 'alone' is properly called love. Just as 'Word' is a *proprium* of the Second Person of the Trinity, so 'love' is a *proprium* of the third person – both are not used *essentialiter*, for the entire Trinity. To prove his point, he repeats what has been said earlier that the Son proceeds as a concept known by God: 'when a thing is understood by anyone, there results in the one who understands a conception of the thing understood, which conception we call a word.'[44] Subsequently, when a knower 'loves' what he knows, his will receives 'a certain impression' of 'the object loved' and 'the object loved is said to be in the lover, just as the thing understood is in the one who understands.' So it follows that when someone knows and loves himself, 'he is in himself not only by real identity, but also as the thing understood is in the one who understands, and the thing loved is in the lover.'[45] Unlike Anselm, Aquinas remains sympathetic towards the pneumatology of the Eastern formula: 'The Spirit rests on the Son.' For Aquinas, the Spirit rests not only 'on' the Son, but most deeply 'in' the Son 'as the love of the lover abides in the beloved.'[46]

> The Holy Ghost is said to be the bond of the Father and Son, inasmuch as He is Love; because, since the Father loves Himself and the Son with one Love, and conversely, there is expressed in the Holy

Ghost, as Love, the relation of the Father to the Son, and conversely, as that of the lover to the beloved. But from the fact that the Father and the Son mutually love one another, it necessarily follows that this *mutual Love*, the Holy Ghost, proceeds from both. As regards origin, therefore, the Holy Ghost is not the medium, but the third person in the Trinity; whereas as regard the aforesaid relation, He is the bond between the two persons, as proceeding from both.[47]

To add, if love is the proper name of the Holy Ghost, the word 'Gift' is most fittingly his. Again, he approves of Augustine's saying, 'As "to be born" is, for the Son, to be from the Father, so for the Holy Ghost, "to be the Gift of God" is to proceed from the Father and Son.'[48] The Holy Spirit is called Gift because he proceeds from another and he is given to us personally. As gratuitous Love, he has the nature of the 'First Gift', through which every other gift is freely given.[49] And because Holy Spirit receives his proper name from Father and Son, 'Gift', taken personally in God, is his proper name too.

> Because the Son proceeds as a word, whose nature it is to be the likeness of its principle, He is properly called the Image, even though the Holy Ghost is also like the Father; so also, because the Holy Ghost proceeds from the Father as love, He is properly called Gift, although the Son, too, is given. For that the Son is given from the Father's love, according to the words, God so loved the world, as to give His only begotten Son (Jn. iii.16).[50]

To be a gift within the Trinity, the Spirit cannot merely be a reality given by only the Father to the Son, for that would deny the Son's positive role in the Spirit's procession. Nor is it only by the Son to the Father, for that would compromise the idea that the Spirit is the Father's gift to us. Therefore it must be, in Aquinas, by both to each other so that the Spirit is the mutual gift of Father and Son to each other. The mutuality of this gift is best understood if the Spirit is the mutual love of Father and Son. The mutual love is the mutual gift. So if we identify the Spirit with the mutual love of Father and Son for each other as Aquinas does, then the gift is ontologically constitutive of the Spirit's personality, not simply an addendum to an already constituted reality.[51] This is how Aquinas seeks to establish speculatively the *processus a patre filioque*, by understanding the Spirit as the Father's and the Son's mutual love. The Spirit, as Gift of both the Father and the Son, is love, and thus he discloses to us the common love by which the Father and the Son mutually love each other. Thus, the Spirit is the 'gift' eternally bestowed by the Father on the Son, through whom it is imparted in time to us. By the Holy Spirit or 'Love proceeding', says Aquinas, 'Father and Son love both each other and us.'[52] Trinitarianly speaking, the Son is known and loved by the Father and the Spirit is the love which consequently proceeds. The Spirit is the Father's love for the Son; conversely, the Spirit is the Son's love for the Father. Which is the dominant motif – the Spirit as the fruit of the mutual love of the first two for each other, or the Spirit as the fruit of the love which the divine essence has for itself, or both? We shall return to this question in the concluding section.

As regards the immanent Trinity, Aquinas speaks of the relation of the Holy Spirit to the Father and the Son, again showing that he belongs essentially to the same Godhead as the others.[53] These attributes or qualities – knowledge, power and operations – possessed by all three persons, compose God's Essence. Because the Spirit's Divinity is the Divinity of God himself which both the Father and the Son are, i.e., the Spirit is of one being with the Father and the Son, then he must be eternally of the Father and the Son. If the full unity of the Trinity is to be maintained, then the Spirit's Divinity must proceed both from the Father and the Son. Like Anselm, the principle of unity is logically prior to the differentiation of persons. The origin of the Spirit is rooted not in the differentiation between Father and Son, but in their fundamental unity of essence. Father and Son together as One God constitute the one single principle of the Spirit, and in one spiration confer their being or divinity to the Spirit. This is 'by reason of the unity of divine power, and by one production they produce the Holy Spirit.'[54] In article 2, chapter 10 of *de Potentia Dei*, Aquinas disposes of the argument of the Greeks, that the distinction between the Son and the Spirit is grounded, not so much in either the distinction of origin from which processions occur or in the terms in which processions have their product as 'in the very process by which they are produced, that generation and procession are intrinsically different from one another as acts just as generation and creation are agreed to be.'[55] He insists that a process or act 'has its species' not from itself, but from either its origin or its term. In God, all three persons possess, as their own, all divine attributes and divine operations because they coinhere in essence and acts. So what differentiates them does not hinge on what they have or how they have it, but 'that the one has same things from the other.' Daley intimates: 'It is the source from which each is God, and the order in which they are or spring from that source, that determines both their relationships and their personal identities.'[56]

The Eastern opponents of the *filioque*, Aquinas says, wrongly hold the Latins of anathema for adding this to the Creed. Scripture does not provide explicit evidence against it, unless, he argues, one sees John 15:26 as entirely 'frivolous.' By reason of the unity of the essence, what is said of the Father must also be said of the Son insofar as it does not infringe the distinct characteristics of the individual persons. The procession of the Spirit from the Son is 'implicitly' found in the original Greek of the Creed of Constantinople. In this, Aquinas dispels Photius' argument that *filioque* would contradict the primordial unity of God, thereby dividing the Godhead into two separate sources of the Spirit.[57] Then he points to the Spirit's mission, by which the Son is sent visibly and invisibly. The Spirit, in the form of dove, descends upon Christ at His baptism, and in fiery tongues upon his apostles. These are visible manifestations of the Spirit's mission from the Father and the Son, without implying any inferiority to them. For the Holy Spirit is not excluded from the Godhead, even when occasionally he is not mentioned together with the Father and the Son. 'For neither can God the Father be comprehended without the Word and Love, nor conversely; and for this reason all three are understood to be Three in One.' Matt. 11:27 reads: 'Neither does any one know the Father except the Son'; although both the Father and the Holy Spirit know the Son. Basing on these passages (Matt. 11:27; John 17:3; Rom. 1:7; I Cor. 8:6, etc.,), Aquinas concludes that any divine attribute which pertains to one of the Persons is to be attributable to the other two, as required by the Oneness of God.

Romans 8.9 speaks of him as 'the Spirit of the Son', showing that the Spirit has his source from the Son, but not alone. For added to the same text are these words of the same Apostle: 'If the Spirit of God dwells in us', which proves that the same Spirit is of the Father and the Son. 'Yet it cannot be said that the Holy Spirit is the Spirit of

Christ in this sense alone that He as Man possessed Him (Luke iv. I, 3), for from the statement in Gal. iv. 6, the Holy Spirit makes us sons of God inasmuch as He is the Spirit of the Son of God. ... But the Holy Spirit cannot be in any sense be called the Spirit of the Son of God except in respect of source, because this distinction alone is met with in the Godhead.' Again, John 15:26 speaks of the Spirit as 'sent' by the Son. The word 'sent' refers to an authority of the Son in regard to the Spirit, one that is 'not of lordship or of superiority, but according to source only.' Therefore, the Spirit proceeds from the Son.[58]

The New Testament links the Spirit closely with Christ in such a way that the Person and work of the Spirit are defined through the Person and work of Christ, not vice versa. However Luke 4:18, where Christ himself claims that 'the Spirit of the Lord is upon me', seems to say the contrary, that the Son likewise is sent by the Holy Spirit. This suggests that Christ is 'of the Spirit', indicating that the Spirit is the source of the Son. To this objection, Aquinas replies that the work of the Spirit in this connection has to do with the incarnate mode of the Son's existence, that 'the Son is sent by the Holy Spirit in regards of the nature which he assumed.'[59] It remains, therefore, that the Spirit, in respect of the eternal Son, is 'of Christ.' Furthermore, John 16:14 accentuates that the Spirit receives his essence from the Son. Governed by the doctrines of *communicatio essentiae* and *communicatio operationem*, he argues, "If all things that belong to the Father belong also to the Son, the authority of the Father, in accordance with which is the source of the Holy Spirit, must also belong to the Son.'[60] Hence, just as the Holy Spirit receives from the Father that which is the Father's, he too receives from the Son that which is the Son's. But that the Spirit, as true God, receives his essence from the Father and the Son, does not make him their Son.

Opposition of Relation or Relation of Origin

How does Aquinas resolve the problem of the Trinity, God being one in the absolute sense, while at the same time several in the relative sense? The solution is to be found in the idea of divine relationship of origin. It is antecedently elaborated by Anselm who states: 'Everything in God is one where there is no opposition of relation.'[61] In the One undivided Godhead, distinctions between persons rest solely on their mutual relations. Their being three in God is required by them being genuinely related to each other *via* processions.

> When something springs from a principle which has the same nature, then necessarily both that which issues and that from which it issues belongs to the same order; and so must have real relationships with each other. Since processions in God are in the identical nature … the relations arising from the divine processions must be real relations.'[62]

A Divine Person is not distinguished from another, says Aquinas, except by the 'opposition of relation.'[63] This teaching, in Anselm and Aquinas, has its roots in Augustine: 'God is everything that he has except for the relations through which each person is referred to each other.'[64]

> Nothing is predicated of God as an accidental category since nothing in him can undergo change. Yet not every predicate belongs to the category of substance. For we use also 'relation', as when we speak of Father-Son or Son-Father. This is not accidental predication because the one has always been Father and the other Son… Hence although being Father and being Son are different, there is no difference in substance, for our predication refers to relation, not to substance. However, relation is not used as an accidental category since there can be no change in God.[65]

This, Aquinas says, conforms to 'straight reasoning. For even among things, with material distinction gone (and in the divine Persons such can have no place), one discovers no differentiation except by such opposition.'[66] Divine processions constitute Persons who are identical with the divine essence, yet different from each other. For the Divine Persons, since they are one in Essence, are recognized as distinct only by relation of source. Each procession consists of two terms: the principle from which proceeds and that which proceeds. These two terms are related to each other as one is the origin from the other, thereby establishing an ontological distinction between persons. To quote Aquinas:

> The idea of relation, however, necessarily means the reference of one to another, according as one is relatively opposed to another. So as in God there is a real relation, there must also be a real opposition. The very nature of relative opposition includes distinction. Hence, there must be real distinction in God, not, indeed, according to that which is absolute – namely, essence, wherein there is supreme unity and simplicity – but according to that which is relative.[67]

Analogously, the word 'relation', when applied to creatures, signifies 'another' thing; whereas, when applied to God, signifies not another but the 'absolute' God, the one self-same unity which cannot be 'perfectly expressed' by the word itself.[68] Aquinas, henceforth, thinks of the divine three in relation to one another as the one self-same unity, which indeed is his dogmatic starting point.

Aquinas accepts Boethius' definition of 'person' as 'an individual substance of rational nature.'[69] Davies doubts if Boethius' definition of person is thoroughly embraced by Aquinas.[70] He argues that Aquinas invokes Boethius' definition in view of asserting the distinction between Son and Spirit by way of the modes of understanding and love (implying intellect). Aquinas, like Boethius, does affirm that the persons are individual, distinct and rational. But he moves beyond it, for later in *Summa Theologica,* when dealing with question 39, he describes *person* as '*relatio subsistens in divina natura,* the Persons of the Godhead being distinguished really by reason of an "opposite real relation".'[71] The same appears in his *de potentia,* where person is defined as 'nothing else than a relationally distinct subsistent in the divine nature.'[72] Fortman rightly comments, 'And if this is broadened so that "it becomes a divine subsistent in an intellectual nature", it is the best definition of person that has been produced so far. It is easy to see in it the three essential notes of a person, incommunicability, substantiality, intellectuality.'[73] Even though the word 'person' does not appear in the Bible, what it signifies is borne out by it. Bray elucidates, '*Person was an aspect of a nature which signified what was distinct in that God.* Because distinction in God is only by relations of origin, a divine person is defined by Aquinas as a *subsistent relation.*'[74] That which defines the Person is his relation of origin.[75] Such definition certainly is at odds with the view that person is essentially a distinct center of consciousness. These immanental relations in God are what Aquinas later calls, in the *Summa*, 'subsistent relations', that which exist in themselves, not an aspect of that which is related.[76] All three persons possess, indeed are, the one and same divine nature. But each is equally God, in a relatively unique manner. God's being is simply relation. Each relation is God existing in a distinct manner, as a distinct opposing relationship to the other. This means: the divine nature in the relation of 'paternity' is the Father, in the relation of 'filiation' is the Son, and in the relation of 'spiration' is the Spirit. Speaking analogously, each person experiences being the one and same Godhead but in a relatively unique way peculiar to his distinctiveness as Father, Son or Spirit.

The *filioque* is justified in the fact that the Father is the principle of two functions, *paternitas* (paternity) and *spiratio* (spiration). The Son proceeds from the Father, so does the Holy Spirit. This Aquinas elaborates by way of four subsistent relations. The Father thus must be related both to the Son and the Holy Spirit as 'the source (*principium*) to that which is from the source.' The Father relates to the Son by way of paternity, but does not relate to the Spirit as such, otherwise the Spirit would be a Son. For paternity constitutes the Father but pertains exclusively to the Son, not the Spirit. The Father is not the Son; nor is the Son the Father. But the Father is everything that the Son is, namely God, except for the opposition of the relationship itself, that which differentiates one from the other within the unity of both. This means there must be another relation in the Father by which he is related to the Spirit, this he calls a 'breathing-forth.' Likewise, just as there abides in the Son a certain relation by which he relates to the Father, this he calls filiation, there must be another relation in the Spirit by which he relates to the Son, this he calls 'procession.' In the origin of the Son from the Father, there are two relations: paternity and filiation, one as 'originating' as regards the Father, the other as 'originated' as regards the Son. In the origin of the Spirit from the Son, there are two relations too: breathing forth and procession, one as spirated from the Father, the other as proceeded from the Son. Yet these two functions do not constitute two persons, but their mutually opposed relations, 'as touching source between the Son and the Holy Spirit, so that the One is from the other.' So if they are to be regarded as distinct persons, the 'passive' process of the Spirit must differ with that of the Son, since no genuine opposition between the 'active' processes of generation and the spiration in the Father arises as to split the Father, the source of Son and Spirit, into two distinct persons. Active spiration, which belongs to the Father whose spirative power is shared with the Son, does not form a new person. If the sources and modes of origin of the Son and the Spirit oppose each other so that the two define each other as persons by relationship between them, then the assertion that the Son himself must be, along with the Father, the source of the Spirit's proceeding is established. The ontological distinctions between the second and third persons rests solely upon their mutually opposed relations, thus making *filioque* a necessity. As regards the relation between the Son and the Spirit, there are two options: either the Son comes from the Spirit or the Spirit comes from the Son. Nobody accepts the former. Something must distinguish the Son from the Spirit, and this, Aquinas argues, is a relation other than that of proceeding from the Father. Only his relation as begetter distinguishes the Father as Father. By the same token, only the Spirit's relation as 'proceeding from the Son' distinguishes the Spirit from the Son. He reasons further, 'if the Father alone be the Source of the Holy Spirit, the Holy Spirit would thus not be distinct from the Son.' Then the principle of the procession of the Spirit would be identical to the generation of the Son. And this is to commit what Aquinas calls the 'Sabellian impiety' of collapsing the distinctions of persons. 'Therefore, that there may be otherness in processions and otherness in those proceeding', Aquinas concludes, 'one of necessity says that the Holy Spirit is not from the Father alone, but from the Father and the Son.'[77] This is why Aquinas insists that it is 'necessary to faith and salvation' to adhere to *filioque* doctrine, and 'that those who deny that the Spirit proceeds from the Son are in no way tolerated.'[78]

The only distinguishing characteristics of the divine Persons consist in the manner in which they give and receive being. However these characteristics which we ascribe to them do not separate the divine essence, for God is indivisibly One. The unity is in the *communicatio essentiae* of God, according to which the Son receives his essence from the Father, and the Spirit his essence from the Father and the Son, all of these take place within the same Godhead. Insofar as the Persons 'face' each other as principle and term, origin and recipient, are they truly recognized as differentiated, thus distinct persons.[79] The towardsness of beings is the essence of relation. Thus the only thing distinguishing Son from Spirit is this: the Son acts, together with the Father, in the spiration of the Spirit. Aquinas agrees with Plato who holds that no distinction is found in immaterial substances except that of order. In respect of the divine persons who are immaterial, there can be no other order except that of origin.[80] The communication of substance occurs by means of the fact that the one Person is the origin of the other, as the Father is the origin of the Son, the Son is the origin of the Spirit, and both the Father and Son together as one spirative power constitutes the one principle of the Spirit.

> Moreover, the Father and the Son, unity of essence considered, do not differ save in this: He is the Father and He is the Son. So anything other than this is common to the Father and the Son. But to be the principle of the Holy Spirit is not included in the notion of paternity and of sonship, for it is one relation by which the Father is Father, and another by which He is the principle of the Holy Spirit, as was said above. Therefore, to be the principle of the Holy Spirit is common to the Father and the Son.[81]

Therefore if the Spirit is distinguished from the Son, he is necessarily 'from' the Son, not vice versa. The Son cannot be said to come 'from' the Spirit, since the Spirit is 'of' the Son, and is 'given' by the Son, just as the Son, as distinguished from the Father, is given by him. The same line of thought resurfaces in his *Summa*, where he argues that should the Spirit not proceed from the Father and the Son as a single principle, there are no grounds for distinguishing him from the Son.[82]

Furthermore Aquinas' distinction between the essential union and hypostatic union also underscores the *filioque* doctrine. Failure to observe this distinction also results in an abolition of the trinitarian distinctions. Incarnation is exclusively of the Son, not of the Father and the Spirit. Only the Son, not the others, is connected through hypostatic union with the 'term' of the incarnating action.[83] Incarnation does not happen in respect of the One Essence in which all three Persons consist, but in respect of '*hypostasis* and individual character (*suppositum*) according to which three Persons are distinguished.'⁸⁴ God acts in full unity with himself *ad extra* so that the Trinity is the subject of the incarnation, but being attired is irreducibly peculiar to the Word.

Why only three? Chapter 26 of his *Contra Gentiles* states two reasons. The first lies in the conception of the relation of origin, which as regards procession does not extend to things without, 'for what proceeds in this manner would not be co-essential with its own source.' The process must remain within (*interius*) its own source, which can be found only in the action of understanding and will. "Therefore there can be in God only two Persons proceeding, One by way of understanding, as the Word, or Son; and the Other by way of love, or as Holy Spirit; there is also one Person not proceeding, namely the Father. Hence there can be only three Persons in the Trinity.' The second lies in the implications of the modes of procession, according to which the Persons are distinguished. 'The mode of a Person (*modus personae*) as regards procession can only be threefold', he explains, 'for instance, it may be one of not proceeding at all, which belongs to the Father; or one of proceeding from One who does not proceed, which belongs to the Son; or one of proceeding from One who does proceed, which belongs to the Holy Spirit.'⁸⁵ Therefore, the divine multiplicity ends with the third person, completing the triune identity.

Relation and Procession: Their Logical Priority

In article 3, Question 10 of his *De Potentia*, Aquinas affirms a real identity between divine relations and divine essence. The divine relations, though distinct among themselves, are each of them identical in essence. No distinction occurs between relations as regards essence which all three distinct persons possess equally and indivisibly. This assertion emerges also in his *Summa Theologica*:

> While relation in created things exists as an accident in a subject, in God a really existing relation has the existence of the divine nature and is completely identical with it ... (thus) a real relation in God is in reality identical with nature and differs only in our mind's understanding, inasmuch as relation implies a reference to the correlative term, which is not implied by the term 'nature.'⁸⁶

Therefore there cannot be a real distinction between persons as divine relations and divine nature, except in a virtual or logical sense, since the two constitute one reality. Human persons, in order to experience relationship, must first subsist as individuals, since with them relation is always an aspect of that which is related accidentally. 'But in God', Aquinas writes, 'relation constitutes a person, inasmuch as it is a divine relation: because it is identical with the divine essence, since in God there cannot be any accidents. Therefore relation, being in reality the divine essence, can constitute a divine *hypostasis*.'[87] In God, relation is constitutive of the divine substance, 'as ways in which that substance is given and received; as givers and receivers, as "subjects" or *supposita* whose whole distinctiveness consists in their giving and receiving what God is, the persons in God are identical with both their processions and their relations.'[88]

Concerning the logical connection between relation and procession or origin, Aquinas deals with these questions: does one presuppose or precede the other? Must the persons first be there in order to form relations to each other? Or do they find their being simply in relation? Here Aquinas makes a helpful distinction: when relations are considered as such, they do logically presuppose the processions that they manifest. But when relations are considered as constituting the persons, relation is logically prior to procession in respect to the person from whom the procession comes: the Father must precede in order to generate the Son. The Person, constituted by relation, is logically first and precedes its act. Aquinas says, '*quia Pater est, generat*', meaning this: he is not the Father because he begets, but he begets because he is the Father.[89] This subtle distinction preoccupies the Scholastic theologians, who seek to establish the famous *modus significandi*, an order in which human thinking and speaking are done. Congar explains, 'In the relationship itself, if what it is in God is considered, the *esse in*, which makes it subsistent, logically precedes the *esse ad*, which distinguishes it from another Person by opposing it relationally.'[90] As regards the person who proceeds, origin is logically prior to relation: the Son is related to the Father as Son because he proceeds from the Father as generated; the Spirit, because he proceeds from both, is related to them as passive spiration.

Per Filium and Historical Antecedents

Aquinas evidently belongs to the Western tradition; nevertheless, he tries to effect an ecumenical consensus between the East and the west. In the beginning of his *De Potentia*, he indicates that the differences between them on the Spirit are not really a matter of substance, but really that of terminology and meaning. 'If we take careful note of the statements of the Greeks, we shall find that they differ from us in words, not in thoughts.'[91] In accordance with Scripture, the Greek fathers are ready to acknowledge the Spirit as 'the Spirit of the Son.' And in seeking to rule out the suggestion that the Spirit is dependent for its being on the Father and the Son, they too are more than ready to accept *per filium* doctrine, that the Spirit proceeds from the Father 'through' the Son. However both concessions, Aquinas argues, entail that the Spirit's procession is 'not entirely independent of the Son', even if the Son and the Father are still mutually related in their unique way as they join, as a single and identical principle, to spirate the Spirit. Some even concede that the Spirit is 'from' the Son as well as 'flows from' the Son, but he does not 'proceed' from the Son.[92] For Aquinas, this is ridiculous, for the verb 'to proceed' denotes origin of any kind. So, if the Spirit 'is' from the Son or 'flows from' the Son, then the Spirit, too, proceeds from the Son. Therefore the Greeks' denial of the *filioque* Aquinas attributes, as his ecumenical conclusion, to 'ignorance, obstinacy' and not to any theological reasons.[93]

Aquinas is more positive than Anselm before him towards *per filium*. With John Damascene, he teaches that the Spirit proceeds from the Father 'through' the Son. He accepts that the Spirit 'abides' in the Son 'as a lover rests in the beloved.' When the Son is said to abide in the Father, it means that the Son proceeds from the Father. Likewise, the Spirit proceeds from the Son, because the Spirit is said to abide in the Son.[94] He further clarifies the preposition 'through', which must not be understood in the creaturely sense as in Arius, referring to temporal and successive order. Aquinas denies temporality to the eternal order, because all three persons are coeternal in the same Godhead. In every action, there are two things: 'the *suppositum* acting, and the power whereby it acts; as, for instance, fire heats through heat.' So on the one hand, if we consider the power whereby the Father and the Son spirate the spirit, there is 'no mean', for this is achieved by one and the same power. On the other hand, if we consider the *suppositum* spirating, then, as the Spirit proceeds both from the Father and the Son, the Spirit proceeds from the Father 'immediately', but from the Son 'mediately.' Aquinas accepts *Per Filium*, interpreting it as referring to a 'principle from a principle' (*principium de principio*), the Son deriving from the Father the one Godhead and hence the power to spirate the Spirit. The Spirit is said to proceed from the Father 'through' the Son, this takes place not in created order but within the uncreated order. In light of the aforesaid, the example of a material procession, that Abel proceeds immediately from Adam his father, and mediately from Eve as his mother, Aquinas says, is inapplicable to the immaterial procession of the divine Persons. The Spirit thus cannot be said to proceed from the Father 'before' he proceeds from the Son, for in God there is no 'before' or 'after' as Athanasius and Augustine assert.[95] Aquinas, then, joins with Anselm in repudiating any thought of inequality in the divine order of procession, for therein no temporal or privileged priority is implied. By the idea that 'whatever causes a thing to be such is yet more so', some argue that the Spirit proceeds 'more' from the Father than from the Son. But Aquinas argues for the opposite: because both the Father and the Son possess equally the same spirative power, 'the Holy Ghost proceeds equally from both, although sometimes He is said to proceed principally or properly from the Father, because the Son has this power from the Father.'[96]

Aquinas is keenly aware of the unity issue imposed by the Eastern fathers, according to whom *the formula ex Patre Filioque* compromises it, resulting in two origins. To them, the unity of God is preserved by their insistence upon the formula *ex Patre* – only one origin in the Godhead, that of the Father, from whom alone both Son and Spirit proceed equally and eternally. Pelikan observes that Aquinas has to confront the imprecise, even careless expressions of some Western fathers, among whom the most embarrassing ones are Hilary and Augustine.[97] For Hilary's imprecise statement, 'the Holy Ghost is to be confessed as proceeding from the Father and Son as authors', could be misconstrued as a denial of *filioque* doctrine, for it could be read solely economically, '*The Father, Son, and Holy Ghost are called one Creator, because they are the one principle of the creature*' (*Pater et Filius et Spiritus Sanctus, quia sunt unum principium creaturae dicuntur esse unus Creator*), and not immanently, that '*the Father and the*

Son are not one, but two spirators' (Patre et filius non sunt unus spirator, sed "due spriatores".[98] From this, it follows that the Father and the Son are not one principle of the Holy Spirit. Hilary's may be taken as an affirmation of the Eastern charge that *filioque* doctrine necessarily implies a positing of two origins in the Godhead, thereby destroying the oneness of God. Not so in Aquinas. He insists on one origin, arguing that Hilary's formula '*a Patre et Filio auctoribus*' needs clarification. To do this, he makes a distinction between 'adjective' and 'substantive' sense: 'spirating is an adjective, and spirator a substantive', and argues that Hilary's formula takes on the former sense.

> The Father and the Son are two spirating, by reason of the plurality of the *supposita*, but not two spirators by reason of the one spiration. For adjectival terms derive their number from the *supposita*, but substantives from themselves, according to the form signified. As to what Hilary says, that the Holy Spirit is from the Father and the Son as His authors, this is to be explained in the sense that the substantive here stands for the adjective.[99]

To add, there is only one Creator substantively, even though it is said adjectively that the creature proceeds from all three persons, yet 'not as distinct persons, but as united in essence.'[100] Likewise there is only one principle, even though it is said adjectively that the Spirit spirates from the Father and the Son, yet not as distinct persons but united in one essence. The Father, as *auctor*, bestows the faculty of spiration to the Son, but he does so by constituting him as a single principle, along with himself. The Spirit 'is said to proceed principally or properly from the Father, since the Son has this capacity from the Father.'[101] The Spirit's being is grounded in the One essence shared equally by the Father and the Son which underlies and is ontologically prior to their differentiation. This means *filioque* guarantees the full unity of the Trinity, which is understood to be grounded in the perichoretic sharing by all three of their common essence.

Aquinas also draws from Augustine's definition of *filioque* to refute the Eastern accusation of the Western positing of a double source in the Godhead, which consequently compromises the monotheistic confession of the Church. Augustine's axiom, '*facendum est patrem et*

Filium principium esse Spiritus Sancti, non due principia' contributes to Aquinas' defense of *filioque*.[102] But to him, Augustine's axiom, '*Pater est principium totius deitatis*', lacks theological precision. This is a reference not to the source of essence, but to the order of nature, which is traditionally named as Father, Son and Spirit. As regards order, the Father (the name of God) is the *principium* of the Godhead, not the source of essence. He alone is not from another but unbegotten; he is the unoriginate source of the Trinity. But in what sense is the Father '*principium*' both of the Son and the Spirit '*generando et spirando*'?[103] In his counterattack against the Greeks, he is able to point out that the imprecision lies in the Greek trinitarian terminology, not in Latin: 'The Greeks use the words *cause* and *principle* indifferently, when speaking of God; whereas the Latin *Doctores* do not use the word *cause*, but only *principle*.' It is because the Greek word 'cause', if applied to the relation between the Father and the Son, gives way to ontological subordinationism, which is not implied in the word 'principle.' For the same reason, while it is customary for the Greeks to say that the Son and the Spirit are 'principled', the Latins avoid such language to escape 'any occasion of error.' 'Although we attribute to the Father something of authority by reason of His being as principle', Aquinas writes, 'still we do not attribute any kind of subjection or inferiority to the Son, or to the Holy Ghost.'[104] He quotes Hilary favourably: 'By authority of the Giver, the Father is greater; nevertheless, the Son is not less, to whom oneness of nature is given.'[105] However inconsistency occurs in his exegesis of the formula, '*a Patre per Filium*', where he uses 'cause' and 'principle' interchangeably; thus he admits that '*haec praepositio "per" designat in causali aliquam causam seu principium illius actus.*'[106] Despite this, the Augustinian use of the word 'principle', commonly translated as origin, referring to 'one principle', lends support to his *filioque* doctrine.

Finally, in refuting those who think of *filioque* as anathema, Aquinas resorts to the historical sources found in Church councils, specifically those of the Council of Ephesus and Chalcedon. 'The Nestorians were the first to introduce the error that the Holy Ghost did not proceed from the Son, as appears in a Nestorian creed condemned in the Council of Ephesus.'[107] As examples of critics of Nestorian heretics, he cites Theodoret of Cyril, and Damascene after him. Thomas' historical judgment, though accurate, may not be convincing to the Greeks for some, he notes, may still contend that Damascene does not admit the *filioque*. They may also claim that his text, 'We say that the Holy Ghost is from the Father, and we name Him the Spirit of the Father; but we do not say that the Holy Ghost is from the Son, yet we name Him the Spirit of the Son', is an outright denial of it.[109] Damascene's text is interpreted neither as confessing nor rejecting the *filioque*. For *Filioque* is a much later disputed phrase, and is not in view when he says that the Spirit does not proceed from the Son.[108] This Aquinas acknowledges, but only after claiming that Damascene is following Nestorians in his denial of the *filioque*. This indicates that Aquinas is very much in conversant with history.

Historically, doctrinal formation came through councils. In every council of the Church a symbol of faith was drawn up to combat some prevalent errors condemned in the council at that time. Then subsequent councils emerge, not as making a new symbol of faith, but rather explain, against the rising heretics, what was 'implicitly contained in the first symbol' by some additions. Such is the case with the council of Chalcedon, where it is declared that those who were there in the council of Constantinople 'handed down the doctrine about the Holy Spirit... (without implying) that there was anything wanting in the doctrine of their predecessors who had gathered together at Nicea; what they were doing was rather to explain, against the heretics, what those fathers understood on the matter.' So the addition of the *filioque* is not regarded as anathema, 'because at the time of the ancient councils the error of those who said that the Holy Spirit did not proceed from the Son had not yet arisen, it was not necessary to make any explicit declaration on that point, ... (n)evertheless the truth was contained implicitly in the belief that the Holy Ghost proceeds from the Father.'[110] Pelikan summarizes:

> ... this historical information from Chalcedon about Constantinople was intended to justify the Western interpolation; as it was legitimate for Constantinople to expand the brief formula of 325, "*Et in Spiritum Sanctum*," into the amplified form that was now used in both Eastern and Western liturgies, so it was legitimate for later generations to expand this, in turn, by adding the *Filioque*. ... the comment of Chalcedon upon the use of Nicea by Constantinople gave Thomas

the occasion to elaborate a more general theory of doctrinal development.[111]

Concluding Reflections

Theology, in Aquinas' estimation, is primarily concerned with the knowledge of God as he is in himself, *secundum quod est principium rerum et finis earum*.[112] Logically, Aquinas begins with God, not God as he relates to us in the economy of salvation, but with God as he is in himself, the immanent Deity. His procedural method is justified by the economy of revelation itself, in virtue of which God as he is in himself communicates his goodness freely in the mystery of creation and redemption. This explains his procedural method, with the opening section of the *Summa*, Book 1, Questions 2-43, devoted to a discussion of God as God, simply as 'the one God', and followed by Questions 44-49, devoted to a discussion of God's outward relation with Creation. Since God's action *ad extra* is an exercise of the divine nature, it is logical for Aquinas to make the common divine essence his *prolegomena*, his starting point. Following Augustine and John Damascene, Aquinas proceeds from the one God, whose unity he apprehends in the concept of the common divine essence, only after that moving towards the concept of the trinitarian persons.[113] Put it differently: the common divine essence as the foundation of trinitarian persons is logically primary in comparison. This in no way means that Aquinas relegates to secondary importance the persons in that essence. To Aquinas, 'Theology is both speculative and practical.'[114] Unfortunately, an over-emphasis upon Aquinas' philosophy, O'Meara argues, has led to a misreading of the medieval Dominican as a logician or an essentialist.[115] Any attempt to present him as such is to betray the balance of his theology.[116] Such an interpretation is too often precipitated by a failure to see his *Summa* as a unified, harmonious whole, thereby treating particular sections as isolated, independent units.[117] The structure of his *Summa* is such that his study of the Trinity of persons and their intra-relations is preceded by a study of the existence, nature and attributes of the one God. Likewise the sequence of topics in the *Prima pars* follows the same pattern, moving from the divine unity to the multiplicity. So regarding the question of the relationship between the treatment of God's being and the consideration of God's Trinity, Hankey explains: 'the *de deo trino* communicates with the *de deo uno* in virtue of the gradual development toward greater distinction in the terms of the various forms of self-relation in the divine.'[118] Henceforth Aquinas scholars propose reading the *Summa* in light of the Neoplatonic scheme of *Exitus-Reditus*, dealing with Creation as coming forth from God as principle and then, through God's redemptive providence, returning again to God as the ultimate end.[119] The *Exitus-Reditus* model constitutes 'two inverse movements', but strictly linked in their unity.[120] Aquinas' theological construct is governed by what Seckler calls '*ordo salutis*':

> In a surprising way, there appears here, in strict correspondence with one another, the origin and end of history, the source and the completion of being, the first and last cause of understanding, so that not only can theology turn itself into a 'science' of the history of salvation, but the history of salvation itself bears within itself the fundamental theological design. It is not therefore, according to Thomas, the theologian who brings order into the tangled events of salvation, but it is the order of salvation that structures theology.[121]

Historically Aquinas' procedural separation between the one divine nature and the trinitarian persons leads to an unfortunate development in later scholastic theology of a real separation. As Moltmann identifies, '… ever since Thomas, the article on God has been divided into the treatise *de Deo uno* and the treatise *De deo trino*.'[122] 'Even in Protestant orthodoxy, first a general doctrine of God "*de Deo*" was outlined, after which there followed teaching on the "*mysterium de sancta trinitate*".'[123] This configuration prejudices subsequent reflections on the Trinity, resulting either in an undue stress on the unity of the Trinity or a reduction of the triunity to the One God. It leads unintentionally but inevitably to a dissolution of trinitarian theology into abstract monotheism.[124] It must be borne in mind that Aquinas' procedural separation does not intend such unhappy legacy. Hill elucidates:

> In the *Commentary on the Sentences* of Peter Lombard, there is no differentiation at all between considering God as One and as Three.

Later, in a second attempt in the *Summa contra gentiles*, he opted for a radical separation of the two tracts, treating God as One in Book I and leaving God as Three for Book IV. In both cases, extrinsic factors were determinative: the order already chosen by Lombard in the *Sentences*, and the audience addressed in the *Contra gentiles*, i.e., non-believers. But when free to follow the exigencies of his own notion of the theological task, in the *Summa Theologiae*, the result is two sets of questions which, while distinguished, are not separated from one another but coalesce to form one theologically integral treatise on God. The order between the two is clear and represents a *demarche* from God under the concept of nature to God under the concept of person(s). But revelation is at work in the earlier treatise as much as it is in the later. The entire work is unified as a *summa* of theology, ...'[125]

The relationship *ad extra* must be grounded in the relationship of Father, Son and the Spirit *ad intra*, the latter is the presupposition or ground of the former. The economic relations of the Trinity correspond to the ontological relations of the Godhead, thus making accessible to us the knowledge of God as he is in himself. What we say about the economic Trinity must also be said of the immanent Trinity, for there are only one Trinity. In the eternal self-differentiation, God's being the Father is ontologically the ground of his being the Son and the Holy Spirit. This does not mean that there is any temporal priority, implying that the Son and Holy Spirit are in any sense less than the Father. Nor does it imply a diminution of deity, for God is wholly existent in all three persons, each of them is fully God. As regards divine processions, Scripture speaks of the sending of the Son and the Spirit with reference to events in history. The Son is sent with the birth of the Christ, whereas the Spirit is sent by the incarnate and risen Christ. 'Jesus said to them again, "Peace be with you. As the Father has sent me, even so I send you." And when he breathed on his disciples, he said to them, "Receive the Holy Spirit" '(Jn 20:21f). Does the sending of persons in history relate to the eternal procession in the Trinity? Does it have any bearing upon the immanent Trinity? If God is One, the immanent Trinity being the abiding presupposition of the economic Trinity, then the sending of the Son and Spirit in history mirrors what is immutably in God apart from the historical revelation in time. There is a correspondence between an eternal and temporal sending and proceeding. Accordingly, Aquinas could say there is a coming forth of the Son and the Spirit in eternity. The temporal sending of the Son reflects changelessly the eternal sending of the Son; the temporal procession of the Spirit reflects changelessly the eternal procession of the Spirit. He relates the eternal generation of the Son and eternal procession of the Spirit on the one hand to the temporal missions of the Son and the Spirit in the world on the other. The Spirit is of the Father, since he comes from him. But he is also of the Son since he is called the Spirit of the Son whom the Father also sends just as he sends the Son himself. Just as the Spirit is of the Father ontologically, prior to his being sent by the Father economically, so too the Spirit is of the Son ontologically prior to his being sent by the Son economically. The Son, who is born in the world, and the Spirit who proceeds into the world are born and proceeded beforehand eternally in God himself. The temporal missions of being sent and given are rooted in the eternal processions of generation and spiration. This approach is most notably that of Augustine, who starts with the economic Trinity, focusing on God's manifestation in time as the self-revelation of the immanent Trinity. Such approach Aquinas also embraces, as is evident in his doctrine of the Trinity which he derives from the teaching of Christ. 'Finally', he writes, 'at the time of grace, the mystery of the Trinity was revealed by the Son of God himself, as is said (Matthew 16:18), Go therefore and make disciples of all nations, baptizing them in the name of the Father and of the Son and of the Holy Spirit.'[126] This means the knowledge of God as he is in himself is accessible to us. God is only known to us in the economy (*oikonomia*), as grounded in the temporal missions of the Son and Spirit. Then from these economic acts in history – the sending of the Son and the gift of the Spirit, Aquinas penetrates back into the eternal processions within the Godhead. The motivation is that 'we may have the right view of the salvation of mankind, accomplished by the Son who became flesh and by the gifts of the Holy Spirit.'[127] Thus the weight of Aquinas' theology falls on the discussion of the economic Trinity, from which the immanent Trinity can be deduced. The economic Trinity throws light on what may be known of God as he is in himself, the immanent Trinity. Aquinas, like Augustine, reasons *a posteriori* from biblically-witnessed salvation history in time back to God's eternal essence. God's historical revelation in three Persons mirrors God in his eternal essence. Statements on the immanent Trinity could be derived through inferring the essence of the Father, Son and Spirit from the way they are revealed to us. We know the triune God only because we see God acting in Jesus and the Holy Spirit, i.e., through the economic Trinity. Though he distinguishes, with the tradition, the immanent Trinity from the economic Trinity, he insists on their unity. So what we encounter in revelation in the economic Trinity corresponds to what God is in eternity, the immanent Trinity. In view of this, the modern discussions of the relationship between the immanent and economic Trinity, though helpful, certainly are not novelties.[128]

As personal, subsistent Love, the Spirit is both the cause and content of love both in God's divine life and in his relation with us. Just as the Spirit is the unitive source of the oneness of love of the Father and the Son, he is also the unitive principle of the oneness of believers with God and so with each other. The essence of personhood is defined by relationality – this is achieved by the Spirit both vertically and horizontally.[129] We become true persons, not in isolated life but only in relationship, and therefore only in the Spirit whose very presence through love 'binds us to the Father through Christ and thereby to one another.'[130] The Spirit is the way to our unity with Christ and with one another. Fatula writes of Aquinas' contribution:

> Just as the Father and the Son's self-communication within the Trinity issues in the Spirit who is their love, their self-communication outside the Trinity into creation constitutes the very bestowal of the Spirit. In the primacy of this love lies the reason for the Spirit's pre-eminence in the economy of salvation: we arrive at participation in the joy of the triune life only by union with the Spirit given to the world as the very content of the Father's and Son's love and joy.[131]

That the Father has a Word in himself by way of self-knowledge 'implies', Aquinas asserts, 'a relation to creatures. For God, by knowing himself, knows every creature.'[132] Likewise God, by loving himself, loves his creatures in himself by the love eternally bestowed by the Father and the Son on each other, namely the Holy Spirit as a distinct person. This he assures us of in his *Contra Gentiles*:

> Since the Holy Spirit proceeds by way of the love by which God loves himself, and by that same love and for the sake of his own goodness God loves both himself and other things, manifestly that love is proper to the Holy Spirit – the love by which God loves us. So also does the love by which we love God, for he makes us lovers of God.[133]

The work of the Spirit thus is to constitute us as 'friends of God', drawing us into the circle of divine love and the intimacy of divine communion. 'Therefore, since by the Holy Spirit we are established as friends of God, fittingly enough it is by the Holy Spirit that human beings are said to receive the revelation of divine mysteries.'[134] The Holy Spirit communicates to our hearts the gospel about a God who, in his knowledge and love of us, summons us into being, and includes us in his inner life as his affectionate 'lovers.' Love unites affections, and makes one heart of two, sharing with us all the riches of God's innermost being. Daley explains:

> This work of the Spirit, this manifestation of divine love, is not simply something superadded to his existence as a distinct person within the life of God; it is a living out, in temporal, created terms, of what the Holy Spirit is as a divine person – a flowing out from the other two, whose very act of breathing him forth brings their own union to perfection, creating unity by way of gift, giving personal reality to the self-spending action of love.[135]

What truly constitutes the Spirit's identity? Here we must observe Aquinas' technical conceptuality that differentiates between constitution and the distinction of persons. That the Spirit is 'distinct' from the other two is established in Aquinas' *filioque* doctrine *via* what he calls *communis spiratio*, that both Father and Son share in the characteristic of breathing the Spirit. But on Aquinas' account, *communis spiratio* is not the identity-condition for the Spirit. Instead the identity-constituting for the Spirit (or any persons) lies in his incommunicable uniqueness, in what he calls *relationes oppositae*. *Communis spiratio* is not among the identity-constituting conditions for any divine person, he says, since it does not belong uniquely to any person: 'Common spiration is not a property, since it belongs to two persons.'[136] The Spirit is known by procession, by the fact that he proceeds from another, and not another proceeds from him, as no divine person proceeds from him. Thus the Spirit's identity itself is unaffected by the *filioque*, in that the Spirit remains the same person even if he proceeds from the Father alone as he is proceeding from the Father and the Son. Conversely, the Father's and the Son's identity are unaffected by *filioque*, in that the Father and the Son remain the same person even if the Spirit proceeds from the Father alone as they together as one spirative power produce the Spirit. Aquinas' view is at odds with Lossky, who says that relations are not the cause of the intra-trinitarian distinctions, but 'serve to express the hypostatic diversity of the Three.'[137] For him, relation is not only their manifestation, but the very basis of the distinction of persons. For Aquinas, *Filioque* doctrine establishes the ontological distinction of the Spirit from the Father and the Son, but does not establish the personal identity of the Spirit. Marshall explains adequately:

> ... knowing what the Spirit's identity is, and so being able to refer to the Spirit, does not depend on accepting the *filioque*. Put differently: for Thomas the identity of the Spirit explicitly floats free of his own technical means for conceiving the constitution and distinction of the divine persons. Accepting his technical conceptuality (divine persons as constituted by *relationes oppositae*, and the like) seems to require accepting the *filioque* in order to uphold the *fides Trinitatis* attested in Scripture and creed, which of course includes the personal distinction of the Spirit from the Son and the Father. But on the grounds of that technical conceptuality itself, it is not necessary to accept the conceptuality in order to identify (or account for the identification of) the Spirit.[138]

Aquinas' major success lies in his ability to steer in between an extremely essentialist, and an extremely interpersonal approach to speaking of the divine persons in God. With Augustine, he is fully conscious of the risk the term 'person' has. He uses it because he too, like Augustine, has to answer the question, '*Three what?*'[139] In addition he uses it because person signifies 'what is most perfect in all nature', a subsistent rationality.[140] With Augustine, Aquinas says that the love involved in the spiration of the Spirit is the mutual love of the Father and Son for each other.[141] But he moves beyond Augustine, and along with Anselm, he affirms that the Spirit proceeds from the love of the Infinite Being for itself. Aquinas thus goes for the single spiration of love, which stands as a dogma for the Catholic Church considering the Fourth Lateran Council. In this, Congar quotes H. F. Dondaine in favour of Aquinas' objection to mutual-love theory:

> What two friends have in common to unite them is not the reality experienced in their act of love. Each experiences his own act, which makes two loves, two acts of loving. What they have in common is the object and their common good. ... But it is to this one object, their community in good, that they adapt their two hearts and their two wills by two loves. ... It is clear that this mystery contains only one act, only one spiration and only one 'loving' that is common to both loving Persons, but this is so because of *the unity of essence*, not because of friendship as such. ...[142]

But Aquinas' theology of the Trinity, in Malet's estimation, is not a theology of essence as in Anselm. He contends that Aquinas maintains what is most precious in Anselm's theology, namely, the doctrine of relations and love as essence, but completes what is most lacking in Anselm:

> that the word *persona* is perfectly acceptable; that the Word is something else than simply consubstantial sharer in supreme spirit; that relation in God is something subsistent; that one can say not simply *that* there is a Son and a Spirit, but also *what* they are (i.e., persons); that it is not the Essence which begets and is begotten in the Persons, but that it is the Person who begets another Person by means of the essence; and that there is not simply a knowledge and a love within the Trinity, but also three knowers and three lovers; ... finally, that the Holy Spirit is not the fruit of the love that the divine essence has for itself, but the fruit of the love of two subjects.[143]

At the outset, it seems that Malet is correct in affirming the mutual love as the dominant motif in Aquinas. Like in Richard of St. Victor, this love, which proceeds from the two subjects not because of the unity of essence, but because of the friendship of them as distinct from each other, is personal. He is like the Greeks in being personalist, but unlike them in affirming that the Spirit proceeds from the Father and the Son. With Augustine, he speaks of the Spirit as proceeding from the mutual love of the first two persons for each other. Love is basically interpersonal, thus Aquinas writes in his *Summa* that the Spirit 'proceeds from the two, uniting them as distinct persons.'[144] With reference to spiration, Aquinas writes in his *De Potentia*: 'The procession of intellect is from only one; but *friendship, which is mutual love*, proceeds from two loving each other.'[145] No doubt the mutual love is present in Aquinas' writings. However Malet's estimation, that the Spirit is the fruit of the love of two subjects, is the very antithesis of Aquinas' *Summa*, which is predominantly Anselmian, while making passing references to the mutual love. The *Summa* presupposes a doctrine of divine Being, the oneness of which is the context of the articulation of Aquinas' Trinity and *filioque*. As proof of this, Aquinas writes:

> The Father loves not only the Son, but also Himself and us, by the Holy Ghost; because ... to love, taken in a notional sense, implies not only the production of a divine person, but also the person produced by way of love, which love has relation to the thing loved. Hence, as the Father speaks Himself and every creature by His begotten Word, inasmuch as the Word begotten adequately represents the Father and every creature, so He loves Himself and every creature by the Holy Ghost, inasmuch as the Holy Ghost proceeds as *the love of the primal goodness* whereby the Father loves Himself and every creature. Thus it is evident that relation to the creature is implied both in the Word and in the proceeding Love, as it were in a secondary way, inasmuch as the divine truth and goodness are a principle of understanding and loving all creatures.[146]

Earlier in his *Contra Gentiles*, we find an Anselmian saying, 'The Holy Spirit proceeds by way of love by which God loves Himself.'[147] The same also appears in his *De Potentia*, where it is stated, 'God with his will naturally and of necessity loves his own goodness, and such love proceeding is the Holy Ghost.'[148] That which the mutual love of the Father and the Son brings forth is not two, but one identical love. This is the very crux of Anselm, according to whom the love which proceeds from the Father and the Son is the love which the divine essence has for itself. Anselm thought of the Spirit as proceeding from the Infinite Being, i.e., indeed, the first two persons considered as being one in essence. The duality in spiration, because of the unity of essence, constitutes only one act of spiration. The mutual love of the Father and the Son is a single reality, because it is the divine love of the Infinite Being for itself, identical with the divine essence, but only as found in the immanent Trinity.[149] Cowburn audaciously but rightly attributes to Aquinas a full-blown Anselmian theory, according to which 'the love involved in spiration is primarily that of the Infinite Being, which may be subsequently considered as including an interpersonal love': 'the Infinite Being is in fact two persons, so that the love is at the same time the love of the Father for himself as God, the love of the Son for himself as God, and the love of each for the other as God: that is, it includes a love of the Father and the Son for each other.'[150] Both his *Summa* and *Compendium theologiae* give priority to solitary love as the *ratio formalis* of spiration; they do not abandon reciprocal love altogether, but grant it a 'secondary' place in the process.[151] To quote Slipyi's words: 'This love is mutual, but as it were only on reduction. The Father loves himself and his essence. But this essence is that of the Son and is identical with the Son.... Therefore the Father, loving himself, loves the Son also, and vice versa.'[152]

Nevertheless Aquinas does not shrink from using the person-language to speak of God, and of the relational dynamism in God's triune life. Augustine's idea of the Spirit as the mutual love of the first two persons for each other is not discarded, even though it is not considered in his *Summa* as having priority. An elaborated explanation of question 10 of his *De Potentia*, where he draws upon Damascene to propose an additional order, i.e. an order *to*, will bring out Aquinas' relational dynamism:

> The Holy Spirit proceeds both from the Father *to* the Son and from the Son *to* the Father not as recipients but as *objects* of love. For the Holy Spirit is said to proceed from the Father *to* the Son inasmuch as he is the love whereby the Father loves the Son; and in the same way it may be said that the Holy Spirit proceeds from the Son *to* the Father inasmuch as he is the love whereby the Son loves the Father. He may be understood, however, to proceed from the Father inasmuch as the Son *receives* from the Father the power to spirate the Holy Spirit, and

in this sense He cannot be said to proceed from the Son to the Father, seeing that the Father receives nothing from the Son.[153]

This text discloses two different ways of speaking of the Spirit's procession, first in relation to the *'terms'* from and to whom he proceeds; second in relation to the 'power' by which he proceeds. The first way necessarily entails the personalist way of speaking of the Spirit, that he is the mutual Love of the Father and the Son for each other as in Augustine. Torre writes, 'For the Son *receives* the Spirit from the Father and *returns* the Spirit to the Father, who *receives* the Spirit in His turn from His beloved. The Spirit is not spoken of merely in *passive* terms, as being from Father and Son; rather, He is spoken of *actively*, as proceeding *to* the Son, abiding in Him, and returning from Him to the Father.'[154] Such a conception spells the death of an ontological subordinationism of the Spirit to the other two persons. With Damascene, Aquinas teaches that the Spirit proceeds from the Father 'through' the Son, and that the Spirit 'abides' in the Son 'as a lover rests in the beloved.'[155] For this reason, the Spirit is said to proceed from the Father *to* the Son 'inasmuch as he is the love whereby the Father loves the Son.' Finally, the Spirit returns from the Son *to* the Father 'inasmuch as he is the Love whereby the Son loves the Father', thereby also returning the love he receives from the Father. The Spirit proceeds from the Father *to* his only-begotten Son, and returns from the Son *to* the Father, thereby completing the circle of love, which is to be explained *via* Damascene's personal *circumincessio* (*perichoresis*).

> In God there is a certain *rotation* in the acts of intellect and will: for the will *returns* to that whence came the beginning of understanding.... Thus someone has said that a monad engendered an atom and reflected its own heat upon itself. And the circle being closed nothing more can be added.'[156]

Aquinas here also follows Richard of St. Victor in affirming the Father's love for the Son as the supreme, 'personal' love for another.[157] The Son derives from the Father Love as well as the power to love reciprocally. And the Love the Father receives from the Son is precisely the very Love he bestows upon Him. Yet the Father, the unoriginate source of the Trinity, does not receive being or power from the Son. Nevertheless the Father receives the Spirit from the Son as the Love of the Son – this is seen in the way he understands the notion of image. Aquinas incorporates Damascene's view, that 'the Spirit is the Image of the Son.' This is alien to the Latin tradition, which attributes the notion of image to the Son alone. Despite the differences that 'love' and 'word' are as image, Aquinas argues that the Spirit could be properly the image of the Son 'since He is the divine love.'[158] He thereby moves beyond the narrow confine of the psychological analogy, and thus finds a way to assimilate Damascene's view within his own tradition. In Damascene's language, 'the Spirit is joined *to* the Father *through* the Son.'[159] The Spirit, as an image of the Son, radiates or reveals the Son eternally, but *to* none other than the Father. This sets him apart from his procession from the Father, since the Spirit manifests the Son because he abides in the Son. *Filioque* delivers the fact that the Spirit is from Father and Son, thus the order is an order *from*, but not an order *to*. Although the latter is not stated, it is implied so that Aquinas, in conceiving the Spirit as the mutual love of the first two persons, could understand the Spirit as the Love of the Father *for* the Son and the Love of the Son *for* the Father. The dynamism of Spirit, conceived in personal term, is the infinite surplus of love of the Father for his beloved Son and the infinite return of that love from the Son *to* his beloved Father. The Spirit is none other than the dynamism of the infinite interpenetrative (perichoretic) love of the first two persons for each other. This idea is an implicate of, if not causally linked to, Aquinas' understanding of the circle of love, that the Spirit flows from the Father *to* the Son and from the Son *to* the Father.[160] By the statement, 'the Father and the Son love each other by the Holy Spirit', Aquinas does not mean that the Spirit is the formal or efficient cause of the mutual love of the Father and the Son; rather it points to the Spirit as the formal or contingent effect of that mutual love.[161] 'It is reasonable', Anselm Min writes, 'to believe that in the eternal simultaneity of *perichoresis* such a formal effect also exercises an impact, however derivative, on the agents themselves, the impact of reinforcing that mutual love, just as the relations and acts of human love reinforce and mediate the mutual love of the human agents, although only analogically.'[162]

There abides in Aquinas an intra-trinitarianly relational dynamism, in which there is a pole of bestowing (the Father), the pole of receptivity (the Son), and the pole of reciprocity or communion (the Spirit). Since the Spirit proceeds as a *hypostasis* from the Father and the Son, he must be in his Person the ontological communion of love that exists between them. This shows Aquinas' interpersonal approach to speaking of divine persons in God, which is not found in Anselm. However his personal emphasis must be understood not apart from the one Divine Being from which statements about the divine processions in God are made. The divine essence, which is not left out of account, forms the background, from there Aquinas moves to a discussion of relational dynamism in God's triune life. The elements of essentialism and personalism are held together in a synthetic balance so that it can be said that for Aquinas 'the Spirit proceeds by essential love (being)'... 'but *as* the mutual love (personal) of the Father and the Son' – 'the essential love being the ultimate ground', whereas 'the mutual love being the proximate ground' of the procession of the Spirit; the former relates to the 'fact' of the personhood of the Spirit; the latter, the 'manner' of that personhood.[163] This may pave the way for further ecumenical discussions.

Finally, a significant contribution of Aquinas is his ontologizing relation, making it constitutive of persons – each of them is a possessor of the whole divine nature. Aquinas does not address the relationship between God being *ipsum esse* or *actus purus* and being a trinity of persons. But he does assert this: 'in God relation and essence do not differ from each other, but are one and the same.'[164] He admits no distinction between the one nature of God and the Trinity, thus this brings him closer to the Eastern view. The ontologically undifferentiated being of God is the inter-relationality of three persons. 'We speak of one essence of the three persons, and three persons of the one essence.'[165] Accordingly God's being is constituted by 'friendship' as is proper to the relations of Father, Son and Spirit. For there are in God a pole of bestowing, a pole of receptivity and a pole of communion or reciprocity. Aquinas conceives of relation in God as the 'facing' of beings towards each other, thus divine persons do not exist in isolation from each other. The import of ontologizing relation lies in a capacity of each person for the other, an opening of each to the other. In Marsh's words, 'Relationship signifies the activity of this capacity, the enriching and fulfilling of this openness. Relationship, therefore, is something dynamic, creative.... Relation in God signifies the achievement of greatest being, divine Being.'[166] If Marsh's description of Aquinas is accurate, then indeed God can be spoken of as pure relational activity. The emphasis here is not on static essence of the Greeks, but on dynamic relating act of the Triune God.[167] This casts light on his doctrine of God, that God, unlike the static and impassive deity of the Greeks, is essentially dynamic and relational.[168] Nevertheless the relational dynamism in God does not need to change his understanding of impassibility, since, in Aquinas, God is pure act, impassibility may still be predicated of God if it is interpreted as an affirmation of divine freedom, which in turn constitutes the basis for God's relation to the world.[169] Thus insofar as God is pure relational activity, there is an infinite surplus of an inner-relationality that now intimately embraces the world, not from divine deficiency, but from a supra-abundance of his love.

Chapter Five

Fecundity, Mutual Love and *Filioque*

Bonaventure

Rightly, Etiene Gilson observes that in order to fully appreciate Bonaventure's theology in its depth and breadth, no one part of his thought is to be extracted in isolation from the whole.[1] That being so, this chapter does not attempt an overall synthesis of his theology, but focuses more specifically on how the doctrine of the Holy Spirit, especially the *filioque* idea, receives its theological defence in Bonaventure (d. 1274), the 'Seraphic Doctor' of the Franciscan tradition. Bonaventure synthesizes Augustine's personalist strands of the Trinity with the thought of Anselm, Pseudo-Dionysius and Richard of St. Victor, to enable him to identify God as ultimate goodness and perfect love.[2] Both concepts are integrally related, and are constitutive of the intra-divine life. In Anselm, God is the all-perfect good, that than which no greater could be conceived. He links the Anselmian notion of perfection with the Dionysian metaphysics of the Good as self-diffusive, affirming that God being the highest good is most self-diffusive. He completes his thought with the Victorine emphasis on love as the highest good. He takes from Richard the concepts of beloved (*dilectus condignus*) and co-beloved (*condilectus*), the distinction between gratuitous love and received love, and the mixture of the two. The theme of emanation by mode of nature and mode of will, together with the idea of *condilectus*, enable Bonaventure to account for the necessity of the third person of the Trinity. With Augustine, he does not deny the essential sense of love, that love is attributed to all three persons. He contends that the Spirit is the mutual love of the Father and the Son in the notional sense, that the Spirit is the immanent fruit of both the Father and the Son joined together in a fecundity of will. The Father is the fountain-fullness, the fecund source from which flow all goodness and immanent processions. He communicates his fecundity to the Son, who together with the Father, spirates the Spirit so that the multiplicity ends with the third. In the Western pneumatological scheme to which Bonaventure belongs, the Spirit is the *vinculum amoris* between the Father and the Son, but he is the bond of a genuine, ex-centric love. Like Richard, his trinitarian language is this: the Father is lover, the Son is beloved, and the Spirit is co-beloved. By this he moves beyond Augustine, thereby accentuating the distinct personality of the Spirit and communion or relationality as an ontological category. This in turn brings him closer to the Eastern view, although his work remains distinctively Western, scholastic both in language and contents.[3]

The First Cherub and Metaphysics of Being

Bonaventure's most significant, yet often-overlooked achievement, in Zachary Hayes' estimation, is his theological metaphysics.[4] Inspired by the mystical life of St. Francis, Bonaventure introduces it in the context of his spiritual journal, which he calls *Itinerarium mentis in Deum*, the journey of the soul into God.[5] He envisions two ways of reflecting on the mystery of the invisible God, which are symbolized by the two angelic beings facing each other on the top of the ark of the covenant in the Holy of Holies. The two Cherubim in the temple image represent what Cousins calls 'the rhetorical structure' of contemplating God.[6] Bonaventure writes:

> By these Cherubim we understand the two modes or stages of contemplating the invisible and eternal things of God: one is concerned with the essential attributes of God and the other with those proper to the Persons.[7]

The Cherubim are the vivid symbols of Bonaventure's fifth and sixth levels of contemplation, the former gazes on God as Being and Unity, and the latter gazes on God as Goodness and Trinity. Bonaventure begins with the attitude of the first Cherub, who 'fixes the gaze primarily and principally on Being itself, saying that God's primary name is *He who is*.'[8] Along with Augustine, he takes as his departure point the unity of divine essence. He wants his readers to begin contemplating God in the unity of his essence. Thus he entitles his fifth chapter: '*On Contemplating the Divine Unity through its Primary Name which is Being.*'[9] This he believes is borne out by the Old Testament, where God reveals himself as Being: 'I am who Am' (Ex. 3:14). Bonaventure writes: 'Damascene, therefore, following Moses, says that *He who is* is God's primary name.'[10] The *telos* of the spiritual journal he embarks at this level is the contemplation of the first principles.[11] More specifically, the journey to God is indeed the journey to a being like God who 'is first, eternal, utterly simple, most actual, most perfect and supremely one.'[12] The absoluteness of God's being consists in the fact that 'it is the universal efficient, exemplary, and final cause of all things ... it is the most sufficient cause of all essences whose power is supremely infinite and multiple in its efficacy because it is supremely unified in its essence ... therefore it is the origin and consummating end of all things.'[13] Quoting Augustine favourably, he intimates: '(The final cause) is "the cause of being, the basis of understanding and the order of living".'[14]

Bonaventure directs us to contemplate what Cousins calls 'the coincidence of opposites' in the divine nature through 'a dialectic of being and non-being.'[15] Echoing Anselm's ontological argument, he affirms that God as the Primary being is so certain that 'it is impossible that he be thought not to be or to be other than unique.'[16] Being and non-being are juxtaposed as absolute opposites, and are in full flight from each other. He elaborates:

> Therefore, just as absolute nothing has nothing of being or its attributes, so contrariwise being itself has nothing of nonbeing either in act or potency, either in objective truth or in our estimation. Since nonbeing is the privation of being, it does not come into our understanding except through being; but being does not come to us through something else because everything which is understood is understood as nonbeing or being in potency or being in act. If, therefore, nonbeing can be understood only through being and being in potency only through being in act, and if being signifies the pure act of being, then being is what first comes into the intellect and this being is pure act. But this is not particular being, which is limited because mixed with potency; nor is it analogous being because that has only a minimum of actuality because it has only a minimum of being. It remains that being in question must be divine Being.[17]

Ironically, a coincidence of opposites also occurs in 'the blindness of the intellect', which confounds being with non-being, and vice versa, and often mistakens the highest being for nothing.[18] The mind's eye, conditioned to particulars and universals, does not see Being itself which is beyond every genus. Borrowing an analogy from Aristotle, Bonaventure explains: 'Hence it is most truly apparent that "as the eye of the bat is in regard to light so is the eye of our mind in regard to the most evident things of nature".'[19] Hence the intellect, accustomed to the darkness of beings and the images of material things, seems to see nothing when gazing upon the light of the supreme Being. And we are not cognizant of the fact that 'this very darkness is the supreme illumination of our mind (cf. Ps. 138:11), just as when the eye sees pure light, it seems to itself to see nothing.'[20]

From the darkness of the human condition, Bonaventure bids us to look at the pure light of being itself. From there he derives divine attributes through a *via negativa*, i.e., by denying God the negative characteristics of the material world. By refusing to predicate of God all forms of non-being, he deduces that being itself must be first, pure, eternal, most simple, most actual, and most perfect and supremely one. Embodied in these attributes is a coincidence of opposites:

> But you have something there to lift you in wonder for Being itself is first and last; it is eternal and most present; it is utterly simple and the greatest; it is most actual and most unchangeable; it is most perfect and most immense; it is supremely one and yet all-inclusive. If you wonder at this with a pure mind, you will be flooded with a greater light when you see further that it is last because it is first. For because it is first, it does all things for itself; and therefore it must necessarily be the ultimate end, the beginning and the consummation, the *Alpha and Omega*.[21]

These opposites are juxtaposed, but strikingly, each is derived from the other. Being itself is most present precisely because it is eternal. As eternal, it does not proceed from another nor of itself cease to be; it has neither past nor future, but only present. It is the greatest precisely because it is the most simple. As such, it possesses the greatest power, hence is the greatest. It is most changeless precisely because it is most actual. As pure act, it can acquire nothing new or lose nothing it already has. Because it is most perfect, it is measureless. Since it possesses all perfections, one can think of nothing better, nobler or more worthy, and consequently of nothing greater than a being like God. Finally, it is the all-embracing principle of all aspects of the multiplicity, precisely because it is supremely one. For the one is the universal efficient, exemplary and final cause of things. These polar attributes coincide as opposites within the Godhead itself.

Second Cherub: Metaphysics of Goodness and the Trinity

Having considered God in the unity of his nature, Bonaventure turns to the opposite, viewing God in the plurality of persons in the Trinity. This is beautifully portrayed in the image of the two Cherubim, placed opposite each other. There abides in the same Godhead a mysterious coincidence of the trinitarian unity of one nature and plurality of persons. The second Cherub speaks of the second method of contemplation, which 'fixes the gaze on the Good itself, saying that this is God's primary name.'[22] While the first method mainly looks to the Old Testament, to Moses and the revelation of God as Being, the second method chiefly looks to the New Testament, to the revelation of the Trinity, and Christ's statement to the rich young man, 'No one is good but God alone' (Lk. 18:19; Matt. 19:17). While Damascene, following Moses, asserts that God's primary name is *He who is*, Dionysius, following Christ, asserts that God's primary name is Good.[23] The same position is provided in his *Commentary on Book I of the Sentences*:

> If we speak of the names that God has given to Himself when He has understood Himself in a proper sense, then the names of this type are proper names. Such are said to be the names "Good" and "He Who Is". Wherefore, Dionysius seems to want that the name "Good" alone is proper to God and His principal name. Damascene, on the other hand, seems to want that the name "He Who Is" alone is proper to God and His principal name.[24]

Bonaventure accepts the Anselmian principle of the *Proslogion*, 'that than which no greater can be thought', accentuating that what is absolutely the best 'cannot rightly be thought not to be, since to be is in all ways better than not to be.'[25] He then unites the Anselmian ascent to the all-perfect Good with the Dionysian principle of the Good as 'Self-diffusive.'[26] Subsequently he writes: 'And this good exists in such a way that it cannot rightly be thought of unless it is thought of as triune and one. For good is said to be self-diffusive; therefore the highest good must be most self-diffusive.'[27] By contemplating God as the Good, as *diffusivum sui*, one can arrive at the Blessed Trinity with awesome admiration.[28] However this exercise must not be construed as proving the Trinity by natural reason. 'Saint Bonaventure is not claiming here the possibility of proving the Trinity by natural reason', Stephen Brown remarks aptly, 'but merely of indicating proofs of fittingness. The necessity he speaks of in regard to these proofs is the "necessity of suitableness".'[29] From a consideration of the Good and its utmost communicability, he demonstrates conceptually how the greatest self-diffusion of the divinity necessarily requires the procession of the Son and the Holy Spirit. This he further explains by means of divine fecundity, the concept of fountain-fullness (*fontalis plenitudo*) taught in his *Commentary on the Sentences of Peter Lombard*.[30] The supreme fecundity allows the supreme communication, from which follows supreme sharing and intimacy, all of these occur within the Divinity itself. The following is Bonaventure's account of the proofs of fittingness for the trinitarian processions, which he derives from a consideration of the Good.

> By reason of Their supreme goodness, the three Persons must necessarily have supreme communicability; by reason of that, supreme consubstantiality; and by reason of supreme consubstantiality, They must have supreme conformability. Then by reason of all these, They must have supreme coequality, and hence supreme co-eternity. Finally, from all the foregoing taken together, they must have supreme mutual intimacy, by which one Person is necessarily in the other by reason of Their supreme interpenetration, and one acts with the other on absolute indivision of the substance, power, and activity of the Most Blessed Trinity.[31]

Bonaventure bridges the two disciplines between philosophy and theology, proceeding from a consideration of God as absolute being to a consideration of God as ultimate goodness. Being is the name of the Old Testament God, whereas Good is the name of the New Testament God. The progression from the former to the latter is indicative of a shift in metaphysics, from that of being to that of the good. This, in turn, casts light on his doctrine of God, that God 'is not simply absolute being but moreover absolute goodness. [Therefore] [o]ne can no longer talk about being as the ground of reality without talking about God, and one can no longer talk about God who is Trinity without talking about the good.'[32] The root of Bonaventure's thinking could also be traced to Francis of Assisi who frequently speaks of God as good in his writings, often referring to God's goodness in the superlative: 'all good, supreme good, totally good, You Who alone are good.'[33] From the Neoplatonic philosophy, *via* Dionysius, Bonaventure identifies the Good as a perfect name of God. Goodness is the supreme attribute of God; it is that which defines the very Godhead, the essence of what God *is*. It also forms the deepest basis for God's creative activity *ad extra*. It is precisely the dynamism of the Good to impart itself, thus giving rise to being. This Dionysius states in the *Divine Names*: 'The first gift of the absolutely transcendent goodness is the gift of being, and that goodness is praised from those that first and principally have a share of being. From it and in it are being itself, the source of beings, all beings and whatever else has a portion of existence.'[34] The good by nature is self-diffusive, sharing itself freely with an other. Since God is Good, it follows that God is necessarily self-communicative.

Victorine's Love and Trinitarian Emanations

However goodness alone, for Bonaventure, cannot justify for the Trinity of persons 'since it specifies neither the mode nor the number of divine emanations.'[35] Thus he completes the picture by resorting to Richard of St. Victor, according to whom the supreme form of good is love which by its very nature seeks to give of itself freely to an other. Bonaventure combines the Dionysian model of the good with the Victorine emphasis on love to work out his doctrine of the Trinity. The crux of Richard's argument for a plurality of divine persons, which Bonaventure accepts, is not the Dionysian axiom of the good *per se* but of charity.[36] Charity is the content of the good, the sovereign form of the good. And if God is good, it follows that God is also love. Where there is fullness of divinity there is fullness of goodness, and where there is fullness of goodness there is fullness of charity. Essentially, perfect charity which is God means other-directness, not self-love. Charity cannot exist without plurality, which he locates on the level of person. There must be a 'thou' in God's life; otherwise God would not be perfect charity. If God were simply one person, there would be no communication of goodness (love) to another, in which case God's love would be private self-love, not perfect love. Thus, if God is perfect love, there must be at least two persons in God. Furthermore if there are only two divine persons, he argues, there could be only love for each other. Such love could become curved-in-upon-itself, in which case it would be neither the fullness nor the perfection of love, for the supreme perfection of love requires that each of the two persons in love shares that love with another. Thus Richard concludes that there must be three divine persons in the Godhead, for perfection of love requires a lover, a beloved, and the fruit of their mutual love expressed in a third as the co-beloved.

Using Richard's analogy of 'supreme happiness', Bonaventure proceeds to provide the 'reason of necessity and fitness' that there are only three Persons in the Deity:

> There cannot be fewer than Three for supreme happiness requires love (*dilectio*) and mutual love (*condilectio*).... Whence, the first Person, since He cannot be begotten (*innascibilis*) and breathed forth (*inspirabilis*), begets and breathes forth; the second, since He cannot be breathed forth, but is begotten, does not beget, but breathes forth; the third Person however, since He is breathed forth and proceeds from One who begets, neither begets nor breathes forth. And therefore it is impossible that there are more than three.... There will be only three Persons, ... One who only gives in whom is Love by nature (*amor gratuitus*); Another, who only receives, in whom is Love by indebtedness (*amor debitus*); and One mediating, who gives and receives, in whom is Love mingled (*amor permixtus*) from Both.'[37]

That there is a mutuality of love in three divine persons of equal dignity meets the status of what constitutes sovereign perfection. Each person is loved equally, is equally perfect, and each has the fullness of wisdom, goodness, and every divine perfection. Bonaventure links the idea of communication or emanation with that of *condilectus* to justify as necessary the existence of the third person. The same idea recurs in his *Journey of the Soul into God*:

> If, then, there were not eternally in the sovereign good a present and consubstantial fertility and a hypostasis of equal dignity, as the fertility by mode of begetting and spiration is, so that it is from an eternal principle that is in eternity doubly principle, with the result that there is a Beloved (*dilectus*) and a loved Companion (*condilectus*), begotten and an outcome of spiration, in other words, Father, Son and Holy Spirit, there would never have been a sovereign good, because that good would not have diffused itself sovereignly.
>
> If you can, then, with the eye of the spirit, seize hold of (*contueri*) the purity of goodness which is the pure act of charity that loves with a gratuitous love and a due [love] and [a love] that is a mixture of the two which constitutes the fullest diffusion by mode of nature and [by mode] of will – it is a Gift, in whom the other gifts are given – then you will see through the sovereign communicability of the good that it is necessary for the Trinity of the Father, the Son and the Holy Spirit to exist.[38]

The principle of plenitude requires that the self-diffusion must not be merely potential, and cannot be less than supreme. For the highest good must be self-diffusive in the highest degree. Hence the highest self-diffusion must be 'actual and intrinsic, substantial and hypostatic, natural and voluntary, free and necessary, lacking nothing and perfect.'[39] Only in the Trinity can there be an eternal, actual and sovereign diffusion, which results in the generation of the Son and Spirit from the Father's fecundity. Otherwise we would not find in the divinity the highest good, 'because it would not be supremely self-diffusive.'[40] Perfect mutual love demands divine persons of equal dignity so as to avoid a disordered love of a created person. In no way could the finite creation be the infinite, perfect self-communication of God, for then creation would, of necessity, be equal to God, in which case it would be divine like God is. God must be sovereignly self-diffusive in a way that is intrinsic and organic to the mystery of the Trinity, prior to and totally independently of creation. Along with Richard of Victor, he argues that the maximum of self-diffusion can be realized only in the Trinity, and not in creation since creation is incapable of meeting the demands of divine fecundity: 'The diffusion in time in creation is no more than a center or point in relation to the immensity of the divine goodness.'[41] This is Bonaventure's vision of the triune God, that God is the purest and primordial self-communicative love which is productive within the Godhead before his *ad extra* activities in the created order.

The Primacy of the Father and Trinitarian Emanations

The mystery of the Trinity is rooted in the mystery of the Father who is the source and goal of all reality. With the Greek tradition, Bonaventure emphasizes the dynamism of the Father as the fountain source of the Trinitarian processions. The primacy of the Father is already taught in his early work, *Commentary on the Sentences of Peter Lombard*, where he bases his position on the Neoplatonic principle of the fecundity of primacy:

> ... but the more primary a thing is, the more it is fecund and the principle of others. Therefore just as the divine essence, because it is first, is the principle of other essences, so the person of the Father, since he is the first, because from no one, is the principle and has fecundity in relation to persons.[42]

In his *Breviloquium*, he equates the Neoplatonic One with the Father, the first person of the Trinity: 'The Father is properly the One without an originator, the unbegotten One; the principle who proceeds from no other; the Father as such.'[43] In his last work, *Collations on the Six Days of Creation* (1274), the year before he dies, he expounds: 'The Father begot His own likeness, that is, the Word co-eternal with Himself, and expressed a similitude of Himself, and in so doing He expressed all that He could.'[44] Abiding in the mystery of the Father is the coincidence of opposites – his unbegotteness and generativity. The Father alone is *innascible*, indicated by a privation of birth or origin, not position.[45] For Aquinas, God begets because he is Father. Contrarily, Bonaventure affirms that God is Father because he begets: '*Ideo Pater, quia generat*.'[46] The Father is first, the sourceless source, and is distinguished by his incommunicable property of *innascibilitas*, a negative quality which is positively his. He explains: 'this *innascibilitas*, under a negative form, is a perfect and positive reality. The Father cannot be born because he does not proceed from another. Not to proceed from another is to be the first, and primacy is a noble affirmation.' Consequently, because the Father is first, he is the principle. As principle, 'there is, in act or in potency, a term that proceeds from that principle (*Quia primum, ideo principium; quia principium, iedo vel actu vel habitu est principiatum*).'[47] 'By reason of his quality of first, one person is, by nature, inclined to produce another. I call here a "quality of first" the *innascibilitas*, the fact that he cannot be born, by virtue of which ... there is in the Father the fullness of a source from which everything emanates.'[48] This is also in congruence with what he says in his *Disputed Questions on the Mystery of the Trinity*: 'The more a being is prior, the more it is the fontal cause of production. Therefore, whatever is produced emanates necessarily from that being which is absolutely first (i.e. the Father).'[49] Because this *innascibilitas* implies fertility, that there is no antecedent, we must stop at the first, and not question why the Father is *innascibilis*. Being the first principle, the Father is therefore first in the order of begetting as *innascibilis*, while at the same time also first in the order of spiration but as *improcessibilis*. The *innascibility* of the Father is the generative and spirative power of the Father. In affinity with the Cappadocians, Bonaventure declares: '*Pater est principium totius divinitatis quia a nullo*.'[50]

'Person' Bonaventure, in agreement with Boethius, defines as 'the *suppositum* of a reasonable nature that is distinguished by a property', and that property is relation.[51] Here he corrects Boethius by including relationality as part of his understanding of a divine person, for 'a relative property can import both relation and origin.'[52] Contrary to Aquinas, he does not exploit the Anselmian principle, that in God all is one except where there is an opposition of relation, to establish the ontological distinctions of the trinitarian persons. For him, Persons are distinguished not by anything absolute as essence but by their different properties, each is identical with the origin, thus each is with and capable of relationship. The three persons are constituted by their origins; the originating relations manifest personal distinction. Origin, which is pre-eminent to being, becomes the ontological basis of emanation and trinitarian relations of persons in the Godhead. Although innascibility is the peculiar attribute of the Father, it does not yet fully define the hypostatic identity of the Father. Rather, this innascibility, that which characterizes the Father in the most excellent way, is the negative complement to generation, precisely because the Father is innascible he is 'a flowing fullness' (*fontalem plenitudinem*), therefore constituting the principal source of origin of the other two emanations. 'The Father's *innascibilitas* pointed to a flowing fullness, [which] is afterall, a productive fullness', he writes, 'however... this flowing fullness is not attributed to the Father because he produces the creatures, since that is an act ... common to all three Persons. Nor is it attributed to him because he produces the Holy Spirit, because that act is common both to him and the Son.' The constitution of the Father, therefore, is understood inevitably in connection with the coincidence of opposites – innascibility and fecundity. Because he is known as innascible he is known as Father, but he is Father in the fullest sense in the act of generating the Son. For Hilary as it is for Bonaventure, the Father is the 'author' of the Son, 'then by what constitutes authority in the Father' to beget, not to create. 'Thus, it is by reason of innascibility that the *hypostasis* of the Father begets.' Paternity is thus exclusively the Father's personal property, denoting his 'positive' relation to his Son, a term which he himself produces.[53]

That the divine life is seen as a good that is communicated, according to Bonaventure, occurs in two ways – by mode of nature (*per modum naturae*), which is the begetting of the Son, and by mode of will (*per modum voluntatis*), which is the procession of the Spirit.[54] This he expounds in a strain reminiscent of Alexander of Hales, according to whom the Father as primal goodness begets the Son by the mode of nature.[55] Returning to the Victorine notion of love as the highest good, he argues that the Father's self-diffusion is not a general kind; rather it is the highest kind, that love diffuses itself personally to one other than the Father, the Son who is at once of equal dignity with the Father. Since good must be communicated, there must be in God the communication of the divine nature or goodness from the Father to the Son. 'The most powerful reason' for putting generation in God is that

> every nature is communicable, and there is in God an aptitude for this by reason of His nobility ... so that His nature must be communicated to several. But there cannot be several from one nature unless one of these is from the other or both are from a third. Since, however, before the divine persons there is nothing, one must be from the other. And since they are conformed in nature and generation is emanation according to conformity of nature, I believe that it is necessary to put generation in God.[56]

In the Deity alone where there is 'substance having supreme simplicity' can there be 'generation of absolute perfection', which imparts 'the same substance in its entirety', yet in a manner that the supposit 'does not to add to the essence ... nor limit it nor multiply the form.'[57] The Son is that person who is eternally generated by the nature of the Father's self-diffusive goodness. As such, the Son is the total self-expression of the Father as Word, and the perfect likeness to the Father as image. The Son/Word is the divine exemplar. The Son is all that the Father is in One other than the Father. The second procession refers to the communication of goodness as a voluntary volition, that the Father produces the Spirit by mode of will. While the Son is generated naturally, the Spirit is spirated voluntarily. This does not imply that the difference between the two processions is that the former is necessary whilst the latter is contingent. Of the precise difference between will as nature (*voluntas ut natura*) and will as will (*voluntas ut voluntas*), Cowburn explains: '[T]he medieval scholastics, following Aristotle, customarily divided agents into those whose acts are determined by natures and those whose acts are freely willed, and instead of talking about necessary acts on the one hand and free acts on the other, they talked about the former as "natural" and the latter as "voluntary".'[58] But for Bonaventure, the will as will means 'personal' will, which does not carry Aristotelian concept of 'free' vs. 'necessary.' Thus the distinction between the will as nature and the will as will is one between nature and person.

The Spirit which proceeds by way of fecundity of will must also proceed by way of love. Any form of procession in the Divinity must be a voluntary liberal one. The most liberal of all human givings is done out of love; similarly with God. 'For an emanation by way of love', Bonaventure writes, 'is the first and noblest ... emanation by way of will.' Quoting Augustine, he elaborates:

.... For the affection of love is the first among all affections and the root of all the others, as Augustine shows (*Civ.* 14.7). And that affection is the noblest of all since it holds more of the element of liberality. This is the Gift in which all other gifts are given... There is nothing in creatures that is considered so delicious as mutual love and without love there are no delights.... If there is, therefore, emanation by way of liberality in God, this must be first and supreme and so by way of love.[59]

Predication of Love

Proceeding from the Father and the Son by way of perfect liberality, the Spirit is the bond and unity of both. The Spirit is the voluntary generous giving of the first two persons to each other: Their mutual love is gift of self. As fruit of their mutual love, the Spirit is 'Gift', from which all other gifts proceed. The Son is generated by the Father and together with the Father spirates the Spirit who is the eternal bond of love between them. In demonstrating this, Bonaventure amplifies his explanation of love in three senses.[60] First, love exists in God as essential love, that by which each of the persons loves by himself. This Bonaventure calls 'complacency', the essential affection predicated commonly of all three persons since they are one God. He illustrates this type of love with the example of the bride and groom, whose social love is directed towards living together. Secondly, love in the notional sense refers to a love by which the Father and the Son are in concord in spiration. Their concord he calls 'love' (delection), the notional affection predicated of the first two persons in spirating the third. The notional predication points to his fecundity which concerns only the Father and the Son. It expresses, in Quinn's words, 'the habitude of spiration pertaining to Father and Son in their relation of procession with respect to the Holy Spirit.'[61] This is illustrated by the example of the mutual conjugal love of bride and groom for each other directed towards begetting a child. It is in this second sense that the Spirit is the mutual love of the Father and the Son. Bonaventure returns to this point again and again:

> Love has the perfection of its delectable value and of its value of union and uprightness from its character of reciprocity. As a consequence of this, we have either not to speak of a person in God

> who proceeds by mode of love or, if there is such a procession, it must be by mode of reciprocal charity.[62]

> The love that the Holy Spirit is does not proceed from the Father insofar as he loves himself, nor does he proceed from the Son insofar as he loves himself, but he proceeds insofar as the one loves the other, because he is a nexus (a bond or unity).[63]

Thirdly, love in the personal sense refers to a love which is the Spirit himself because he who is co-produced by way of perfect generosity cannot be other than love (*amor*). This he illustrates by the child, who can be called love (*amor*), because he is produced by the mutual conjugal will of bride and groom. As the fruit of their will in concord, the child is only a 'loved one' (*amatus*), although he may be called 'love' by virtue of an emphatic mode of speech. Having recognized the limitation of his example, Bonaventure hastens to say that there is no correspondence between what occurs in the created order and what occurs in God. Whereas what proceeds in created love is not a person, he argues, in God, that which proceeds in the concord of Father and Son is

> truly and properly love (*amor*), having the reason of both love and person (*hypostasis*). He is love because he first proceeds from a most liberal will by way of perfect liberality; he is person because, being distinguished from those who produce him and yet being unable to be distinguished essentially, he is distinguished personally; this is not the case in created love.[64]

This sheds light on the question of the precise relation of Father and Son to Spirit. The Spirit is personal love which proceeds from the mutual love of the first two persons.

Bonaventure uses synonymously of the Spirit the three common terms of affection, *amor*, *dilectio* and *caritas*, whose respective connotations he refines. *Amor* signifies a unifying love; *dilectio* goes beyond this to signify a chosen beloved, as in the Song of Songs 5:10: 'My beloved is chosen out of thousands'; *Caritas* goes beyond that to signify a beloved of an inestimable value, as St. Paul speaks of Timothy: 'My dear and faithful son' (I Cor. 5:17). All three terms combined express fully a loving relational dynamism in the Trinity.

By his identification of the three terms with respect to the Spirit, Bonaventure could speak of the Spirit as at once the unitive, choice and dear love of the Father and the Son.[65]

Furthermore Bonaventure differentiates terms that are proper from those that are appropriated to the divine persons. An argument arises as to whether love is proper to the Spirit: just as 'wisdom' is to the Son, so is love to the Spirit; but wisdom is not proper to the Son, so love is only appropriated to the Spirit. In response, Bonaventure rejects the parallel of wisdom and love. For wisdom is not predicated with respect to another person, but essentially of God. The statement, 'the Father is wise by generated wisdom' is false, because wisdom, of itself, is always meant essentially, unless appropriated. Augustine once upholds this saying, but he later rejects it as untrue: if the Father is without the Son, who is the Father's wisdom, the Father is not wise. Bonaventure follows Augustine, holding that wisdom pertains to all three persons, not just the Son.[66] For him, the true parallel for the Son with respect to the Spirit as love is not wisdom but the Son's name, 'word.' Just as Word is proper to the Son, so love is proper to the Spirit. Whereas wisdom implies no relation, both word and love imply a relation; the former implies a relation to the one speaking the word (i.e., Father); the latter implies a relation to those joined by love, that which is proper to the Spirit. The Spirit proceeds by way of love, as the Son proceeds by way of word. Therefore the saying, 'Father and Son love each other *by* the Holy Spirit', is true, but not this, 'The Father is wise *by* generated wisdom.' The Father and the Son love themselves by the Spirit without the Father's being wise by his generated wisdom. To clarify further, Bonaventure draws a distinction in the expression 'wisdom of another' between the subject of wisdom and its origin, signified by the genitive 'of.' Thus it is true to say that 'the Son is the Father's wisdom', since he proceeds from the Father as wisdom. But the expression, 'the Father is wise *by* generated wisdom' is false, for the ablative 'by' conveys origin, indicating that the Son is the principle of the Father. But wisdom is predicated essentially; 'to be wise' is not understood notionally, because it in no way conveys origin. Nevertheless in the Trinity, the Spirit proceeding is not appropriated love but properly love. Thus notionally the expression, 'Father and Son love each other *by* Holy Spirit', is true. For the ablative 'by' conveys origin, and as such, love is predicated notionally with respect to the persons who are joined by love, in which case the Spirit is their common fruit.[67] This theme will recur later.

The second procession is the production of a person who proceeds by way of mutual love. Because this production is by way of fecundity of will, not by way of fecundity of nature, it is not generation. Thus the person who proceeds is not a Son, but the Spirit of Love. However Bonaventure's vision of *filioque* cannot be understood apart from his synthesis with the Victorine themes of love and the Spirit as *Condilectus*.

Trinitarian Love and the Spirit as *Condilectus*

In analyzing the trinitarian dynamism of love, it becomes obvious that he follows Richard in arguing that the three persons represent three modalities of love. The first is a love that is purely communicative and gratuitous. At the other extreme is a love that is purely receptive and responsive. And in between these two is a modality of love that is a mixture of the two, which constitutes the fullest diffusion by the two modes of emanation. With the theme of *condilectus*, Bonaventure completes the trinitarian circle of love. The relationship between the first two persons, essential to Boanventure's thought, is completed in the divine person of the Holy Spirit. The perfection of love demands three divine persons: the Father being the sourceless source of boundless love, the Son being the emanation of love proceeding from the nature of the Father's goodness to diffuse itself, and the Spirit being the sharing of that love which proceeds as an act of full freedom. '(T)he fertility by mode of begetting and spiration', Bonaventure writes, 'is from an eternal principle that is in eternity doubly principle, with the result that there is a Beloved (*dilectus*) and a loved companion (*condilectus*)', a third loved by the first two in harmony.[68] This is indeed the Trinity of love in which, from an eternal principle eternally co-producing, there is a beloved and co-beloved. As image, the Son shares in the positive aspect of the Father's fecundity to produce another, without sharing the negative attribute of innascibility. Thus the Son, like the Father and together with him, is the principle of the Spirit to whom, with the Father, he communicates the divine nature. In affirming the unity of essence

Bonaventure gives special place to Damascene's doctrine of circumincession, that communication of life occurs from person to person. There in the intra-trinitarian life is 'a supreme interpenetration' (circumincession) of a dynamic life of distinct persons, who exist in intimate union and loving relationship.[69] The love of the Father and the Son is of such great intimacy that the Spirit proceeds from them as from one principle – this justifies *filioque*. He clarifies:

> And if you are the other Cherub and contemplate that which is proper to the persons, and if you are amazed that communicability coexists with personal identity, consubstantiality with plurality, a unity of nature with personality, coequality with order, coeternity with production, and *mutual intimacy with emanation – for the Son is sent by the Father, and the Holy Spirit by both the Father and the Son*, yet *the Holy Spirit sent from both* ever remains with them and never departs from them.[70]

Keenly aware of the Greek position on this issue, Bonaventure provides arguments both from the Scripture and from theological reasoning. The biblical texts he focuses are Jn. 15: 16; 16: 14; Gal. 4:6 – these texts indicate that the Spirit is the Spirit of both the Father and the Son. His theological argument for *filioque* reflects a correspondence between the economic missions and the eternal emanation, in virtue of which the one who is sent by the Father and Son in history is the one who proceeds from them eternally. The visible mission of the Spirit from the Father and the Son is seen in the sending of the Spirit on the Church in the form of tongues of fire and of a dove. He explains, 'This is not because of some new link or identification with the symbolic species, but by reason of the union between the thing signified and the sign specifically destined, both in manner and origin, to express it.'[71] Considering the properties of the divine persons, the Father, the unoriginated principle, is the fontal fullness of origin as regards the Son and the Spirit. As the primordial principle of personal fecundity, the Father is the author of the other two persons and the principle of divine authority given them according to their proper modes of origin. The Son receives authority solely from the Father, from whom alone he emanates, and so the Son is sent to us by the Father's authority. The

Spirit has authority from both the Father and the Son, from whom the Spirit emanates, and thus the Spirit is sent to the Church under both authority. 'To be sent' implies eternal emanations. In the case of the Son, he is sent by the Father, who proceeds from no one, for nowhere is it said that he is sent. By this temporal sending, God thus shows that the Son proceeds from the Father eternally. 'But since the Son both produces and is produced, He both sends and is sent. And since the Holy Spirit is eternally produced but does not produce, except in time, it is proper to Him to be sent; but to send applies to Him only in regard to the creature.'[72] Thus the following proposition, 'the Holy Spirit sends the Son', refers to the Son in his incarnate mode of existence, Christ as a man born of a Virgin; it cannot refer to the eternal Son, in which case the Spirit would be the source of the Son.[73] Likewise, there is a congruence of an immanent Gift and a temporal gift; so if the Spirit is given to us in time by the Son, he too must proceed eternally from the Son. Hence the temporal mission of the Spirit from the Father and the Son has a beginning in time, which corresponds to the immanent mission of the Spirit from the Father and the Son in eternity. God communicates himself in history as he is in himself in eternity. The immanent trinitarian mystery of God is the ontological ground of the economy of a trinitarian history, the former being the abiding presupposition of the latter.

In order that the mutual love of the first two persons not be turned into a private self-love, it must necessarily go out into another, thus the third is spirated. Yet it is not the love of the first two turned towards each other as in Augustine, but of them turned towards the third, their co-beloved. Alike Richard, Bonaventure's trinitarian configuration is this: the Father is the lover, the Son is the beloved, and the Spirit is the co-beloved. If God is love, the highest love, and since love cannot be private self-love but other-directed, then love in God implies a community. Because this love in God is the most perfect of loves, it must be very liberal and common. As a liberal love, it naturally tends towards another; as a common love, it must be shared, loving and being loved, giving and receiving. One person gives or loves gratuitously; another receives this love that is his due; and yet another both loves and is loved, that is, a mixture of the first two. This is precisely consonant with the intertrinitarian relationship of love, according to which there is 'the gratuitous love of the Father for both the Son and the Spirit – He receives nothing in return from them; the well-merited love of the Spirit since He proceeds from the Father and the Son; and finally the mixed love of the Son, a love due to his Father but given gratuitously to the Holy Spirit.'[74]

Filioque means, for Bonaventure, the Father and the Son are united in breathing forth the Holy Spirit in a special manner: 'The Spirit is properly called the link or unity of the Father and Son. Spirit taken in relation to spirituality is common to the whole Trinity, as it is said in regard to spiration it is proper to the Holy Spirit....The Holy Spirit proceeds from the Father and the Son, not insofar as they are distinct Persons, but insofar as there is in them one fruitfulness of the will, or one active spiration.'[75] The bond which Bonaventure speaks of refers to the Spirit as the agreement of the Father and the Son in being the origin of the Spirit. 'Although the Son and the Holy Spirit have Their Source from the Father in a different manner', he further explains, 'on the contrary the Father and the Son breathe forth the Holy Spirit in the same manner.'[76] However the Spirit does not exercise any active role with respect to the Father and the Son; rather the Spirit proceeds in a passive manner from the first two acting in concord, not giving anything to them but receiving everything from them.[77] Thus the Spirit as the mutual love is understood not as a kind of cause, but as effect of the Father and the Son in their love. This is what he means by the expression, 'The Father and the Son love each other by the Holy Spirit.'[78] Here he takes great care in fleshing out the expression by applying his distinction of essential and notional love. If the verb 'to love' (*diligere*) takes on the essential sense, it refers to the complacency of the will commonly attributed to all three persons, in which case it would be wrong to say that the Father and the Son love each other by the Spirit, because then they would be *by* the Spirit.[79] Therefore taken essentially, the statement, 'The Father and the Son love each other by the Holy Spirit', really means 'The Father loves himself, and the Son loves himself by the Holy Spirit', since this essential sense would indicate the very essence that is identical with the persons and by which each person loves himself. This, he argues, is unacceptable. If, however, love is understood notionally, it then refers to the fecundity of will to produce from itself a person, and this fecundity is only in two, though the will is in all three. Taken notionally, the statement is true, because Father and Son are construed with love 'retransitively.'⁸⁰ Thus the statement, 'Father and the Son love each other by the Holy Spirit', means: 'the Father loves the Son, and the Son loves the Father, by the Holy Spirit.' This saying is true, because the love which is the Spirit is a love binding the Father to the Son, and the Son to the Father. This love is mutual, unique and also undivided (*substantificus*).⁸¹ The Father and the Son are distinct, but also connected. Connection suggests a unity that arises from an already existing distinction.⁸² By reason of the act of connecting, the Father and the Son are said to love each other by the Holy Spirit. They are mutually connected in spirating the Spirit. Thus the Spirit is the bond of love between the Father and the Son. When the Father and the Son are said to be joined together, 'being joined' either refers to the Spirit as the causal principle from which the Father and the Son come, or to the Father and the Son from whom the Spirit proceeds. The former is impossible because it would mean the first two persons receive from the Spirit; in fact, by reason of the simplicity of God, they would receive everything, including their being, from the Spirit, in which case it is false. Thus the second alternative is right, that the Father and the Son's 'being joined' expresses that they together form a co-principle of the Spirit.⁸³ 'Therefore the Holy Spirit is related to their joining as to his own principle and not in any way by the notion of a form (i.e., principle) that could give them something.'⁸⁴ This is his intimation of the *filioque* doctrine. Love is unique to the Spirit because it is the expression of the mutual love of the Father and the Son. Only the Spirit is *that* love.⁸⁵

Concluding Reflections

The afore-mentioned shows that Bonaventure's model of the *filioque* is uncompromisingly Western, that the Spirit proceeds from the Father and the Son. He writes, 'the Greeks and the Latins agree upon the authority of Scripture, which says that the Holy Spirit is of the Son and is sent by the Son; but they differ over reason and revelation.... the Greeks have compared the Spirit to the breathing forth of an outer breadth, but the Latins to the breathing forth of an inner love.'⁸⁶ Although the early Greeks do not confess the *Filioque*, he says, they do not outrightly deny it. However 'their scurrilous progency have added to the paternal madness and say that he proceeds from the Son only temporally. And therefore the Roman Church condemns them as so many heretics and schismatics.'[87] For Bonaventure, eternally the Spirit proceeds from the Father 'before' (*prius*) the Son. However 'before' does not mean before in 'duration', nor does it mean before in 'causation' – both are false. But if it means before in 'authority', so that 'before' is the same as 'more prominently' (*principalius*), this is true.[88] 'The Holy Spirit proceeds from the Father before the Son in regard to authority, but not in regard to duration or causation or origin ... to be first in causality would be contrary to the unity of essence.'[89] In the eternal self-differentiation, God's being the Father is ontologically the ground of his being the Son and the Spirit. In the divine processions, no temporal priority is implied, suggesting that the Son and Spirit are in any sense less than the Father, for each of them is fully God. Bonaventure's emphasis on origin removes every tint of ontological subordinationism. The Father and the Son are 'one Source' (*principium*) of the Spirit.[90] The Son is thus given a role to play in the spiration of the Holy Spirit. The Spirit proceeds from the Father through the mediation of the Son, and also immediately *per se*: '*Dicendum quod Spiritus dicitur procedere a Patre principaliter, et per se: principaliter, quia auctoritas est in Patre; per se, quia non tantum mediante Filio, sed etiam immediate. Non tamen plenius procedit a Patre, nec perfectius.*'[91] Hayes comments:

> The Spirit would be bond in a more perfect sense if He stood in an immediate relation to both of the other persons than if he stood in an immediate relation to one and in a mediate relation to the other...The relation between two productive persons is more intimate if, in the act of production, they are not independent of each other, but mutually related in a productive act. Such an intimate interrelation would include a greater degree of unity between them, and consequently a greater degree of bliss.[92]

Love has 'the perfection of delight and union and rectitude from mutuality', therefore 'the person proceeding by way of love must proceed by way of mutual love.'[93] Here Bonaventure makes extremely clear that the love involved in the second procession is not the solitary love of the Infinite Being for itself as in Anselm, but is essentially mutual:

> For a procession, two things are necessary: that it be from one, and that it tends to another. But the love that is Holy Ghost does not proceed from the Father as he loves himself, nor from the Son as he loves himself; it proceeds from the Father and the Son as they love each other, since it is the link between them. Hence the Holy Ghost is a love that is from one and tends to another, and so fulfills the requirements of procession.[94]

One may argue, as Cowburn does, that if the love involved in spiration is the essentially mutual love of the first two persons for each other, then they, as two loves, spirate the Holy Spirit as two persons.[95] Contrarily, Bonaventure stresses that the love must be single, as the Holy Spirit himself is, that the Father and the Son spirate the third in so far as they possess one nature, one will and one volition ('*affectus*').

> It is objected: if mutual (the love), then not unique (the love, and hence the third person). The answer is: this is true in lovers whose wills are distinct, but not in God.[96]

> The Holy Spirit proceeds from the Father and the Son in as much as they are one in the fruitfulness of the will.[97]

> The Father and the Son spirate as one in essence, nature or will.[98]

Hence the mutual love of the first two persons, for Bonaventure, is a single reality, i.e., one active spiration in God. This is rooted in the fact that the Spirit proceeds from the Father and the Son, not insofar as they are distinct persons, but insofar as there is in them one fecundity of will. Endorsing Bonaventure's solution, Coffey writes:

> In the Godhead, so perfect is the adaptation of Father and Son to each other in their mutual love that they become *unus spirator* of the Holy Spirit, remaining, however, always distinct as Father and Son, *duo spirantes*. It is in this adaptation, based on the personal likeness

between Father and Son arising from generation, that, to use St. Bonaventure's word, the divine will becomes 'fecund.'[99]

Fairly speaking, Bonaventure takes as his departure point Augustine's unity of divine essence, upon which his meditation is fixed. However he neither follows Augustine's model of the Trinity all the way; nor does he develop an independent treatment of the 'one God.' Instead he develops one that has its roots in the Greek patristic tradition, in which divine persons occur as the ontological priority. Rather than putting the stress on the unity of substance as in Augustine, Bonaventure places the emphasis on divine persons, which undergirds relationship since to be a person is to be in relation to another. Like the Cappadocians, each person is understood according to origin, and thus each is a relation of origin. Damascene's idea of circumincession (interpenetration) is woven into Bonaventure's theory, and by way of Richard's he develops his model of the Trinity based on the good.[100] Richard's doctrine of trinity as a community of love finds its fullest intelligibility in Boanventure, whose starting point is Neo-Platonic and Augustinian one of God as the *Summum Bonum*. That which characterizes the inner life of God is the fountain-fullness of fecundity and the fullness of the self-diffusion of the good. For Richard, the highest Good is love, the nature of which is personal and communicative. As such the Trinity is grounded in mutual relationships of love. Divine persons of the Trinity are not only related to each other, but they coinhere in each other, and draw life from one another. Bonaventure's model highlights the personal nature of God as a dynamic one constituted by a community of intrinsically-related persons. His emphasis on distinct personhood and relationality is contributive to the development of social doctrine of the Trinity, which is prevalent in the twentieth century.

Bonaventure understands the Father as unoriginated origin, sourceless source and inner ground of unity in the Trinity. This sets him apart from Augustine who grounds the unity principle in the One Essence. He starts with the Father as the groundless ground of a self-communicative love, which produces the Son and the Spirit. Because he takes love as the starting point and focus of unity in the Trinity, he is moving, unlike the predominant Latin tradition, not from the essence of God but like the Greek tradition, from the

Father who originally possesses the being of God that is constituted as love. Kasper's words echo Bonaventure's view: 'For love cannot be thought of except as personal and inter-personal love. The person, therefore, cannot exist except in self-communication to others and in acknowledgement by others. For this reason, once God is thought of from the start as personal, the oneness and unicity of God cannot be conceived as meaning a solitary God.'[101] The basic presupposition at work in Bonaventure's view is that trinitarian relations need not necessarily be relations of origins or processions as in Augustine. Noteworthy is his affinity with the Eastern tradition, according to which persons as persons are capable of being the subject of acts that relate one to the other; they are capable of loving relationships within the one substance of God who is love. As such the Son and the Spirit can be eternally related, even without having their eternal origin in one another. The possibility of genuinely interpersonal relations of love is dependent not upon origin, but their individual concreteness and dynamic personalities. For 'a relative property can import both relation and origin.'[102] Like his predecessor, Richard, his view, too, is an alternative in Western theology to the predominant Augustinian position, according to which the only relations are the processions.

For Bonaventure, it is precisely the dynamic nature of the divine to communicate itself. An important point to be drawn from this is that the love of the Father, Son and Spirit is an open love, not a love curved in upon itself; it is not a self-enclosed love, but an overflowing love, a love that is wide enough to embrace the entire universe. The image of divine life as a flowing fountain expresses a dynamic character of God, that the Christian God is not the impassive and disinterested deity of the Greeks who has nothing in common with creation. Rather, the triune God is the infinite, dynamic, supra-abundant fountain-fullness of self-diffusive love, who, by the nature of being love, is at once Most High and most intimately related (*altissime et piisime*).[103] That God is personal also spells the death of the theistic notion of a unipersonal God because, Kasper reasons, '(s)uch a view will be compelled to look for a counterpart for God, find it in the world and man, and, by setting up a necessary relation between God and the world, be unable any longer to preserve the transcendence of God and his freedom in love.'[104] The trinitarian God is neither the supreme object over against humanity nor the supreme subject contingent upon humanity for fulfillment. O'Donnell's words reflect Bonaventure's thought: 'God is in his own life interpersonal communion, and because God in his own being is love, God can be love for us, a love which is free and gratuitous. The love which God is overflows into creation and time.'[105]

Another significant contribution of Bonaventure is his idea of *kenosis* which is ontologically constitutive of God's triune life. It is precisely Godlike to empty himself. The Father, being the first principle of the Godhead, is not only the fountain-fullness of love but also totally self-communicative love, or self-emptying by the nature of the good. In the act of generating the Son, the Father, who is infinitely rich in love, communicates his total self, and thus becomes poor. Whatever is given is given absolutely and completely, since the self is diffusive goodness. 'Because the whole is communicated and not merely part, whatever is possessed is given, and given completely.'[106] Here lies another pair of opposites that coincide in the Father: the Father as the fountain-fullness of love, and as self-emptying, the latter contingent upon the former. The mystery of the Father, therefore, is the coincidence of fullness and emptiness (by the nature of self-diffusion); richness (in goodness) and poverty (by the nature of *kenosis*).[107] *kenosis* is ontologically rooted in the nature of the Father's goodness to diffuse itself. The Father empties himself from the infinite surplus of goodness. Only because the Father is infinitely rich in goodness can he be poor. Humility pertains to the Father who gives himself totally as an infinite gift of goodness. The totality of self-gift characterizes the Father as a true, poor and humble servant, an image radically different from that of a controlling despot. Bonaventure's understanding of God the Father as the kenotic self-giving thus pre-empts the absolute hierarchical rule of the Father as the first principle. So the power of God the Father is defined not as monarchical power 'over' another but as the power of the kenotic total self-sharing of love 'with' another. This is what Delio calls an 'inverted patriarchy, in which power is diffusive love.'[108] Bonaventure's understanding of God's Fatherhood as diffusive love could therefore meet the modern objection of the Father image as invalid in describing the life of the Trinity.

The Father is hidden in the object of his love, namely the Son who is the true and perfect expression of the Father. This he states in his *Collations on the Six Days*, 'From all eternity the Father ... expresses himself and a likeness similar to himself, and in so doing he expresses the sum total of his potency.'[109] Later in the same, he writes, '(t)he Word expresses the Father and the things he made, and principally leads us to union with the Father who brings all things together; and in this regard he is the Tree of Life for by this means we return to the very fountain of life and are revived by it.'[110] In the self-communication of the Father to the Son, the Son receives from the Father the nature of self-diffusive goodness. Thus, just as the Father is kenotic, so too, is the Son; just as the Father is poor, so too, is the Son. Just as the Father's humility is expressed in being totally turned towards the Son, so too, the Son's humility is manifested in being turned towards the Father. From the Father, the Son receives the property of being the origin of others, since together with the Father, the Son produces the Spirit. Like the Spirit, the Son is produced by the Father's self-diffusive goodness; but with the Spirit, the Son also shares the property of receptivity. Whereas it is by way of receptivity to the Father's self-diffusive goodness that the Son, the equal other, is generated, it is by way of receptivity to the mutual self-communicative love of the first two that the Spirit, their co-beloved, is spirated. The Trinity is, therefore, not a substance with personhood added on; rather it is personal love, totally self-giving, and dynamically self-emptying. Bonaventure's model of the Trinity shows its maximum affinity with that of the Cappadocians. This Delio elaborates:

> Thus the rule of the Father is not only self-giving, but the very gift of the Father is given in the Son who, as Son, is both receptive to the Father's goodness and like the Father, generates or diffuses the good as self-gift to the Father, the union of which is expressed in the person of the Holy Spirit. The Son, therefore, is both receiver and giver of the good. In this respect the Son shares in the Father's rule of self-giving so that the Son, like the Father, is not a self-sufficient monarch but what we might call a 'servant,' giving all to the other. Because the Spirit is the gift of self-donation between the Father and the Son, the Spirit, too, shares in the rule of self-giving and, indeed, is the gift par excellence. Thus we see that patriarchy, or the rule of the Father, is self-gift, which is the basis of the shared rule of the three divine persons based on the nature of the good as relational.[111]

Love is equally predicated of all three persons, this essential sense which is commonly shared by Augustine, Aquinas and Bonaventure. Yet the essential predication of love presents for Augustine difficulties in distinguishing the procession of the Spirit. Contrarily, Aquinas and Bonaventure restrict love to the Spirit, that the Spirit alone is properly love. Both distinguish between the essential predication and personal predication. For Bonaventure, the personal love is unique because it is the expression of the mutual love of Father and Son. As the immanent fruit of the mutual love of the first two persons joined together in a fecundity of will in spiration, love is a *proprium* of the third person. Aquinas, on the other hand, based on his parallel between acts of knowledge and acts of love, considers 'love proper to the Spirit as residing in the hypostasized *terminus* of an act of divine love (essence). Just as the divine mind produces a Word, and just as that Word (but not the ability to know) is proper to the Son alone (indeed is the Son); so too the divine will produces a Love (Thomas does not use the word like that, confessing a lack of vocabulary at this point), which Love (and not the divine ability to love) is proper to the Spirit alone (indeed is the Spirit).'[112] For Bonaventure, the Spirit does not proceed from the Father and the Son according to the unity of essence; nor does it proceed according to the differentiation of persons, but rather in accordance with the fact that although they are different, they are still indivisibly One. Their unity is one of essence as hypostasized in the Father and the Son in a personal way so that they together, as distinct persons, in a concord of will (love) spirate the Spirit. Here Bonaventure distances himself from Augustine, who fails to see the relations between the divine persons as grounded in the ontology of God. For him, relation is an ontological predicate, by reason of which there is no divine substance behind, supporting the person. By this, he is able to make claims about the being of the particular persons and their distinguishable identity, without absorbing them into the all-embracing oneness of God, and thereby also avoid the heresy of modalism.

Finally, beyond dispute, Bonaventure's thought differs with Augustine's, that the Spirit is not the mutual love of the first two lovers turned towards each other, but rather of the first two lovers turned towards the third as in Richard. Although Bonaventure stands within the Latin tradition, his view shows affinity with the

Greek tradition, accentuating the identity of the Spirit as the one who opens up the relationship of the other two, although it is not clear why must there be only three. That 'why three?' has been answered in Augustine's idea of the Spirit as the bond of love, for in God, there are two, and the reciprocity of the two. But Augustine's mutual love-theory has been criticized for depersonalizing the Spirit, and Bonaventure seeks to avoid this. In an 'I-Thou' relationship, the love that the Father and the Son bestow upon each other is not a distinct person; at least, it does not give concrete particularity to the Spirit as distinct from the 'I' and 'Thou.' Thus in Augustine, the Spirit has little function, if any except as a link between the Father and the Son. On the contrary, Bonaventure's view of God as the perfect communion of love allows the distinctiveness of the Spirit to come through far more strongly than Augustine's mutual-love theory. Bonaventure develops Augustine's love analogy along the vein of Richard, conceding that mutual love, to be perfect, must be shared with the third. Therefore in God, not only would we find an I-thou relationship of reciprocal love, but also the third as co-beloved, thereby completing the trinitarian circle of love. He is successful in deducing the immanent-Trinitarian dynamic from the nature of God's self-diffusive love, but he fails to derive God's unity from the reciprocity of persons. He tends to overemphasize the independence of persons at the expense of God's unity. Like Richard, Bonaventure does not develop his theory from the perspective of the economy of salvation, and thus the immanental relations are really emptied of any definite contents. How God might be in and for himself is Bonaventure's preoccupation, not how God might be for us.

Notes

Introduction

[1] For a thorough, but more philosophical study of the different kinds of love, including the love between the divine persons in the Trinity, see J. Cowburn, *Love and the Person* (London: Geoffrey Chapman, 1967).

[2] Y. Congar, *I Believe in the Holy Spirit*, 3 vols., (London: Geoffrey Chapman, 1983), 3: 96, his preface.

[3] C. Gunton, *Theology Through the Theologians* (Edinburgh: T. & T. Clark, 1996), 127.

[4] See W. Kasper, *The God of Jesus Christ*, M. J. O'Connell (tr.), (New York: Crossroad, 1984), 298, concedes that Aquinas' synthesis strikes a balance between the various conceptions, ending with a position not far removed from that of John Damascene, whose writings Aquinas esteems highly.

[5] B. Gaybba, *The Spirit of Love* (London: Geoffrey Chapman, 1987), 81.

Chapter One: The *Filioque* Question

[1] V. Lossky, 'The Procession of the Holy Spirit in Orthodox Trinitarian Doctrine', in J. Erickson and T. Bird (eds.), *In the Image and Likeness of God*, (Oxford: Mowbrays, 1974), 71; T. R. O'Connor, '*Homoousios* and *Filioque*: An Ecumenical Analogy', *Downside Review* 83 (1965): 1-18. For Eastern view of the Holy Spirit, see S. Burgess, *The Holy Spirit: Eastern Christian Traditions* (Peabody: Hendrickson, 1989); J. McIntyre, 'The Holy Spirit in Greek Patristic Thought', *Scottish Journal of Theology* 7 (1954): 353-75.

[2] For history, see D. Ritschl, 'The History of the *Filioque* Controversy', and M. Fahey, 'Son and Spirit: Divergent Theologies between

Constantinople and the West', in H. Küng and J. Moltmann (eds.), *Conflicts About the Holy Spirit*, (New York: Seabury, 1979), 3ff and 15ff.
3. B. Bobrinskoy, *The Mystery of the Trinity. Trinitarian Experience and Vision in the Biblical and Patristic Tradition* (New York: St.Vladimir's Seminary Press, 1999), 283, makes mention of Tertullian, Marius Victorinus, Hilary and St.Ambrose, all speak of the procession of the Spirit from the Son, and the communication of the Spirit by the Father and the Son.
4. J. N. D. Kelly, *Early Christian Doctrines* (London: Adam & Charles Black, 1968^4), 110.
5. B. de Margerie, *The Christian Trinity in History*, E. J. Fortman (tr.), (Massachusetts: St. Bede's Publications, 1982), 78.
6. *Adv. Praxean* 4. Cf. A. McGrath, *Christian Theology. An Introduction* (Oxford: Blackwell, 2001^3), 323; A. Harnack, *History of Dogma*, vol. II (London: Williams & Norgate, 1897), 257ff.
7. For a study of Irenaeus, see R. Olson, *The Story of Christian Theology. Twenty Centuries of Tradition and Reform* (Illinois: InterVarsity, 1999), 68-78; Kelly, *Early Christian Doctrines*, 110.
8. G. L. Prestige, *God in Patristic Thought* (London: S. P. C. K, 1952), 98-9. See G. Watson, 'The *Filioque* - Opportunity For Debate?', *Scottish Journal of Theology* 41 (1988), 318: 'The idea of unity expressed by Tertullian has been aptly described as "organic" in that the unity of God is established by an organizing principle which administers its authority in a threefold manner... Tertullian proposes a structural analogy between the essence of God and the history of the world whereby the dispensations of the Father and the Son are followed by the Spirit. World history is here structured according to the nature of deity in a manner which would be unthinkable for St. Basil... To adopt such a structural analogy as proposed by Tertullian is to do precisely what was later achieved by the *filioque* addition'.
9. Tertullian, *Adv. Praxean 4* as cited in B. E. Daley, 'Revisiting the "*Filioque*": Roots and Branches of an Old Debate, part One', *Pro Ecclesia* vol. X (2001), 37.
10. *Ibid.*, 2 as in Daley, 'Revisiting the "Filioque"', 37 & Kelly, *Early Christian Doctrines*, 113; T. F. Torrance, *The Christian Doctrine of God. One Being, Three Persons* (Edinburgh: T. & T. Clark, 1996), 176.
11. *Ibid.* Cf. Kelly, *Early Christian Doctrines*, 113.
12. *Ibid.*, IX as in Margerie, *The Christian Trinity*, 81 (translation is his).
13. *Ibid.*, 4; B. Gaybba, *The Spirit of Love* (London: Geoffrey Chapman, 1987), 46; G. Bray, 'The *Filioque* Clause in History and Theology', *Tyndale Bulletin* 34 (1983), 113; J. H. S. Burleigh, 'The Doctrine of the

Holy Spirit in the Latin Fathers', *Scottish Journal of Theology* 7 (1954), 124

[14] *Ibid.*, 3.

[15] *Ibid.*, 8.6-7 as in Margerie, *The Christian Trinity*, 79 (translation is his); Olson, *The Story*, 97.

[16] H. B. Swete, *On the History of the Doctrine of the Procession of the Holy Spirit* (Cambridge: Deighton, Bell, and Co, 1876), 122.

[17] E. J. Fortman, *The Triune God. A Historical Study of the Doctrine of the Trinity* (Philadelphia: Westminster, 1972), 115, where he indicates that Tertullian knew of the immanent Trinity, certainly not less than the Apologist.

[18] Hilary, *De Trinitate* XII.55-57. The English translation is from vol. IX of the second series of Nicene and Post-Nicene Fathers, 18 vols., P. Schaff (tr.) (Grand Rapids: Eerdmans, 1886-1900), 233. Cf. *De Trinitate* ii. 29, where the question of '*per quem sit*' is answered; H. B. Swete, *The Holy Spirit in Ancient Church* (London: Macmillan, 1912), 304, footnote 2.

[19] *Ibid.*, ii.29; Y. Congar, *I Believe in the Holy Spirit*. 3 vols., D. Smith (tr.), (London: Geoffrey Chapman, 1983), 3:50, where he argues that this text points not to the procession but to the witness borne by Father and Son.

[20] *Ibid.*, 8.20 as cited in Daley, 'Revisiting the "*Filioque*"', 38.

[21] *Ibid.* Cf. Daley, *ibid.*, 38; Congar, *I Believe in the Holy Spirit*, 3:50.

[22] *Ibid.*, ix.73 as in Fortman, *The Triune God*, 132.

[23] *Ibid*; cf. viii. 19.

[24] *St. Hilary of Poitiers*, in E. W. Watson *et al* (tr.), A Select Library of Nicene and Post-Nicene Fathers, Second Series, (Grand Rapids: Eerdmans, 1899), 9:60. The same is found in Fortman, *The Triune God*, 131. Cf. Daley, 'Revisiting the "*Filioque*"', 38, footnote 17, where he identifies a possible, but unlikely alternative translation of *qui Patre et Filio auctoribus confitendus est:* 'who is to be professed on the authority of Father and Son'.

[25] Cf. Augustine, *De Trinitate* vi.11 as cited in J. Pelikan, *Development of Christian Doctrine. Some Historical prolegomena* (New Haven: Yale University Press, 1969), 123. This author is indebted to Pelikan's discovery.

[26] Cf. Augustine, *De Trinitate* 5.14; Anselm 3.202-204 (*De Processione Spiritus Sancti*).

[27] Hilary, *De Trinitate* vii.41 as in Pelikan, *Development of Christian Doctrine*, 140.

[28] *Ibid.*, ii. 1; 29 as in Fortman, *The Triune God*, 131. Cf. Augustine, *De Trinitate* vi. 11 as in Pelikan, *Development of Christian Doctrine*, 134; Bobrinskoy, *The Mystery of the Trinity*, 284, footnote 36.

29. B. Altaner, *Patrology*, H. C. Graef (tr.), (New York: Herder & Herder, 1961), 445.
30. J. Pelikan, *The Christian Tradition*. 3 vols. (London: University of Chicago Press, 1971), 1: 203.
31. Ambrose, *On the Holy Spirit*, in R. J. Deferrari (tr.), *Saint Ambrose: Theological and Dogmatic Works*, (Washington: Catholic University of America Press, 1963). See R. P. C. Hanson, *The Search for the Christian Doctrine of God* (Edinburgh: T. & T. Clark, 1988), 756, where he dismisses this treatise as a 'pot-boiler', since it makes too much use of the great Greek fathers. Similarly, but more amicably, Swete, in his *The Holy Spirit in the Ancient Church*, 317-18, undermines the significance of the treatise because of Ambrose's unoriginality. Both of these comments, Badcock reasons, are unfair to Ambrose: 'It is true that his argument for the divinity of the Spirit is derivative and unoriginal, but it is also true that there is little that *can* be added to the claims of the Eastern theologians of the fourth century on this question; to ask Ambrose to say more is to ask him to do what practically all subsequent theologians of the Spirit have, like him, found either impossible or unnecessary. ... More importantly, ... (t)here is to be found in Ambrose, more than in any of his Greek sources, a real sense of the vital place of the Spirit in revelation, history, theology, the church, and the Christian life. In these matters he exceeds in a refreshing way the normal expectation one brings to the reading of patristic theology'. Cf. G. D. Badcock, *Light of Truth & Fire of Love* (Grand Rapids: Eerdmans, 1997), 64.
32. Ambrose, *On the Holy Spirit*, in H. De Romestin (tr.), NPNF Second Series, vol. 10, (Peabody: Hendrickson, 1994), book 3, chapter 18, 154.
33. *Ibid.*, 155.
34. Ambrose, *On The Christian Faith*, in H. De Romestin (tr.), NPNF Second series, Vol. 10, (Peabody: Hendrickson, 1994), book 1, chapter 1, para. 6, 202.
35. *Ibid.*, 202-03.
36. Ambrose, *On the Holy Spirit*, 2.12.
37. *Ibid.*, 1.9, 12; 3.1.
38. *Ibid.*, 3.1.
39. *Ibid.*, 1.12.
40. *Ibid.*, 2.8.
41. Ambrose, *De Spiritu Sancto* 1.11 (Hereafter as *De Sp. S*) as cited in Daley, 'Revisiting the "*Filioque*"', 39; Swete, *On the History of the Doctrine*, 120.
42. Swete, *On the History of the Doctrine*, 120.

43 Ambrose, *De Sp. S* 2.5 & 11; 3.1; *Comm. in Luc.* VIII as in Congar, *I Believe in the Holy Spirit*, 3:50.
44 Swete, *History of the Doctrine*, 120.
45 *De Sp. S.* 1. 152-54 (*PL* 16, 769). For English translation, see volume 44 of the *Fathers of the Church*, ed., P. Schopp (New York, 1947ff.), 90.
46 *De Sp. S.* 1.15.
47 *Ibid.*, II. 12 as cited in Swete, *History of the Doctrine*, 120-21.
48 *Ibid.*, III. 1 as cited in Swete, *ibid.*
49 *Ibid.*, II. 11 as cited in Swete, *ibid.*
50 Cyril, *Adversus Nestorii* 4.1-3 (*PG* 76. 132; 173; 184) as cited in Bobrinskoy, *The Mystery of the Trinity*, 283 and Daley, 'Revisiting the "*Filioque*"', 44. Cf. *Commentary on John* (*PG* 74, 541) as cited in R. Haugh, *Photius and the Carolingians: The Trinitarian Controversy* (Belmont: Nordland, 1975), 193. Swete, *The Holy Spirit in the Ancient Church*, 269, argues that Cyril would have had no problem with the formula *ex utroque* if it is understood to mean *ex Patre per filium*.
51 *Ibid.*
52 Theodoret, (*PG* 83. 148) as in Bobrinskoy, *The Mystery of the Trinity*, 284.
53 Cyril, *Adversus Nestorii* (*PG* 76. 433) as cited in Haugh, *Photius*, 194.
54 Augustine, *De Trinitate* VI.11, in P. Schaff (ed.), *A Select Library of the Nicene and Post-Nicene Fathers of the Christian Church. St. Augustine: On the Holy Trinity, Doctrinal Treatises, Moral Treatises*, (Grand Rapids: Eerdmans, 1956), 3:84. NPNF translation is used unless otherwise indicated. H. Bettenson (ed. & tr.), *The Later Christian Fathers*, (Oxford: Oxford University Press, 1970). The reference will be followed by Bettenson; J. Burnaby (ed.), *Augustine: Later Works, Library of Christian Classics*, (London: SCM, 1955), 8: 88ff. The reference will be followed by LCC.
55 *Ibid.*, 5.16 (Bettenson, 230). Cf. D. Coffey, 'The Holy Spirit as the Mutual Love of the Father and the Son', *Theological Studies* 51 (1990), 197, where he denies the Holy Spirit as the common gift of the Father and the Son in the immanent Trinity 'because it is of the essence of gift that it be bestowed gratuitously'. Such an assessment, Peters contends, results from a wedge which Coffey drives between the economic and immanent Trinity. See T. Peters, *God as Trinity. Relationality and Temporality in Divine Life* (Kentucky: Westminster/John Knox, 1993), 206, footnote 98.
56 *Ibid.*, V.11; XV.17.
57 *Ibid.*, VI.5.
58 G. O'Collins, *The Tripersonal God. Understanding and Interpreting the Trinity* (New York: Paulist, 1999), 136.
59 *De Trinitate.*, XV.19 as cited in D. Ngien, *The Suffering of God according to*

Martin Luther's Theologia Crucis (Bern: Peter Lang, 1995), 170. Cf. K. Barth, *Church Dogmatics*, in G.W. Bromiley (ed.) & T. E. Torrance (tr.), (Edinburgh: T. & T. Clark, 1962-75), I/1, 483: 'As God is in Himself Father from all eternity, He begets Himself as the Son from all eternity. As He is the Son from all eternity, He is begotten of Himself as the Father from all eternity. In this eternal begetting of Himself and begotten of Himself, He posits Himself the third time as the Holy Spirit i.e., as the love which unites Him in Himself'. This shows Augustine's influence on Barth. For a study of Barth's defence of the *filioque*, see Watson, 'The *Filioque* – opportunity for Debate?', 320-25, where Barth, he argues, maintains that the *per filium* doctrine 'disputes the *relatio originis* between the Son and the Spirit, so that the Spirit can only "improperly" be called the Spirit of the Son. Further, the unity of God is called into question by this modified form (from the Father through the Son). It presupposes that in relation to the Spirit, Father and Son do not have all things in common. Instead of the Father being the Father of the Son and so by implication, per the *filioque*, the origin of the Spirit with the Son, the origin of the Spirit is postulated as a second function alongside his Fatherhood'.

60 *The City of God* 11.10.1; *De Trinitate* 5.5-6
61 *De Trinitate* V.6 (LCC, 188); *De Trinitate* VI.5.
62 *Ibid.*, IV. 20.
63 O' Collins, *The Tripersonal God,* 139. Cf. Augustine, *De Trinitate* XV.17, 29, and his *Faith and the Creed* XIX as cited in Badcock, *Light of Truth*, 72; Peters, *God as Trinity*, 207, footnote 105.
64 *De Trinitate* IV. 20 as in Daley, 'Revisiting the "*Filioque*"', 41.
65 *De Trinitate* XV.17, 29. Based on this text, A. Heron, in his '"Who Proceedth from the Father and the Son": The Problem of the *Filioque*', *Scottish Journal of Theology* 24 (1971), 166, argues for the defensibility, not the necessity, of the *filioque*: 'defensible as indicating that the procession of the Spirit from the Father is not separable from the relation between the Father and the Son; not necessary, in that he does not proceed from the Son in the same way as from the Father, and it is not therefore vital that we name the Father and the Son together in affirming his procession'. Thus he sees no need to have to choose between the two triadologies. Most recently, J. Moltmann, in *The Trinity and the Kingdom of God*, M. Kohl (tr.), (Minneapolis: Fortress, 1993), 178-90, seeks to reconcile both Eastern and Western formulations by changing *ex Patre Filioque* to *ex Patre Filiis*, 'from the Father of the Son'. Contra Moltmann, Bray writes: 'This would concede the monopatrism of the East, but recognize, in the Augustinian tradition of the West, that the Father does not subsist or

act apart from the Son. This is an ingenious formula, but fails to answer the question at the heart of the dispute, viz. what role, if any, does the Son in the procession of the Holy Spirit?' Cf. Bray, '*Filioque* in History', 98.

66 Ibid., V.14. Cf. J. P. Mackey, 'The Holy Spirit: Relativizing the Divergent Approaches of East and West', *Irish Theological Quarterly* 48 (1981), 265.

67 Ibid., XV.17. See also M. O'Carroll, *Trinitas: A Theological Encyclopedia of the Holy Trinity* (Wilmington: Michael Glazier, 1986), 42.

68 Kelly, *Early Christian Traditions*, 276; E. Clapsis, 'The *Filioque* Question', *Patristic and Byzantine Review* 1 (1982), 132-33.

69 *De fide et symbol* 18, 19 as in Swete, *The Holy Spirit in Ancient Church*, 324-25.

70 *On Christian Teaching* (Oxford: Oxford University Press, 1997), 10 as cited in R. E. Olson & C. A. Hall, *The Trinity* (Grand Rapids: Eerdmans, 2002), 46; Swete, *The Holy Spirit in Ancient Church*, 325.

71 Olson and Hall, *The Trinity*, 46.

72 Ibid.

73 *Serm.* 71 (Migne, *PL* xxxviii. 354ff) as cited in Swete, *The Holy Spirit in the Ancient Church*, 327, and his *History of the Doctrine*, 126-27; Haugh, *Photius*, 204.

74 Augustine, *Tractatus in Joannis Evangelium* (*PL* 35, 1888ff) as cited Haugh, *Photius*, 204-05.

75 Ibid.

76 Ibid.

77 Ibid.

78 See R. Jenson, *The Triune Identity* (Philadelphia: Fortress, 1982), 137-38; T. Marsh, *The Triune God: A Biblical, Historical, and Theological Study* (Mystic, Conn.: Twenty-Third Publications, 1994), 131; C. Gunton, *The Promise of Trinitarian Theology* (Edinburgh: T. & T. Clark), 38-9; his 'Augustine, The Trinity and the Theological Crisis of the West', *Scottish Journal of Theology* (1990), 45. Like Jenson and Marsh, Gunton contends that Augustine's trinitarian view 'owes more to neoplatonic philosophy than to the economy of salvation'. All accept as Augustine's starting point the divine essence, which is verified as Father, Son and Spirit. Zizioulas, like Gunton, is critical of the essentialist ontology of God, insisting on returning to the insight of the Cappadocians. He writes: 'This would bring us back to the ancient Greek ontology: God first *is* God (His substance or nature, His being), and then exists as Trinity, that is as persons... The significance of this interpretation lies in the assumption that the ontological "principle" of God is not found in the person but in the

substance, that is, in the "being" itself of God... The one God is not the one substance but the Father, who is the "cause" both of the generation of the Son and the procession of the Spirit... And the one divine substance is consequently the being of God only because it has these three modes of existence, which it owes not to the substance but to one person, the Father. Outside the Trinity there is no God, there is no divine substance, because the ontological "principle" of God is the Father'. Cf. J. Zizioulas, *Being as Communion* (London: Darton, Longman & Todd, 1985), 40-41; Gunton, *The Promise of Trinitarian Theology*, 31-57.

79 Augustine, *De Trinitate* XV. 26. Also *Tract*. XCIX is referred to in *De Trinitate* xv. 27, '*de hac re in sermone quodam proferendo ad aures poluli Christiani diximus, dictumque conscripsimus*'. See Swete, *History of the Doctrine*, 126, footnote 3.

80 T. R. Martland, 'A Study of Cappadocian and Augustinian Trinitarian Methodology', *Anglican Theological Review* XLVII (1965), 256; P. Sherrard, *The Greek East and the Latin West: a Study of Christian Tradition* (London: Oxford University Press, 1959.), 67; O'Carroll, *Trinitas*, 42. Cf. P. Carey, 'Historical Perspectives on Trinitarian Doctrine', *Religious and Theological Studies Fellowship Bulletin* (Nov./Dec., 1995), 9ff, proposes that Augustine 'begins where the Cappadocians leave off: accepting their answer to the question "why not three gods?" he proceeds to ask "three what?" His concern is to elaborate the distinctions between the three on the assumption that they are one God. Augustine never uses the divine essence *per se* as his starting point'. Along the same vein, Weinandy and Hill argue that the customary distinction between the Eastern priority of the three persons and the Western priority of the unity of God is not entirely accurate historically. See T. G. Weinandy, *The Father's Spirit of Sonship* (Edinburgh: T. & T. Clark, 1995), 56-60; W. Hill, *The Three-Personed God* (Washington: Catholic University of America Press, 1982), 115-17; Margerie, *The Christian Trinity*, 162-3. Barnes proposes to reread Augustine, not with the presumed neo-platonic context, but within the polemical context of the end of the fourth century, specifically associated with the key themes and terminology of Nicene theology. See M. R. Barnes, 'Rereading Augustine's Theology of the Trinity', in S. Davis, D. Kendall & G. O' Collins (eds.), *The Trinity* (Oxford: Oxford University Press, 1999), 174-75. Whether this counter-proposal is an accurate reading of Augustine is a separate subject for an entire study.

81 Bobrinskoy, *The Mystery of the Trinity*, 284.
82 *De Trinitate* X. 18f (LCC, 88ff.).
83 *Ibid.*, XIV. 8 (LCC, 105ff.). Cf. Gunton, 'Augustine, the Trinity and

The Theological Crisis of the West', 46: '(Augustine's) notion of mind is strongly religious in character, so that of him it could be said as it has also been said of Hegel, that his motto was "I think, therefore I am religious". Nonetheless, it is in categories taken from the inner mental world that he seeks to unpack his analogies for the being of God.'

84 *Ibid.*, 15.38; 41 (Bettenson, 229).
85 *Ibid.*, VIII. 10-14 as in Burleigh, 'The Doctrine of the Holy Spirit', 131-32. His fondness of this love-formula is evident, since it appears at great length in Books IX and X, and reemerges in his concluding book XV.
86 *Ibid.*, XV. 17.
87 *Ibid.*, VIII. 10-14.
88 Badcock, *Light of Truth & Fire of Love*, 74.
89 Haugh, *Photius*, 35.
90 J. N. D. Kelly, *Early Christian Creeds* (London: Longman, 1972^3), 86-90; Fortman, *The Triune God*, 159. From the 7th century, the *Quicunque* is generally attributed to St. Athanasius. But in the 17th century, it is discovered that the date is much later than Athanasius, and it is of Latin origin. Thus the *Enchiridion Symbolorum* simply states that 'the view prevails now that the symbol originated in South Gaul ... between 430-500 from an unknown author'. Cf. Denzinger-Schoenmetzer, *Enchiridion Symbolorum* (New York, 1963^{32}), 75.
91 Denzinger-Schoenmetzer, *ibid.*, 805; 1300-1302 as cited in Fortman, *The Triune God*, 225.

Chapter Two: The Necessary Reasons for *Filioque* in Anselm

1 See F. S. Schmitt, *Opera omnia ad fidem codicum*. 6 vols. (Edinburgh: T. Nelson, 1946-61), 1:104 (*Proslogion* 4). I will use the English edition by J. Hopkins and H. Richardson, *Anselm of Canterbury*, 4 vols., (Toronto: Edwin Mellen, 1976). (Hereafter cited as Anselm.). Occasionally their *Anselm of Canterbury. Trinity, Incarnation, and Redemption. Theological Treatises* (New York: Harper Torchbooks, 1970) will be used. (Hereafter cited as *Theological Treatises*.)
2 Schmitt, I.104 (*Proslogion* 4) as cited in Congar, *I Believe in the Holy Spirit*, 3:96. Cf. *Anselm*, 1.95 (Hereafter cited as Anselm.). Pelikan, *The Christian Tradition*, 3:258-59, writes of Augustine's idea of 'faith seeks, but understanding finds', and its influence on Anselm.

3. Congar, *I Believe in the Holy Spirit*, 3:96ff; Marsh, *The Triune God*, 131ff; Gaybba, *The Spirit of Love*, 72ff; Olson & Hall, *The Trinity*, 55. For an analysis of Luther who stands squarely in the Augustinian tradition, see Ngien, *The Suffering of God according to Martin Luther's 'Theologia Crucis'*, 135-45.
4. Augustine, *De Trinitate* I.4 as in W. J. Jurgens, *The Faith of the Early Fathers*, I-III (Collegeville: Liturgical Press, 1970-79). Cf. H. Bettenson, *The Later Christian Fathers* (Oxford: Oxford University Press, 1970). The following quote, 'Substance is something common to all three persons of the Trinity, but it is not ontologically primary until Augustine makes it so', could be found in J. D. Zizioulas, 'On Being a Person: Towards an ontology of Personhood', in C. Schwöbel and C. Gunton (eds), *Persons, Divine and Human*, (Edinburgh: T. & T. Clark, 1991), 40.
5. *Ibid.*, I.7.
6. Anselm, 3.3 (*De Incarnatione Verbi*).
7. *Ibid.*, 1.4 (*Monologion*)
8. *Ibid.*, 3.37 (*De Incarnatione Verbi*).
9. *Ibid.*, 1.84-5 (*Monologion*).
10. *Ibid.*
11. Augustine, *De Trinitate* 5.8.10 as quoted in O' Collins, *The Tripersonal God*, 141, and R. Cross, 'Two Models of the Trinity', *Heythrop Journal* XLIII (2002), 293, footnote 33. Cf. *De Trinitate* 7.7: '*Dictum est tamen tres personae non ut illud diceretur sed ne taceretur*', as quoted in Gunton, *The Promise of Trinitarian Theology*, 40.
12. Schmitt, I. 85; also cited Congar, *I Believe in the Holy Spirit*, 3: 97.
13. Anselm, 3.37. Cf. S. M. Burgess, *The Holy Spirit: Medieval Roman Catholic and Reformation Traditions* (Peabody: Hendrickson, 1997), 31.
14. Augustine, *The City of God* 2.10.1; cf. his *de Trinitate* 5.5-6 (cf. Bettenson's edition.). See G. R. Evans, *Anselm and Talking about God* (Oxford: Clarendon, 1978), 102 & 105.
15. *Theological Treatises*, 24-5 (*De Incarnatione Verbi*).
16. Augustine, *De Trinitate* 5.x.11 as cited in Evans, *Anselm and Talking about God*, 100.
17. Schmitt, I.11.21-5 as cited in Evans, *ibid.*, 100. (Translation is Evans's.)
18. See R. Cross, *Great Medieval Thinkers. Duns Scotus* (Oxford: Oxford University Press, 1999), 64; Fortman, *The Triune God*, 222.
19. Congar, *I Believe in the Holy Spirit*, 3:99. Aquinas belongs to the Augustinian tradition, affirming that the *filioque* is required for an ontological distinction between the Son and the Spirit. Cf. Gaybba, *The Spirit of Love*, 75; B. Davies, *The Thought of Thomas Aquinas* (Oxford: Clarendon Press, 1992), 193-206.

[20] Congar, *I Believe in the Holy Spirit*, 3:98-9. Fortman, *The Triune God*, 174:'Though Anselm generally followed Augustine closely, he did not approve Augustine's statement that the Holy Spirit proceeds *principaliter* from the Father any more than he approved the Greek view that the Holy Spirit proceeds from the Father "*per Filium*"'. Cf. G. O' Collins, 'The State of the Questions', in Davis, Kendall & O' Collins (eds.), *The Trinity*, 11. One must note this as a historical fact, that the original form of the Nicene-Constantinopolitan Creed (from 381) does not say that the Spirit proceeds from the Father '*alone*'; rather it states that the Spirit proceeds 'from the Father of the Son'. Cf. Augustine, *De trinitate* XV. xvii, 29, where he states that the Spirit proceeds from both the Father and the Son, albeit *principaliter* from the Father. For a study of Photius's doctrine of the procession of the Holy Spirit from the Father '*alone*', see M. A. Orphanos, 'The Procession of the Holy Spirit According to Certain Later Greek Fathers', in L. Vischer (ed.), *Spirit of God, Spirit of Christ. Ecumenical Reflections on the Filioque Controversy*, (London: SPCK, 1980), 21-5; cf. Gaybba, *The Spirit of Love*, 74; Congar, *I Believe in the Holy Spirit*, 3:58. For Photius, being a source of the Holy Spirit is strictly personal, an activity belonging to the Father only, not shared by all three. He retreats from the accepted Greek conception of the Spirit *per filium*, insisting that the Spirit proceeds from the Father 'alone', and the Son and the Spirit is likened unto two branches from a single stem.

[21] Schmitt, II.213:'*Ex eo enim quod pater et filius unum sunt, id est ex deo, est spiritus sanctus, non ex eo unde alii sunt ab invicem.... Et. Quoniam pater non est prior aut posterior filio, aut maior aut minor, nec alter magis aut minus est deus quam alter, non est spiritus sanctus prius de patre quam de filio. Si ergo dicitur quod spiritus sanctus principaliter sit a patre, non aliud significatur, quam quia ipse filius de quo est spiritus sanctus sit de illo, a patre.*' As quoted in Congar, *I Believe in the Holy Spirit*, 3:99. (Translation is Congar's.) Cf. Anselm. 3.198 & 214; Augustine, *De Trinitate* 15.17.29:'... and God the Father alone is he from whom the Word is born, and from whom the Holy Spirit principally proceeds. And therefore I have added the word "prinicpally", because we find that the Holy Spirit proceeds from the Son also. But the Father gave him this too, not as to one already existing, and not yet having it; but whatever he gave to the only-begotten Word, he gave by begetting him. Therefore he so begat him as that the common Gift should proceed from him also, and the Holy Spirit should be the Spirit of both.'

[22] Schmitt, II.202 as cited in Congar, *I Believe in the Holy Spirit*, 3:99.

[23] Anselm, 3.33-4 (*De incarnatione Verbi 13*). For a detailed analysis of

Anselm's images, see G. R. Evans, 'St. Anselm's Images of Trinity', *Journal of Theological Studies* XXVII (1976), 46-57.

[24] See G. Bray, 'The *Filioque* Clause in History and Theology'.

[25] Anselm, 3.212 (*De Processione Spiritus Sancti* 9).

[26] A. I. C. Heron, '"Who Proceedeth From the Father and the Son": The Problem of the *Filioque*', *Scottish Journal of Theology* 24 (1971), 154. It is Heron's judgment that Barth follows the Anselmian line of trinitarian thought. He quotes Barth's concluding remark about the procession of the Spirit: 'This third mode of existence (i.e. the Spirit) cannot result from the first alone or from the second alone, nor yet from a co-operation of the two, but only from their being as God the Father and God the Son, who are not "persons" either for themselves or in co-operation, but two modes of existence of the one being of God. Thus the one Godness of the Father and of the Son is, or the Father and the Son in their one Godness are, the origin of the Spirit.' Cf. K. Barth, *Church Dogmatics* I/1, G. Bromiley (ed.), (Edinburgh: T. & T. Clark, 1975), 486-87 as cited in Heron, ibid., 152-53. See also D. Ritschl, 'Historical Development and Implications of the *Filioue* Controversy', in Vischer (ed.), *Spirit of God, Spirit of Christ*, 63-4; O' Carroll, *Trinitas*, 12.

[27] Anselm, 3.188-92 (*De Processione Spiritus Sancti*). See J. Hopkins, *A Companion Study of St. Anselm* (Minneapolis: University of Minnesota Press, 1972), 109-11.

[28] Ibid., 3.261, footnote 5; *Theological Treatises*, 87, footnote 2 (*De Processione Spiritus Sancti*).

[29] Ibid., 3.196-98 (*De Processione Spiritus Sancti*).

[30] Ibid., as in Fortman, *The Triune God*, 174.

[31] Ibid. Cf. Augustine, *The city of God*, as quoted in O'Collins, 'The State of the Questions,' in Davis, Kendall & O'Collins (eds.), 11. Anselm's remark, which he takes from Augustine, anticipates Aquinas' trinitarian theology of God as subsistent relations. For a discussion of Augustine's inner-trinitarian relations, see his *De Trinitate* 5.5-6.

[32] Fortman, *The Triune God*, 174.

[33] G. Bray, *The Doctrine of God* (Illinois: InterVarsity, 1993), 181-82, where he criticizes Anselm who, having ignored the evidence of both Scripture and tradition, 'subsumed the generation of the Son under the general heading of procession, as if it were analogous to the procession of the Spirit'. See Fortman, *The Triune God*, 174, who also recognizes that the term 'procession' has a double meaning, applying it both to the Son's procession from the Father (which he means generation) and the Spirit's procession from the Father and the Son (which he means spiration).

34 G. R. Evans, 'Anselm of Canterbury', in G. R. Evans (ed.), *The Medieval Theologians. An Introduction to Theology in the Medieval Period*, (Oxford: Blackwell Publishers, 2001), 100. See her *Anselm* (Wilton: Morehouse, 1989), 65; A. I. C. Heron, *The Holy Spirit* (Philadelphia: The Westminster, 1983), 92.

35 Anselm, 1.61-73 (*Monologion* 48-63); Schmit, II.183:22-9 (*De processione Spiriti Sancti* I). Cf. Augustine's *De Trinitate* 15.7.12 who understands the Father as memory, the Son as understanding, and their Spirit as will or love. See W. Hankey, 'The Place of the Psychological Image of the Trinity in the Arguments of Augustine's *De Trinitate*, Anselm's *Monologion*, and Aquinas' *Summa Theologiae*', *Dionysius* III (Dec., 1979), 99-110; M. Levering, 'Speaking the Trinity: Anselm and His 13th Century Interlocutions on Divine *Intelligere* and *Dicere*', in J. R. Fortin (ed.), *Saint Anselm – His Origins and Influence*, (Lewiston: Edwin Mellen Press, 2001), 131-43; E. H. Cousins, 'Fecundity and Trinity', in M. L. Kuntz and P. G. Kuntz (eds.), *Jacob's Ladder and the Tree of Life. Concepts of Hierarchy and the Great Chain of Being*, (New York: Peter Lang, 1987), 77-8.

36 *Ibid*.

37 *Ibid*.

38 *Ibid*.

39 Olson and Hall, *The Trinity*, 56.

40 Daley, 'Revisiting the "*Filioque*"', 48, where he deals with *Monologion* 54 (Anselm, 1.64). See *Summa*, Ia, 37, 1, ad 3 as cited in Gaybba, *The Spirit of Love,* 79. Aquinas, too, accepts the idea of the Spirit as the mutual love between Father and Son. But for him a 'bond' is a connection, which cannot explain the origin of nor can it be identified with Spirit. As such this bond is a medium, not an end product or term (*terminus*).

41 Anselm, 1.64 (*Monologion*).

42 Schmit, 1.13 (*Monologion*) as cited in Pelikan, *The Christian Tradition*, 3:261.

43 D. Coffey, 'The Holy Spirit as the Mutual Love of the Father and the Son', 199: 'In its earliest formulation, Augustine felt some obligation to provide scriptural foundation for the mutual-love theory, though he was unable to do this in a satisfactory way. But by the end of the *De trinitate* it had become for him an almost self-evident variation or extension of the *filioque*, and so did not require any justification beyond mere mention.'

44 Bray, *The Doctrine of God.*, 181; his '*Filioque* in History and Theology', 127-29.

45 Anselm, 3.199-200 (*De Processione Spiritus Sancti*). Cf. Barth, *Church*

Dogmatics I/1, 549, where Barth concurs with Anselm in rejecting the Eastern exegesis' of John 15:26 in isolation from the wider context of texts.

[46] Anselm, 3.200 (*De Processione Spiritus Sancti*).
[47] *Ibid.*, 3.195 (*De Processione Spiritus Sancti*). Cf. S. B. Ferguson, *The Holy Spirit* (Illinois: InterVarsity, 1996), 75-6, where he speaks of the economic Trinity as a true revelation of the immanent Trinity.
[48] *Ibid.*, 3.204-205 (*De Processione Spiritus Sancti*).
[49] *Ibid.* Cf. Burgess, *The Holy Spirit*, 34.
[50] *Ibid.*, 3.205 (*De Processione Spiritus Sancti*).
[51] *Ibid.*, 3.202 (*De Processione Spiritus Sancti*).
[52] *Ibid.*, 3.202-04 (*De Processione Spiritus Sancti*). Cf. D. G. Bloesch, *The Holy Spirit. Works & Gifts* (Illinois: InterVarsity, 2000), 42, where he says that Augustine's distinction between the sign and the reality reflects 'the Platonic polarity between the material copy and the original'. Cf. Augustine's *De Trinitate* 15.26.45, where he says that John 15:26 ought to be interpreted together with John 20.23 so as to show that the Spirit proceeds also from the Son as verified in the Son's breathing on the disciples.
[53] *Ibid.*, 3.202 (*De Processione Spiritus Sancti*).
[54] *Ibid.*, 3.204 (*De Processione Spiritus Sancti*).
[55] *Ibid.*, 3.201 (*De Processione Spiritus Sancti*).
[56] *Ibid.*, 3.209 (*De Processione Spiritus Sancti*).
[57] *Ibid.*, 3.210 (*De Processione Spiritus Sancti*).
[58] *Ibid.*, 3.209 (*De Processione Spiritus Sancti*).
[59] For a discussion of Augustine's influence on Anselm, see F.V. Fleteren, 'The Influence of Augustine's *De Trinitate* on Anselm's *Monologion*', in C. Viola and F.V. Fleteren (eds.), *Saint Anselm - A Thinker for Yesterday and Today. Anselm's Thought Viewed by Our Contemporaries*, (Lewiston: Edwin Mellen, 2002), 411-43.
[60] Marsh, *The Triune God*, 132. For a study of communion as an ontological category in the Eastern fathers, see J. Zizioulas, *Being in Communion: Studies in Personhood and the Church* (London: Darton, Longman & Todd, 1985). He writes: 'Among the Greek Fathers the unity of God, the one God, and the ontological "principle" or "cause" of the being and life of God does not consist in the one substance of God but in the *hypostasis*, that is, the person of the Father. The one God is not the one substance but the Father, who is the "cause" both of the generation of the Son and of the procession of the Spirit' (40-1). For a recent study of the same, see A. J. Torrance, *Persons in Communion: Trinitarian Description and Human Participation* (Edinburgh: T. & T. Clark, 1996) who deals with the question of the ontological

principle – in God the person of the Father or the relational divine being itself. Alan advances the position of his uncle, Thomas Torrance, who writes that the Being of God is 'essentially personal, dynamic and relational Being'. See Torrance, *The Christian Doctrine of God*, 141 as quoted in R. Del Colle, '"Person" and "Being" in J. Zizioulas' Trinitarian Theology: Conversations with Thomas Torrance and Thomas Aquinas', *Scottish Journal of Theology* 54 (2001), 73.

61 Marsh, *ibid*.
62 Moltmann, *Trinity and the Kingdom of God*, M, 16-7; Badcock, *Light of Truth & Fire of Love*, 78-9.
63 Gunton, *The Promise of Trinitarian Theology*, 41.
64 *Ibid*.
65 *Ibid*., 38-9.
66 Anselm, 1.68 (*Monologion*).
67 *Ibid*., 1.69 (*Monologion*).
68 Levering, 'Speaking of the Trinity', 132-33. For Anselm's linguistic analysis of 'uttering' (*dicere*) as an essential property, see Anselm 1.701-72: 'For there ought to be no doubt that the Father and the Son and their Spirit each speaks of Himself and the other two, just as each also understands himself and the other two' (*Monologion*).
69 Anselm, 1.69 (*Monologion*).
70 Bray, '*Filioque* in History and Theology', 127-28.
71 Congar, *I Believe in the Holy Spirit*, 3:100. C. M. LaCugna, *God for Us* (San Francisco: Harper, 1993), 15, 211 & 226-27, where she approves of Kaufman's abandonment of the distinction between the immanent and the economic Trinity. Such distinction, both argue, would drive a wedge between 'God in himself' and 'God for us', rendering God totally irrelevant to the Christian life. Hence the entire trinitarian enterprise is to be found within the soteriological framework. See G. D. Kaufman, *Systematic Theology: A Historicist Perspective* (New York: Charles Scribner's Sons, 1968), 102, n.9. For critical responses to LaCugna and Kaufman, see T. G. Weinandy, *The Father's Spirit of Sonship* (Edinburgh: T. & T. Clark, 1995), excursus two, 123-36; P. D. Molnar, *Divine Freedom and the Doctrine of the Immanent Trinity. In Dialogue with Karl Barth and Contemporary Theology* (London: T. & T. Clark, 2002), where he argues for the purpose of the immanent Trinity.
72 Moltmann, *Trinity and the Kingdom*, 183-85.
73 J. Thompsom, *Modern Trinitarian Perspectives* (Oxford: Oxford University Press, 1994), 154.
74 Barth, *Church Dogmatics* I/1, 486-87. Cf. M. L. Becker., 'THE SELF-

GIVING GOD. The Trinity in Johannes von Hofmann's Theology', *Pro Ecclesia* Vol. XII (2003), 436-37, where he argues that in Hofmann, as it is in Barth and Rahner, 'God's being is best understood in terms of a specific history, namely, the history of God's self-giving in Jesus and his community', and that 'the relationship of God, the Father of Jesus Christ, is an eternal, intra-divine relationship with Jesus the man'.

75 T. Peters, *God – the World's Future* (Minneapolis: Fortress, 1992), 251-52.
76 J. Moltmann, *The Crucified God*, M. Kohl (tr.), (San Francisco: Harper & Row, 1974), 205; E. Jüngel, *God as the Mystery of the World*, D. L. Guder (tr.), (Grand Rapids: Eerdmans, 1983), 300, 343, 379-80; and Barth, *Church Dogmatics*, Vol. IV/1, 246-47.
77 Anselm, 1.97-8 *(Proslogion 8)*. Also quoted in R. B. Edwards, 'The Pagan Doctrine of the Absolute Unchangeableness of God', *Religious Studies* 14 (1978), 13-4.
78 Peters, *God – the World's Future*, 252.
79 Badcock, *Light of Truth & Fire of Love*, 77.
80 Anselm, 1.224-25 *(De Processione Spiritus Sancti)*.
81 See P. T. Forsyth, 'The Divine Self-emptying', *in God and the Father*, (London: Independent, 1957), 42; *Marriage, Its Ethics and Religion* (London: Hodder and Stoughton, 1912), 70-1.

Chapter Three: The Spirit as Co-beloved (*Condilectus*)

1 See Fortman, *The Triune God*, 191; D. Knowles, *The Evolution of Medieval Thought* (Baltimore: Vintage Books, 1962), 145.
2 For primary sources, see *Patrologia Graeca*, J. P. Migne (ed.), vol. 196, (Paris, 1878-90). (Hereafter cited as *PL.*); *De Trinitate: Texte critique avec introduction, notes et tables, J. Ribaillier* (ed.), (Paris: Vrin, 1958). (Hereafter cited as *De Trin.*); G. A. Zinn (ed.), *Richard of St. Victor* (New York: Paulist, 1979). (Hereafter cited as Zinn, *Richard.*). For Richard of St. Victor's mystical theology, see M. W. Blastic, *Condilectio: Personal Mysticism and Speculative Theology in works of Richard of Saint Victor* (Michigan: UMI, 1991); S. Chase, *Angelic Wisdom and the Grace of Contemplation in Richard of St. Victor* (Notre Dame: University of Notre Dame Press, 1995), and his *Contemplation and Compassion. The Victorine Tradition* (London: Darton, Longman & Todd Ltd., 2003).
3 *De Trin.* 3. 10 (Cousins' translation); cf. E. Stiegman, 'Bernard of Clairvaux, William of St. Thierry, the Victorines', in Evans (ed.), *The Medieval Theologians*, 144-46.

4. See Congar, *I Believe in the Holy Spirit*, 3:96; Gaybba, *The Spirit of God*, 78-9. For a comprehensive study of Richard of St. Victor's Trinity, see N. Den Bok, *Communicating the Most High. A Systematic Study of Person and Trinity in the Theology of Richard of St. Victor* (Paris: Brepols, 1996). Bok's main thesis is to read Richard as a medieval rejection of social trinitarianism (458-64.)
5. J. Bligh, 'Richard of St. Victor's *De Trinitate*: Augustinian or Abelardian?', *Heythrop Journal* 1:2 (April, 1960), 126-31. Bligh shows how Richard is indebted to Achard.
6. Cousins, 'A Theology of Interpersonal Relations', *Thought: A Review of Culture and Idea*, Vol. XLV (1970), 56-82. Cf. P. Henry, *Saint Augustine on Personality* (New York: Macmillian, 1960), 10, where he writes of Augustine's personal character, not purely essential, of love, which Richard shares.
7. Zinn, *ibid.*, 384.
8. *De Trin.* 4. 3 (Cousins' translation).
9. See *PL* 196, 889 as cited in Fortman, *The triune God*, 191; Burgess, *The Holy Spirit*, 64.
10. Zinn, *Richard*, 373-74.
11. Zinn, *Richard*, 374.
12. *De Trin.* I:8, 93.
13. *De Trin.*, prologue, 83-4 as cited in Blastic, *Condilectio*, 130.
14. *Ibid*. Cf. B. McGinn, 'The Language of Love in Christian and Jewish Mysticism', in S. T. Katz (ed.), *Mysticism and Language*, (New York: Oxford University Press, 1999), 202-35.
15. *The Twelve Patriarchs*, LXXVII as in Zinn, *Richard*, 136. Cf. R. J. Masiello, 'Reason and Faith in Richard of St. Victor and St. Thomas', *New Scholasticism* 48 (1974): 233-42, who fails to see the contemplative context in which Richard's conception of 'necessary reasons' is understood.
16. Zinn, *Richard*, 374.
17. *Ibid*.
18. Zinn, *Richard*, 375-76.
19. Zinn, *Richard*, 374.
20. *Ibid*.
21. *De Trin.* 2. 16-9 as cited in Stiegman, 'Bernard of Clairvaux...', in Evans (ed.), *The Medieval Theologians*, 146; Hill, *The Three Personed God*, 226.
22. LaCugna, *God for Us*, 161. Aquinas also accepts the Dionysian concept of *boum diffusivum sui*.
23. *De Trin.* 3.2 as cited in Stiegman, 'Bernard of Clairvaux ...', in Evans (ed.), *The Medieval Theologians*, 154.

24. Zinn, *Richard*, 374.
25. See Cousins, 'A Theology of Interpersonal Relations', 68, his footnote 27, where he quotes favorably Gregory the Great. XL *Homilae in Evangelia* 1, 17 (PL 76, 1139A).
26. Zinn, *Richard*, 374.
27. *De Trin.* 3.2 as cited in Pelikan, *The Christian Tradition.*, 3:263.
28. Zinn, *Richard*, 374-375.
29. Hill, *The Three Personed God*, 227-28; A. Nygren, *Agape and Eros*, P. S. Watson (tr.), (Philadelphia: Westminster, 1953), 654.
30. Congar, *I Believe in the Holy Spirit*, 3:103.
31. Zinn, *Richard*, 375. Cf. Anselm, *Proslogion* 1-5 as cited in Zinn, *Richard*, 376.
32. *Ibid.*, 378.
33. *Ibid.*, 376.
34. *Ibid.*
35. *Ibid.*, 376-377.
36. *Ibid.*, 377.
37. *Ibid.*
38. D. Ngien, 'The God Who Suffers', *Christianity Today* (Feb., 3, 1997), 40.
39. C. S. Lewis, *The Four Loves* (London: Collins, 1963).
40. Zinn, *Richard*, 377. Cf. M. A. Meerson, *The Trinity of Love. Modern Russian Theology* (Quincy: Franciscan, 1998), 103-04. Meerson sees influences of Victor's love paradigm on several Russian theologians. Berdiaev, for example, insists that 'God is the lover, and he cannot and does not wish to exist without the loved one'. God longs for the other, not because of 'an impairment, but rather the fullness and perfection of God's existence.'
41. Zinn, *Richard*, 384. Cf. W. C. Placher, *Narratives of a Vulnerable God. Christ, Theology and Scripture* (Kentucky: Westminster/John Knox, 1994), 67-8; J. J. O' Donnell, *The Mystery of the Triune God* (London: Sheed & Ward Ltd, 1988),78-9.
42. *Ibid.*
43. *Ibid.*, 384-85.
44. *Ibid.*, 384. Cf. C. C. Richardson, *The Doctrine of the Trinity* (New York: Abingdon, 1958), 91-2; M. T. Prokes, *Mutuality. The Human Image of Trinitarian Love* (New York: Paulist, 1993), 22-5.
45. *Ibid.*, 392. Also quoted in A. Yong, *Spirit-Word-Community. Theological Hermeneutics in Trinitarian Perspectives* (Hampshire: Ashgate, 2002), 67.
46. *Ibid.*, 385.
47. *Ibid.*
48. *De Trin.* V, 15, 25 as cited in Fortman, *The Triune God*, 194.

49 *De Trin.* V, 23 as cited in Fortman, *ibid.*, 193-94.
50 Zinn, *Richard*, 386.
51 *Ibid.*
52 *Ibid.*
53 *Ibid.*, 388. Also included in A. McGrath (ed.), *The Christian Theology Reader*, (Oxford: Blackwell, 2001²), 203-04.
54 See Boethius, *Liber de persona et duabus naturis*, 3 (PL 64, 1343) as cited in Congar, *I Believe in the Holy Spirit*, 3:107; cf. J. Thompson, *Modern Trinitarian Perspectives* (New York: Oxford University Press, 1994), 132; Gunton, *The Promise of Trinitarian Theology*, 94, where he sees problems in Boethius' view: 'Not only is there stress on individuality – *unrelatedness* – but the tendency that was to play so important a part in modern individualism, of defining our humanity in terms of reason (Descartes again), is given strong prominence'.
55 See *De Trn.* 4.22.24 as cited in O'Collins, *The Tripersonal God*, 143; Hall and Olson, *The Trinity*, 59; C. Welch, *In This Name. The Doctrine of the Trinity* (New York: Charles Scribner's Sons, 1952), 296.
56 *De Trin.* 4.24.
57 *De Trin.*, IV: 7, 169 as cited in Blastic, *Condilectio*, 148.
58 *De Trin.*, 4:7, 170 as cited in Blastic, *ibid.*, 149 (Blastic's translation).
59 *De Trin.* 4.11, 173 as cited in Blastic, *ibid.*, 150 (Blastic's translation).
60 *De Trin.*, 4:12, 175 as cited in Blastic, *ibid.*, 150 (Blastic's translation). Cf. Bray, The *Doctrine of God*, 182.
61 T. F. Torrance, *The Hermeneutics of John Calvin* (Edinburgh: T & T Clark, 1988), 9. Cf. O'Donnell, *The Mystery of the Triune God*, 101: 'The person is constituted not only by substantiality but also by the origin from which he has his being'. Nevertheless O'Donnell argues that Richard preserves the Boethian definition of person, because for him *sistere* refers to the person who has its being in itself, not in another, while *ex* speaks of the relationship of origin by which the person receives its being. Collins argues against O'Donnell, but in favour of Moltmann's interpretation, that existence is in the light of another. Quoting Moltmann: '*Ec-sisting* means "being out of oneself", which is an experience of oneself in the ecstasy of love, to be totally in the other and to understand oneself totally from the other is the ecstasy of love.' See P. Collins, *Trinitarian Theology West and East. Karl Barth, the Cappadocian Fathers, and John Zizioulas* (Oxford: Oxford University Press, 2001), 139.
62 Moltmann, *The Trinity and the Kingdom*, 173-74.
63 *De Trin.* V:6, 201 as cited in Blastic, *Condilectio*, 154 (Blastic's translation).

64 *De Trin.* V:6, 314-315 as cited in Blastic, *ibid.*
65 *De Trin.*, V:6, 202 as cited in Blastic, *ibid.*, 155 (Blastic's translation).
66 Blastic, *ibid.*, 155-156.
67 Bok, *Communicating the Most High*, 333-34.
68 *De Trin.* VI:10, 239.
69 *De Trin.* VI: 14, 245-46 as cited in Blastic, *Condilectio*, 160 (His translation); Congar, *I Believe in the Holy Spirit*, 3:105.
70 See Cousins, 'A Theology of Interpersonal Relations', 81; Burgess, *The Holy Spirit*, 65.
71 *De Trin.* 5.23 as cited in B. McGinn, *The Growth of Mysticism. Gregory the Great through the 12th Century* (New York: Crossroad, 1994), 599.
72 Zinn, *Richard*, 388-89.
73 *De Trin.* 5.13 as cited in Burgess, *The Holy Spirit*, 69.
74 *Ibid.*
75 *De Trin.* 3.11.
76 Congar, *I Believe in the Holy Spirit*, 3:105.
77 *De Trin.* V. 16, 214-15: '*Constat autem quia verus amor potest esse aut solum gratuitus, aut solum debitus, aut ext troque conjunctus, id est, ex uno debitus et ex alio gratuitus. Amor gratuitus est, quando quis ei a quo nichil muneris accipit, muneris accipit, gratante inpendit. amor debitus est, quando quis ei a quo gratis accipit nichil nisi amorem rependit. Amor ex utroque permistus est, quo alternatim amando et gratis accipit et gratis inpendit*' (Blastic's translation).
78 Augustine, *De Trinitate* XII. 4, 8 as cited in Bligh, 'Richard of St. Victor's *De Trinitate*', 120-21.
79 *Tract. in Ioann.*, XIV, 9 (*PL* 35, 1508) as cited in Bligh, *ibid.*, 122.
80 McGinn, *The Growth of Mysticism*, 414. Cf. Augustine, *De Trinitate* 9.2.2 where he speaks of the Spirit as the bond of love between the lover and the beloved.
81 O' Collins, 'The Holy Trinity: The State of the Questions', in Davis, Kendall & O'Collins (eds.), *The Trinity*, 11.
82 C. Gunton, *Theology Through the Theologians* (Edinburgh: T & T Clark, 1996), 126-27.
83 Thompson, *Modern Trinitarian Perspectives*, 127.
84 Gaybba, *The Spirit of Love*, 80. Cf. P. S. Fiddes, *Participating in God. A Pastoral Doctrine of the Trinity* (London: Darton. Longman + Todd, 2000), 266-67.
85 Badcock, *Light of Truth & Fire of Love*, 248.
86 See Gregory, *Ad Ablabium*, NPNF, 2nd ser., V. 334 as cited in S. Coakley, '"Persons" in the "Social" Doctrine of the Trinity: A Critique of Current Analytic Discussion', in Davis, Kendall & O'Collins (eds.), *The Trinity*, 123; cf. R. E. Olson, *The Mosaic of Christian*

Belief (Illinois: InterVarsity, 2002), 140.
[87] See Gregory, *Ad Graecos*, 24-25 as cited in Coakley, *ibid.*, 132.
[88] Hill, *The Three Personed God*, 230-31.
[89] Badcock, *Light of Truth*, 250-52.
[90] W. Pannenberg, *Jesus – God and Man*, L. L. Wilkins & D. A.. Priebe (tr.), (Philadelphia: Westminster, 1977), 181.
[91] Nygren, *Apage and Eros*, 653.
[92] *Ibid.*, 654.
[93] This author is indebted to Robin Parry's comment on this point.
[94] See chapter five of this book.
[95] L. Hogdson, *The Doctrine of the Trinity* (New York: Charles Scribner's Sons, 1944). Hogdson, for one, argues for an 'internally constitutive unity' between the divine unity and organic unity in creation. Moltmann, in particular, has developed his model in some ways similar to Hodgson's. He insists that the unity of the three persons lies not so much in some underlying substance as in communicative love among the persons. His emphasis on perichoretic unity, not substantial unity, accentuates the elements of mutuality and interdependence as ontologically constitutive of God's inner life. The Trinity is no 'self-enclosed circle in heaven', but a dynamic community of fellowship open to creatures: 'To throw open the circulatory movement of the divine light and the divine relationships, and to take men and women, with the whole of creation, into the life-stream of the triune God: the meaning of creation, reconciliation and glorification' (Moltmann, *Trinity and the Kingdom*, 178). For an extensive study of Richard's influence on Russian theology, see Meerson, *The Trinity of Love*.

Chapter Four: *Filioque*, Solitary Love and Mutual Love

[1] G. Leff, *Medieval Thought: St. Augustine to Ockham* (Baltimore: Penguin, 1958), 213; Fortman, *The Triune God*, 204; Watkin-Jones, *The Holy Spirit in the Mediaeval Church,* 154, calls Aquinas 'the first truly great theologian of the mediaeval period'.

[2] For Aquinas' materials, see A. C. Pegis (ed.), *Basic Writings of Saint Thomas Aquinas*, vol. 1, (New York: Random House, 1945); C. J. O'Neil (tr.), *Summa Contra Gentiles. Book Four: Salvation* (Notre Dame: University of Notre Dame Press, 1955). (Hereafter abbreviated as *SG*); *On the Power of God*, 3 vols., (London: Burns, Oates & Washbourne, 1932-34). (Hereafter abbreviated as *De Pot.*); P.

Mandonnet (ed.), *Scriptum super libros sententiarum*, vol. 1 (Paris: Sumptibus P. Lethielleux, 1929). (Hereafter abbreviated as *sent.*). For Latin texts and English translations of *Summa Theologiae*, see English Dominican Fathers (tr.), (London: Blackfriars, 1963-76). (Hereafter abbreviated as *ST*a; Pegis' edition will be abbreviated as *ST*.).

3   T. F. O'Meara, *Thomas Aquinas. Theologian* (Notre Dame: University of Notre Dame Press, 1997), 90.
4   A. D. Sertillanges, *St. Thomas Aquinas and His Work* (London: Blackfriars, 1957), 38.
5   G. E. M. Anscombe & P. T. Geach, *Three Philosophers* (Oxford: Oxford University Press, 1973), 118ff.
6   *ST* I.32,1.
7   *Ibid.* See also Pelikan, *The Christian Tradition*, 3:287.
8   *Boeth. de Trin.* 1:4 as cited in Fortman, *The Triune God*, 205. Cf. Augustine, *Tract. XXVI, super Ioann.*, VI 64 (*PL* 35, 1618) as cited in *ST* I.32,1.
9   *ST* I.32,1
10 *Ibid.*
11 *Ibid.* Cf. Thomas, 'Trinity, Logic and Ontology', in Schwöbel (ed.), *Trinitarian Theology Today*, 66-67.
12 *SG* I. 3, 13 as cited in Davies, *The Thought of Thomas Aquinas*, 191. For *SG* materials, I will use Watkin-Jones' translation unless otherwise indicated.
13 See Alexander of Hales, *Summa Fratris Alexandri*, I. 10 as cited in Davies, *ibid.*, 189. Davies notes that this *Summa*, though attributed to Alexander, may not be his.
14 Congar, *I Believe in the Holy Spirit*, 3:117; Burgess, *The Holy Spirit*, 78.
15 *ST* I.32,1. Cf. F. Copleston, *A History of Philosophy* (New York: Image Books, 1962), 2: 179, where he, speaking specifically of Richard of St. Victor's system of theology, points out that although natural reason fails to discern the necessity fully, it could still provide 'necessary reasons' for what necessarily exists. Since God is necessarily a Trinity, there must be a necessary reason for this assertion. This, in Victor, is done by the analogy of human love.
16 See Richard of St. Victor's *De Trin* (*PL* 196, 892) as cited in *ST* I. 32, 1.
17 See Hilary, *De Trin.*, II (*PL* 10, 58) and Ambrose, *De Fide*, I, 10 (*PL* 16, 566) as cited in *ST* I. 32, 1.
18 See Daley, 'Revisiting the "*Filioque*"', 59; Bray, *The Doctrine of God*, 43.
19 *SG* 4, 17.
20 *Ibid.*
21 *Ibid.*

[22] *SG* 4, 19 where he quotes Aristotle, *Nicomachean Ethics*, III, 5 (1114a32-b1). See Ngien, *The Suffering of God According to Martin Luther's 'Theologia Crucis'*, 103, quoting William Ockham, *Summa Logicae* I. C. XIV.XV (St. Bonaventure: The Franciscan Institute, 1957), 43-49; 98-100. Ngien argues that Luther's position concurs with Ockham's (for our purpose also with Aquinas'). For Ockham, a thing 'as it is in itself' is known through cognition of its 'act'. Thus to know God aright is to know his works.

[23] *SG* 4, 18. See J. Webster, 'The Identity of the Holy Spirit: a problem in trinitarian theology', *Themelios* 9 (1983), 4-5, where he observes contemporary attempts to reformulate the doctrine of God in non-trinitarian terms. For instances, the late Professor G. Lampe wrote: 'the Spirit of God is to be understood, not as referring to a divine *hypostasis* distinct from God the Father and God the Son or Word, but as indicating God himself as active towards and in his human creation'. M. Wiles follows the same approach, affirming that 'God as Spirit is God as present'. See Lampe, *God as Spirit* (Oxford: Oxford University Press, 1976); Wiles, *Faith and the Mystery of God* (London: SCM, 1982), 123.

[24] *Ibid.*

[25] *Ibid.* Cf. H. McCabe, 'Aquinas on the Trinity', *New Blackfriars* 80 (1999), 272-74.

[26] *ST* Ia.36,3.

[27] *SG* 4, 24 (O'Neil's)

[28] Congar, *I Believe in the Holy Spirit*, 3:117.

[29] *ST* 1. qq. 14-15.

[30] D. J. Merriell, *To the Image of the Trinity. A study in the Development of Aquinas' Teaching* (London: Pontifical Institute of Mediaeval Studies, 1990), 154. Merriell observes that Aquinas, in his *Contra Gentiles*, makes no explicit mention of Augustine's psychological triad of memory, understanding, and will. The Father is spoken of as the mind itself, not as memory. Both God the Father and the mind he regards as the principle of their respective processions. See *SG* 4, 26.

[31] Bray, *The Doctrine of God*, 182; S. B. Ferguson, *The Holy Spirit* (Illinois: InterVarsity, 1996), 76.

[32] *SG* 4, 20: '*amor vim quandum impulsivam et motivam habet*'; *ST* 1.27, 4 & 36, 2: '*nomen spiritus impulsionem quamdam et motionem signifare videtur*'. Cf.. *SG* 4, 19 where Aquinas often uses the term '*inclinatio*', which corresponds to '*impulsivam*'. Also cited in Congar, *I Believe in the Holy Spirit*, 3:125 and W. T. Cavanaugh, 'A Joint Declaration? Justification as *Theosis* in Aquinas and Luther', *Heythrop Journal* 41 (2000), 268.

33. *SG* 4, 19 (O'Neil's translation)
34. *ST* Ia. 27.3 as cited in Davies, *The Thought of Thomas Aquinas*, 197;cf G. D. Smith, *The Teaching of the Catholic Church* (London: Burns & Oates, 1952), 148-50.
35. Daley, 'Revisiting the "*filioque*"', 53. The word 'affective' is O'Neil's translation. See *SG* 4, 24. One must bear in mind that like Augustine, Aquinas also holds that the Spirit does not have a proper name, but may be appropriately called Holy Spirit because he is spirated, and like the first two person, is both spirit and holy. See Augustine, *De Trinitate*, V. 12; cf. *ST* I.27,4; 28,4; 36,1.
36. *SG* 4, 24.
37. See *I Sent.* d. 27, q.2, a.1; *ST* Ia, q. 43, a. 5, ad. 2 as cited in Congar, *I Believe in the Holy Spirit*, 126.
38. *SG* 4, 20 (O'Neil's translation).
39. *ST* Ia. 4, ad 3 as cited in Gaybba, *The Spirit of Love*, 83.
40. Gaybba, *ibid.*, notes that the origin of the term 'spiration' is unknown.
41. Davies, *The Thought of Thomas Aquinas.*, 198.
42. *ST* Ia.37,1. Cf. M-R Hoogland, *God, Passion and Power* (Leuven: Peters, 2003), 103-08.
43. See Augustine, *De Trinitate*, 9 & 15.
44. *ST* I.37,1.
45. *Ibid.*
46. *ST* I.36,2.
47. *ST* I.37,2. Cf. R. Del Colle, *Christ and the Spirit. Spirit-Christology in Trinitarian Perspective* (Oxford: Oxford University Press, 1994), 107-08.
48. See Augustine, *De Trinitate* IV, 20 as cited in *ST* I.38,2.
49. B. Bonjoannes, *Compendium of the Summa Theologica of St. Thomas Aquinas Pars Prima*, W. Lescher (tr.), (London: Thomas Baker, 1906), 94.
50. *ST* I.38,2.
51. Gaybba, *The Spirit of Love*, 136-37.
52. *ST* I.37,1.
53. *SG* 4, 16.
54. *SG* 4, 25 (O'Neil's).
55. See *De Pot.* 10.2 as cited in Daley, 'Revisiting the "*filioque*"', 55.
56. Daley, *ibid.*, 55.
57. *Ibid.*, 56.
58. *SG* 4, 24.
59. *Ibid.*
60. *Ibid.*
61. See Anselm, *De Processione Spiritus Sancti*, ch. 1.

62 *ST* Ia. 28.1.
63 *SG* 4, 24 (O'Neil's).
64 Augustine, *de Trinitate* 5.5.
65 *Ibid.*
66 *SG* 4, 24 (O'Neil).
67 *ST* I.28,3.
68 *Ibid.* Cf. C. Wells, 'Aquinas and Jenson on Thinking about the Trinity', *Anglican Theological Review* 84 (2002), 373-375.
69 *ST* Ia. 29. 2. Davies, *The Thought of Thomas Aquinas*, 201, says that by 'substance', Aquinas means 'subject', signifying 'subsistence'. See note 56.
70 Davies, *ibid.*, 201-02.
71 See *ST* Ia. 39.2; also quoted in Watkin-Jones, *The Holy Spirit*, 165.
72 *De Pot.* 9.4 as cited in *Fortman, The Triune God*, 208..
73 Fortman, *ibid.*, 208.
74 Bray, *The Doctrine of God.*, 183. See also Fiddes, *Participation in God*, 34-36.
75 *De Pot.* 8.4 as cited in Congar, *I Believe in the Holy Spirit*, 3:125.
76 *ST* I.28, 1; 32, 2.
77 *SG* 4, 24.
78 *Liber contra errores Graecorum 1, introduction*, H.-F. Dondaine (ed.), *Sancti Thomae de Aquino opera omnia* 40 (Rome, 1969), 71.4-9 as cited in Daley, 'Revisiting the "*Filioque*"', 51.
79 *De Pot.* 10. Cf. T. Marsh, *The Triune God. A Biblical, Historical and Theological Study* (Connecticut: Twenty-Third Publications, 1994), 153.
80 *SG* 4, 24 (O'Neil).
81 *Ibid.* Cf. J-P Torrell, *Saint Thomas Aquinas,* vol. 2. *Spiritual Master*, R. Royal (tr.), (Washington: Catholic University of America Press, 1996), 158-59.
82 Cf. *ST* Ia. 28, 1-4; 36.
83 Cf. *ST* 3a. 3, 1-4. See O' Collins, *The Tripersonal God*, 146, where he proposes to think of distinctive 'terms' rather than 'roles' for the divine action.
84 *SG* 4, 26.
85 *Ibid.* Cf. G. D. Badcock, *Light of Truth & Fire of Love* (Grand Rapids: Eerdmans, 1997), 79.
86 *ST* Ia.23.2.
87 *ST* I.28,2; 29, 3-4; 40, 1; 42, 5 as cited in Congar, *I Believe in the Holy Spirit,* 3:126. Cf. Welch, *In This Name*, 121, noted that Aquinas' distinction between Person (*summa res* relative) and Nature (*summa res* absolute) cannot be a real one, but if any, only a virtual one. Marsh, *The*

Triune God, 152, agrees with Welch's observation.
88. *De Pot.* 10.3 as cited in Daley, 'Revisiting the "*Filioque*"', 56.
89. See *ST* Ia. q.40 as cited in Congar, *I Believe in the Holy Spirit*, 3:126.
90. See Congar, *ibid.*, 125-26, footnote 16.
91. *De Pot.* 10.5 as cited in Daley, *ibid.*, 57.
92. *ST* I.36,2; *SG* 4, 24.
93. *Ibid.*
94. *Ibid.*
95. Athanasius, *Sym. 'Quicumque' (Denzinger, no. 39)* as cited in *ST* I.33, 1. Cf. *ST* I.42,3 where Aquinas approves of Augustine, 'not that one is before the other, but that one proceeds from the other'.
96. *ST* I.36,3. Cf. C. Kiesling, 'On Relating to the Persons of the Trinity', *Theological Studies* 47 (1986), 608.
97. J. Pelikan, 'The Doctrine of *Filioque* in Thomas Aquinas and its Patristic Antecedents. An analysis of *Summa Theologica* Part I, q. 36', in *St. Thomas Aquinas. Commemorative Studies*, I (Toronto: Pontifical Institute of Medieval Studies, 1974), 325.
98. *De Trinitate* 2.29, *(PL* 10.69) as cited in *ST* I.36, 4. See also Pelikan, *Development of Doctrine,* 131-33, for a discussion of Hilary's position.
99. *ST* I.36,4.
100. *Ibid.*
101. *ST* I.36,3.
102. *De Trinitate* V. 14 as cited in *ST* I.36, 4.
103. *ST* I.39,5.
104. *ST* I.33,1.
105. *De Trin.*, IX (PL 10, 325) as cited in *ST* 1.33,1.
106. *ST* I.36,3; cf. Pelikan, 'The Doctrine of *Filioque*', 330, where he says that the distinction between 'cause' and 'principle' may not be maintained consistently. See also M. D. Torre, 'St. John Damascene and St. Thomas Aquinas on the Eternal Procession of the Holy Spirit', *St. Vladimir's Theological Quarterly* 38 (1994), 312-13, who takes issue with Aquinas' linguistic (Greek) deficiency as seen in his discussion of 'cause': '(Aquinas) could have granted that what was "admissible" in Latin was "objectionable" in Greek. He misses this. His mistakes are those of his age: he did not know Greek, and despite all his efforts, his knowledge of the Greek Fathers remained limited'.
107. *ST* 1.36,2.
108. See *De Fide Ortho.*, I, 8 (PG 94, 832) as cited in *ST* 1.36,2.
109. Cf. Torre, 'On the Eternal Procession of the Holy Spirit', 312, esp. footnote 22, where he notes: 'The first stirrings of the *filioque* controversy don't begin until one generation after Damascene's death

and don't become a real issue until more than 50 years after'. See also J. Gregoire, 'La relation eternell de l'Esprit au Fils d'apres les ecrits de Jean de Damas', in *Revue d'histoire ecclesiastique* 64 (1969), 738-43, as cited in Torre, *ibid*. Gregoire argues that John's denial, although a real one, of the procession of the Spirit from the Son may not be aiming here at the Western doctrine of the *filioque*.

[110] *ST* 1.36,2.
[111] Pelikan, '*The* Doctrine of *filioque*', 325.
[112] *ST* 1,2, prologue.
[113] Congar, *I Believe in the Holy Spirit*, 3:116-17; Torre, 'on the Eternal Procession of the Holy Spirit', 303-27.
[114] *ST* I.1, 4.
[115] O' Meara, *Thomas Aquinas*, 89.
[116] Congar, *I Believe in the Holy Spirit*, 3:116-17.
[117] Hill, *The Three-Personed God*, 62-3.
[118] Hankey, *God in Himself*, 131. See also N. Nash, *The Beginning and End of Religion* (Cambridge: Cambridge University press, 1996), 144; A. Nichols, *Discovering Aquinas. An Introduction to His Life, Work, and Influence* (Grand Rapids: Eerdmans, 2003), 39.
[119] See M.-D. Chenu, *Toward understanding St. Thomas*, A.-M. Landry & D. Hughes (tr.), (Chicago: Regnery, 1964), 297-322; Marsh, *The Triune God.*, 144-45; F. Kerr, 'Thomas Aquinas', in Evans (ed.), *The Medieval Theologians*, 212; W. Hankey, *God in Himself. Aquinas' Doctrine of God as expounded in the Summa Theologiae* (Oxford: Oxford University Press, 1987), 10 & 39.
[120] J-P. Torrell, *Saint Thomas Aquinas. Vol. 1. The Person and His Work*, R. Royal (tr.), (Washington: Catholic University of America, 1996), 151.
[121] See M. Seckler, Le salut et l'historie. La pensee de saint Thomas d'Aquin sur la theologie de l'historie, *Cogitatio fidei* 21 (Paris, 1967), 30-31 as cited in Torrell, *ibid.*, 151.
[122] Moltmann, *Trinity and the Kingdom*, 19.
[123] Moltmann, *The Crucified God*, 239.
[124] See Moltmann, *Trinity*, 19; K. Rahner, *The Trinity* (New York: Herder & Herder, 1970), 16; Kapser, *The God of Jesus Christ*, 290-99, where he rejects the separation between *De Deo Uno* and *De Deo Trino*, but begins with *De Deo Trino* as his dogmatic departure point; T. L. Smith, *Trinitarian Theology: A study in Theological Method* (Washington: Catholic University of America Press, 2003), 39-46, reproaches Cajetan for the resultant, especially modern, interpretations that have separated Aquinas' treatise between *De Deo Uno* and *Deo Deo Trino*.
[125] Hill, *The Three-Personed God*, 62-63.

126 *ST* 2a 2ae. 174.6 as cited in Davies, *The Thought of Thomas Aquinas*, 194-95. See also Ferguson, *The Holy Spirit*, 77; Torre, 'On the Eternal procession of the Holy Spirit', 316; D. Coffey, 'A Proper Mission of the Holy Spirit', *Theological Studies* 47 (1986), 148-49.
127 *ST* I, q.32, aa. 1 & 3; also cited in Hill, *The Three-Personed God*, 69.
128 For contemporary examples, see E. Hill, *The Mystery of the Trinity* (London: SCM, 1985); Molnar, *Divine Freedom and the Doctrine of the Immanent Trinity;* D. Coffey, *Deus Trinitas: The Doctrine of the Trinity* (Oxford: Oxford University Press, 1999).
129 Hill, *The Three-Personed God*, 303.
130 M. A. Fatula, 'The Holy Spirit and human actualization through love; the contribution of Aquinas', *Theology Digest* 32 (1985), 222-23.
131 *Ibid.*
132 *ST* I.34,3. Cf. C. H. Pinnock, 'Divine Relationality: A Pentecostal Contribution to the Doctrine of God', *Journal of Pentecostal Theology* 16 (2002), 6-8. Pinnock is fair not to equate Aquinas' divine-human relationship with his '*personal model of God*' (or commonly called 'openness theism').
133 *SG* 4, 23.
134 *SG* 4, 21.
135 Daley, 'Revisiting the "*Filioque*"', 62.
136 *ST* I.32,3; cf. 30,2.
137 Lossky, 'The Procession of the Holy Spirit in Orthodox Trinitarian Doctrine', in Erickson & Bird (eds.), *In the Image and Likeness of God*, 79. Also quoted in Del Colle, *Christ and the Spirit*, 22.
138 B. D. Marshall, 'Action and Person: Do Palamas and Aquinas Agree About the Spirit?', *St. Vladimir's Theological Quarterly* 39 (1995), 406-07. Cf. Hill, *The Three-Personed God*, 72-73.
139 *De Trinitate* 7.4; cf. *ST* I.30,4.
140 *ST* I.29,3.
141 Cf. *De Trinitate* VI. 5; XV 17 & 19.
142 Congar, *I Believe in the Holy Spirit*, I:90.
143 See A. Malet, *Personne et amour dans la theologie trinitaire de saint Thomas d' Aquin. Bibliotheque thomiste* 32 (Paris: Vrin, 1956), 159 as cited in Daley, 'Revisiting the "*Filioque*"', 60. LaCugna, *God For Us*, 156, agrees with Malet's view, that 'the love of God for himself is not egostistical but personal, the love of the divine persons for one another, not love of self or love of essence for essence'. Likewise, Anthony Kelly holds the same position, that 'the Father and the Son, both possessing the divine nature, are one principle of divine love, and of the Spirit associated with it. Yet speaking from within the

interpersonal concreteness of our Christian communion with the Trinity, the Holy Spirit is the mutual love existing between the Father and the Son, the Spirit by which they love themselves and us'. See his *The Trinity of Love. A Theology of the Christian God* (Wilmington: Michael Glazier, 1983), 130. Cf. O' Collins, *The Tripersonal God*, 136-37, 144, who argues that Augustine contributes to the theme of the Spirit as the fruit or reality of mutual love, but Aquinas opts for the Spirit as 'the inner fruit of love'.

[144] *1 Sent.*, 10, a.5, ad. 1 as cited in Cowburn, *Love and the Person*, 265. Cf. *ST*.I.36,4;37: 'The Holy Ghost proceeds from the Father and the Son as being plural'; *ST*.I.37,1;39,8.

[145] *De Pot.* 10.2 as cited in Cowburn, *ibid.*, 266: '*Processio intellectus est ab uno solo; sed amicitia, quae est amor mutuus procedit ex duobus ad invicem se amantibus*'. See also *De Pot.* 9.9: 'What proceeds intellectually must be really distinct from what proceeds by way of the will, for the word which proceeds intellectually proceeds from only one, its utterer, whereas the Holy Ghost, who proceeds by way of the will as love, necessarily proceeds from two mutually loving each other'.

[146] *ST* I.36,2. Also cited in Congar, *I Believe in the Holy Spirit*, I:90.

[147] *SG* 4, 23.

[148] *De Pot.* 10.2 as cited in Cowburn, *Love and the Person*, 266.

[149] See Anselm, *Monologion*, chaps. 49-53.

[150] Cowburn, *Love and the Person*, 267.

[151] *Compendium Theologiae*, cc. 45-50. See also M. T.-L, Penido, 'A propos de la procession d'amour en Dieu', *Ephemerides Theologicae Lovanienses* 15 (1938), 344 as cited in Cowburn, *ibid.*, 267.

[152] J. Slipyl, '*De amore mutuo et reflexo in processione Spiritus Sancti explicanda*', *Bohoslovia* 1 (1923), 3 as cited in Cowburn, *ibid*, 267.

[153] *De Pot.* 10 as dealt with by Torre, 'On the Eternal Procession of the Holy Spirit', 317-19. I am indebted to Torre's discovery.

[154] Torre, *ibid.*, 318.

[155] *ST* I.36,2. Cf. J. Damascus, *An Exact Exposition of the Orthodox Faith, in Writings, Fathers of the Church*, vol. 37, (Washington, D.C: Catholic University of America, 1958), 196, where it says, 'He is the Spirit of the Son, not as being from Him but as proceeding *through* Him from the Father'. Damascus also holds that the Spirit abides in the Son: 'He is the sanctifying force that is subsistent, but proceeds unceasingly from the Father and abides in the Son' (201). Implied here is that the Spirit proceeds from the Father towards the Son, to abide in Him.

[156] *De Pot.* 9.9 as cited in Torre, 'On the Eternal Procession of the Holy Spirit', 310.

[157] *Ibid.*

158 *ST* I.35,2.
159 Torre, 'On the Eternal Procession of the Holy Spirit', 318.
160 *Ibid.*, 319. Gregory of Palamas also speaks of the dynamism of the Spirit as the outpouring of the Father's love spontaneously returned by the Son. He writes: 'The Spirit of the Word from on high is like a mysterious love of the Father towards the Word mysterious only begotten; it is the same love as that possessed by the Word and the well-beloved Son of the Father toward him who begat him; this he does insofar as he comes from the Father conjointly with this love, and this love rests naturally on him'. See his *The Physical Chapters* (PG 150. col. 1144 D -1145 A) as translated by J. Meyendorff, *A Study of Gregory of Palamas* (Alyesbury, England: Faith Press, 1966), 232.
161 *ST* I.37,2.
162 A. K. Min, 'Pneumatology in a Divided World', in B. E. Hinze & D. L. Dabney (eds.), *Advents of the Spirit* (Milwaukee: Marquette University Press, 2001), 442, footnote 16.
163 Coffey, 'The Holy Spirit as the Mutual Love of the Father and the Son', 224-25. Cf. *1 Sent*. d. 10, q.1, a.2 as cited in Coffey, *ibid*, and his *Deus Trinitas*, 50-51, where he speaks of the Holy Spirit as 'precisely the objectification of the mutual love of the father and the Son.... Henceforth according to the taxis the Father's love for the Son and the Son's love for the Father are each to be identified with the Holy Spirit. This latter is also the teaching of St. Thomas. ... It is only as the mutual love of the Father and the Son, or rather its objectification, that the Holy Spirit has his existence. As mutual, the double-bestowal of love, that is, by the Father and the Son on each other, must be coincident and indeed must constitute a single bestowal and a single act'.
164 *ST* I.28,2; cf. *ST* 1.39,1. See G. Emery, *Trinity in Aquinas* (Ypsilanti: Sapientia, 2003), chapter five where he argues that Aquinas' doctrine of subsisting relations represents a synthesis of both essentialism and personalism.
165 *ST* I.39,2.
166 Marsh, *The Triune God*, 153.
167 Hill, *The Three-Personed God*, 73.
168 See C. M. LaCugna, 'The Relational God: Aquinas and Beyond', *Theological Studies* 46 (1985): 647-663; A. Kelly, 'God: How Near a Relation?', *Thomist* 14 (1970): 191-229.
169 *ST* I.14,2 where Aquinas describes God as *actus purus*. Cf. T. Weinandy, *Does God Suffer?* (Notre Dame: University of Notre Dame Press, 2000), 120-29, for his discussion of God as pure act in relation to divine immutability and impassibility. For a recent study of

Aquinas's view of divine suffering, see Hoogland, *God, Passion and Power*; M. Dodds, *The Unchanging God of Love* (Fribourg: Editions Universitaires Fribourg Suisse, 1985), and his 'Thomas Aquinas, Human Suffering and the Unchanging God of Love', *Theological Studies* 52 (1991), 330-44; E. Stump, *Aquinas* (London: Routledge, 2003), chapter 16: 'Providence and Suffering'. This author is also indebted to Ralph Del Colle's wisdom.

Chapter Five: Fecundity, Mutual Love and *Filioque*

[1] E. Gilson, *The Philosophy of Saint Bonaventure*, I. Trethowan and F. J. Sheed (tr.), (New York: Sheed and Ward, 1938), 430. For Latin text of Bonaventure, see *Doctoris Seraphi S. Bonaventurae opera omnia* (Quaracchi, 1882-1902).

[2] I. Delio, *Simply Bonaventure. An Introduction to His Life, Thought, and Writings* (New York: New City, 2001), 13.

[3] Watkin-Jones, *The Holy Spirit in the Medieval Church*, 138.

[4] Z. Hayes, 'Christology and Metaphysics in the Thought of Bonaventure', *Journal of Religion* 58 (Supplement, 1978), 92-95.

[5] *Itinerarium mentis in Deum* 1, 2 (hereafter: *Itinerarium*.). For English translations, see E. Cousins, *Bonaventure: The Soul's Journey into God, The Tree of Life, the Major Life of St. Francis* (New York: Paulist, 1978), 98 (hereafter: Cousins's *Journey*); P. Boehner, *Bonaventure's Journey of the Mind to God* (Indianapolis: Hackett, 1993), 5-6 (hereafter: Boehner's *Journey*). Scholars have seen Bonaventure as the one who raises Francis' mystical life to the level of metaphysical thought. For examples, Gilson, in his *Philosophy of Bonaventure*, 60, remarks: 'What St. Francis had simply felt and lived, St. Bonaventure was to think'; A. Pegis, 'St. Bonaventure, St. Francis and Philosophy', *Medieval Studies* 15 (1953): 1-13; B. McGinn, 'The Influence of St. Francis on Theology of the High Middle Ages: The Testimony of St. Bonaventure', in F. C. Blanco (ed.), *Bonaventuriana*, 2 vols., (Roma: Edizioni Antonianum, 1988), I:97-118.

[6] E. Cousins, 'The Coincidence of Opposites in the Christology of Saint Bonaventure', *Franciscan Studies* 28 (1968), 32.

[7] *Itinerarium* 5, 2; Cousins's *Journey* 94-95.

[8] Ibid.

[9] Ibid.

[10] Ibid. Cf. John Damascene, *De Fide orthodoza*, I, 9: 'It seems that of all the names predicated of God the more proper name is "*He Who Is*"'. As cited in Boehner's *Journey*, 67.

[11] See A. Louth, *The Origins of the Christian Mystical Tradition* (Oxford: Clarendon, 1981), 146-54, where he discusses the soul's ascent in Augustine's *De Trinitate*.

[12] *Itinerarium* 5, 6; Cousins' *Journey* 98.

[13] Ibid., 5, 7-8; *ibid.*, 99-100.

[14] Cf. Augustine, *De civitate Dei*, VIII, 4 as cited in Cousins' *Journey* 99.

[15] Cousins, 'St. Bonaventure's Coincidence of Opposites', 33.

[16] Cousins' *Journey* 99-100. See Cousins, 'The Coincidence of Opposites', 33, footnote 25, where Anselm's *Proslogion* c. 2-4 is cited.

[17] Cousins' *Journey* 96.

[18] Ibid.

[19] Cf. Aristotle, *Metaph. I minor*, t. q, c. (993b 9-11) as cited in Cousins' *Journey* 96.

[20] Cousins' *Journey*, 96-97.

[21] Ibid.

[22] Ibid., 98.

[23] cf. Dionysius, *De divinis nominibus*, III, 1: 'And first of all, if it pleases you, let us consider the name "The Good". This is a perfect name, since it manifests all the emanations of God'. Cited in Cousins' *Journey* 95, Boehner's *Journey* 67. For a summary of Pseudo-Dionysius's writings and thought, see B. McGinn, *The Foundation of Mysticism* (New York: Crossroad, 1991), 157-82; Louth, *The Origins of the Christian Mystical Tradition*, 159-78.

[24] *I Sent.*, d. 22, q. 1, a. 3 as cited in Boehner's *Journey*, 69, footnote 167. 25 *Itinerarium* 6, 2; Cousins' *Journey*, 102. (For *I Sent.*, Congar's, Watkin-Jones', Fortman's translation will be used unless otherwise indicated). See also *Disputed Questions on the Mystery of the Trinity*, 41.

[25] Ibid.

[26] On the influence of Pseudo-Dionysius on Bonaventure's view of the Trinity, see Z. Hayes' Introduction to *Saint Bonaventure's Disputed Questions on the Mystery of the Trinity*, in G. Marcil (ed.), *Works of St. Bonaventure*, vol. III (New York: Franciscan Institute, 1979), 22-25. See also E. Dreyer, 'An Advent of the Spirit: Medieval Mystics and Saints', in B. E. Hinze & D. L. Dabney (eds.), *Advents of the Spirit*, 159, where she observes that of the 240 times in his corpus Bonaventure uses the term, 'self-diffusive goodness', 140 times appear in the *Sentences*.

[27] *Itinerarium* 6, 2; Boehner's *Journey* 33. Also cited in E. Cousins, *Bonaventure and the Coincidence of Opposites* (Chicago: Franciscan Herald, 1978), 105.

[28] C. Carpenter, *Theology as the Road to Holiness in Saint Bonaventure* (New York: Paulist, 1999), 72-73.

[29] Boehner's *Journey* 69, footnote 166. See C. B. Bray, 'Bonaventure's Proof of the Trinity', *American Catholic Philosophical Quarterly* 67 (2003), 201-17 where he shows how Bonaventure works philosophically upon the doctrine of the Trinity, arguing for the necessity of the immanent Trinity.

[30] *I Sent.*, d. 27, p. I, a. un., q. 2, ad 3. Cousins points out that Bonaventure errs in attributing the *Liber de causis* to Aristotle. It becomes evident in the thirteenth century, he claims, that the work is done by an Arabian philosopher familiar with Proculus's *Elements of Theology*. See his 'Bonaventure's Mysticism of Language', in Katz (ed.), *Mysticism and Language*, 242.

[31] *Itinerarium* 6, 2; Boehner's *Journey* 34. Also quoted in Fortman, *The Triune God*, 216; O'Carroll, *A Theological Encyclopedia of the Holy Trinity*, 57.

[32] I. Delio, 'Bonaventure's Metaphysics of the Good', *Theological Studies* 60 (1999), 231.

[33] See R. J. Armstrong, J. A. W. Hellmann, and W. J. Short (trs.), *Francis of Assisi: Early Documents*, vol. 1: *The Saint* (New York: New City, 1999), 162 as quoted in Delio, *Simply Bonaventure*, 41. Delio discovers nine times Francis refers to God's goodness in his writings. See also Z. Hayes, 'Bonaventure: Mystery of the Triune God', in K. B. Osborne (ed.), *The History of Franciscan Theology*, (New York: Franciscan Institute, 1994), 45.

[34] See *Pseudo-Dionysius: Complete Works*, C. Luidheid (tr.), (New York: Paulist, 1987), 99. Also cited in Delio, 'Bonaventure's Metpahysics of the Good', 232.

[35] Hayes, Introduction to *Saint Bonaventure's Disputed Questions of the Mystery of the Trinity*, 33.

[36] Cf. Richard, *De Trinitate* 3.14; Hayes, *ibid.*, 16-17.

[37] *Dist.* ii (of *Lombardus, Sent.* i), *quaest.* iv., *conclusio* as cited in Watkin-Jones, *The Holy Spirit in Medieval Church*, 138.

[38] *Itinerarium* 6, 2 as in Congar, *I Believe in the Holy Spirit*, 3: 110. Also cited in M. O'Carroll, *Veni Creator Spiritus: A Theological Encyclopedia of the Holy Spirit* (Collegeville: Liturgical Press, 1990), 35.

[39] *Ibid*; Cousins' *Journey* 103; also quoted in Congar, *I Believe in the Holy Spirit*, 3: 110.

[40] *Ibid*; Boehner's *Journey*, 33. Cf. Richard of St. Victor, *De Trinitate* I, 4-5; III, 2. See also Cousins, 'Fecundity and the Trinity: An Appendix to Chapter Three of the Great Chain of Being', in M. L. Kuntz & P. G. Kuntz (eds.), *Jacob's Ladder and the Tree of Life*, 78.

[41] *Ibid*; Cousins' *Journey* 103. For a trinitarian theology of creation, see I. Delio, 'Does God "Act" in Creation? A Bonaventurian

Response', *Heythrop Journal* 44 (2003): 328-44. Bonaventure reflects on the creation within the mystery of the Trinity. He teaches that had God not already generated his own Son by his nature he could not have created creatures by his will. See H. U. von Balthasar, *Theodramatik* IV (Einsiedeln: Johannes, 1983), 56, n. 13. Likewise Aquinas holds the same view: 'From the procession of the distinct divine persons every procession and multiplicity of creatures is caused'. Elsewhere he closely links the creation with the eternal processions. Creation is likened unto the streams flowing from the Son into the creation. He explains, 'I understand these streams as currents of the eternal procession, by which the Son proceeds from the Father, and the Holy Spirit from the Father and the Son in an ineffable manner'. As cited in O'Donnell, *The Mystery of the Triune God*, 160.

42 *I Sent.*, d. 2, a. un., q. 2 as cited in Cousins, 'Bonaventure's Mysticism of Language', 256.
43 *Breviloquium* 1, 3. For English translation, see J. de Vinck, *The Works of Bonaventure*, vol. 2: *Breviloquium* (Paterson: St. Anthony Guild, 1963), 39.
44 *Collationes in Hexaemeron*, J. de Vinck (tr.), *The Works of Bonaventure*, 5 vols., (Paterson: St. Anthony Guild, 1970), 5: 9.
45 *I Sent.*, d. 27, p. 1. a. u., q. 2: '*Non quia Deus, quia tunc etiam inesset Filio: non quia innascibilis, quia innascibilitas dicit nativitatis privationem, non positionem: ergo a divisione, quia Deus pater*' as quoted in Delio, 'Bonaventure's Metaphysics of the Good', 234, footnote 24.
46 Ibid. Cf. Congar, *I Believe in the Holy Spirit*, 3:111.
47 *I Sent.*, d. 27, q. 1, a. 1; q. 1, ad 3 as cited in Congar, Ibid., 3:112.
48 *I Sent.*, d. 2, q. 2 as cited in Congar, *ibid.*, 3:111. See also J. F. Quinn, 'The Role of the Holy Spirit in St. Bonaventure's Theology', *Franciscan Studies* 33 (1973), 275; Burgess, *The Holy Spirit*, 71.
49 *Disputed Questions on the Mystery of the Trinity*, 139. Translation is Hayes's.
50 *I Sent.*, d. 27, q. 1, a. 1, ad 3 as cited in Congar, *I Believe in the Holy Spirit*, 3:112.
51 *I Sent.*, d. 23, a. 1, q. 1; d. 25, a. 1, q. 1 as cited in Congar, *ibid.*, 113.
52 *I Sent.*, d. 25, a. 1, q. 2 as cited in Fortman, *The Triune God*, 215.
53 *I Sent.*, d. 27, q. 1, a. 1, ad 3 as cited in Congar, *I Believe in the Holy Spirit*, 112.
54 *Itinerarium* 6,2 as quoted in Congar, *ibid.*, 3: 110. For a study of Bonaventure's Christology, I. Delio, *Crucified Love. Bonaventure's Mysticism of the Crucified Christ* (Quincy: Franciscan, 1998).
55 See Congar, *ibid.*, 3:109; Cowburn, *Love and the Person*, 261, both of

whom observe in Alexander of Hales the two modes of communication.

[56] *I Sent.*, d. iii, p. 1, q. iv., concl. as cited in Watkin-Jones, *The Holy Spirit in the Medieval Church*, 138.

[57] *Ibid.*

[58] Cowburn, *Love and the Person*, 261.

[59] *I Sent.*, d. 13, a. 1, q. 2 as cited in Fortman, *The Triune God*, 215.

[60] *I Sent.*, d. 10, a. 2, qq. 1-2 as cited in J. F. Quinn, 'The *Scientia Sermocinalis* of St. Bonaventure and His Use of Language Regarding the Mystery of the Trinity', *Miscellanea Mediaevalia* 13 (1981), 420-22. See also H. J. Ennis, 'The Place of Love in the Theological System of St. Bonaventure in General', in J. G. Bougerol (ed.), *Sancta Bonaventura, 1274-1974*, 5 vols., (Rome: Collegio S. Bonaventura, 1974), 4: 130-33.

[61] Quinn, *ibid.*, 421.

[62] *I Sent.*, d. 10, a. 1, q. 3 as cited in Congar, *I Believe in the Holy Spirit*, 3:111.

[63] *I Sent.*, d. 13, a. unic., q. 1, No. 4 as cited in Congar, *ibid.*

[64] *I Sent.*, d. 10, a. 2, q. 1 as cited and translated by W. H. Principe, 'St. Bonaventure's Theology of the Holy Spirit with Reference to the Expression: "Pater Et Filius Diligunt Se Spiritu Sancto"', *Sancta Bonaventura*, 4:255-56: '*In divinis vero et proprie amor est, habens rationem amoris et hypostasis: amoris propter hoc, quia ex voluntate liberalissima primo procedit per modum perfectae liberalitatis; hypostasis, quia cum distinguatur a producente et non possit distingui a producente et non possit distingui essentialiter, distinguitur personaliter; non sic autem est in amore creato*'. The same article appears in *Cord* 24 (1974):235-56. See also Congar, *I Believe in the Holy Spirit*, 3:114-15.

[65] *I Sent.*, d. 10, dub. 1, resp. as cited in Quinn, 'The *Scientia Sermocinalis* of St. Bonaventure', 421.

[66] *I Sent.*, d. 32, a. 2, q. 1, Resp., as cited in Quinn, *ibid.*, 422.

[67] *Ibid.*

[68] *Itinerarium* 6, 2 as in Congar, *I Believe in the Holy Spirit*, 3: 110.

[69] Cousins' *Journey* 6, 2.

[70] Boehner's *Journey* 6, 6.

[71] *Breviloquium* I, 5 as in J. de Vinck (tr.), *The Works of Bonaventure*, 5 vols., (Paterson: St. Anthony Guild, 1963), 2: 51-2.

[72] *Ibid.*

[73] *Ibid.*

[74] See *Sermo de Trinitate*, 1 as cited in Ennis, 'The Place of Love', 133, footnote 18.

[75] *I Sent.*, d. 10, a. 1, q. 1 as cited O'Carroll, *Veni Creator Spiritus*, 36. (Translation is hers)

76 *I Sent.*, d. 10, a. 2, q. 3, concl. as cited in Watkin-Jones, *The Holy Spirit in the Medieval Church*, 139.
77 *I Sent.*, d. 10, a. 1, q. 2, ad 4m: '…*Quaedam sunt verba, quae in voce activa significant passionem, ut verba ad sensum pertinentia, ut video, audio et similia; quaedam in voce activa significant actionem, ut facio et percutio, similiter in passiva. Dicendum igitur, quod hoc quod est nectere, cum nectere dicatur Spiritus, quia ab utroque procedit, recte in voce activa passionem significat et in passiva actionem; et iedo non significatur, quod aliquid det Patri et Filio, sed quod magis recipiat*'. As cited in Principe, 'Saint Bonaventure's Theology of the Holy Spirit', 258.
78 *I Sent.*, d. 32, a. 1, q. 1, args. 1-4 f as cited in Principe, *ibid.*, 248.
79 *Ibid.* Also cited in Quinn, 'The *Scientia Sermoncinalis* of St. Bonaventure', 421.
80 *Ibid.*, as cited in Principe, 'Saint Bonaventure's Theology of the Holy Spirit', 249.
81 *I Sent.*, d. 10, a. 2, q. 2 as cited in Ennis, 'The Place of Love', 132.
82 Ennis, *ibid.*
83 *I Sent.*, d. 32, a. 1, q. 2 as cited in Principe, 'Saint Bonaventure's Theology of the Holy Spirit', 251.
84 Principe, *Ibid.*
85 See Congar, *I Believe in the Holy Spirit*, 3: 111; Gaybba, *The Spirit of Love*, 84.
86 *I Sent.*, d. 11, a. unicus, q. 1., concl. as cited in Watkin-Jones, *The Holy Spirit in the Medieval Church*, 140.
87 *Ibid.*
88 *I Sent.*, d. 12, a. unicus, q. 1, Concl., as cited in Watkin-Jones, *ibid.*
89 *I Sent.*, d. 10, a. 1, q. 1 as cited in O'Carroll, *Veni Creator Spiritus*, 36. (Translation is hers)
90 *I Sent.*, 24, a. 2, q. 1, concl. as cited in Watkin-Jones, *The Holy Spirit in Medieval Church*, 140.
91 *I Sent.*, 12, a. unicus, q. 2; see also q. 3, concl. as cited in Watkin-Jones, *Ibid.*
92 Hayes, Introduction to Bonaventure's *Disputed Questions on the Mystery of the Trinity*, 57.
93 *I Sent.*, d. 13, a. 1, q. 3 as cited in Fortman, *The Triune God*, 215.
94 *I Sent.*, d. 13, a. 1, q. 1 as cited in Cowburn, *Love and the Person*, 262.
95 Cowburn, *ibid.*, 263. Cowburn rejects Bonaventure's reply: 'A defender of the mutual-love theory cannot have it both ways. If the love involved in spiration is the essentially mutual love of the first two persons for each other, then they spirate the Holy Ghost as two persons and not as one in nature and will'.
96 *I Sent.*, d. 10, a. 1, q. 3 as cited in Cowburn, *ibid.*, 263.

97. *I Sent.*, d. 11, a. 1, q. 2 as cited in Cowburn, *ibid*.
98. *Ibid*.
99. Coffey, *Deus Trinitas*, 58.
100. *I Sent.*, d. 19, a. 1, q. 1, concl., as cited in Fiddes, *Participating in God*, 72. See Bougerol's introduction to *Sancta Bonaventura*, 25, where he claims that Bonaventure quotes Damascene in his corpus over two hundred times. Cf. Damascene, *Expositio fidei orthodoxae* 8. 17;
101. Kasper, *The God of Jesus Christ*, 299.
102. *I Sent.*, d. 25, a. 1, q. 2 as cited in Fortman, *The Triune God*, 215.
103. *Breviloquium* 1. 2.
104. Kasper, The God of Jesus Christ, 229.
105. O'Donnell, *The Mystery of the Trinity*, 161.
106. *Itinerarium* 6, 3; Cousins' *Journey* 105
107. Delio, 'Metaphysics of the Good', 236-37.
108. *Ibid*. Cf. LaCugna, *God For Us*, 91, where she argues that a metaphysic based on being results in substance ontology, which cannot overcome the bedrock values of patriarchy, autonomy, non-determinism by another or self-possession.
109. *Collations on the Six Days* 1, 13.
110. *Ibid.*, 1, 17.
111. Delio, 'Bonaventure's Metaphysics of the Good', 238. Cf. LaCugna, *God For Us*, 391, where the same conclusion based on the Cappadocian model of the Trinity is reached.
112. Gaybba, *The Spirit of Love*, 84-85.

Bibliography

Books

Almagno, R. S. & Harkins, C. L. (eds.), *Studies Honoring Ignatius Brady, Friar Minor* (New York: The Franciscan Institute, 1976).

Ambrose., *Some of the Principal Works of St. Ambrose*, in H. De Romestin (ed.), NPNF Second Series, Vol. 10, (Peabody: Hendrickson, 1994).

....., *On the Holy Spirit*, in R. J. Deferrari (tr.), *Saint Ambrose: Theological and Dogmatic Works*, (Washington: Catholic University of America Press, 1963).

Anscombe, G. E. M & Geach, P. T., *Three Philosophers* (Oxford: Oxford University Press, 1973).

Aquinas, T., *Summa Theologiae* (London: Blackfriars, 1963-76).

......, *Summa Theologica*. 5 vols. English Dominican Fathers (tr.), (Westminster: Christian Classics, 1948).

......., *Summa Contra Gentiles. Book Four: Salvation*, C. J. O'Neil (tr.), (Notre Dame: University of Notre Dame Press, 1955).

......, *On the Power of God*. 3 vols. English Dominican Fathers (tr.), (London: Burns, Oates and Washbourne, 1932-34).

......, *On the Power of God*, L. Shapcote (tr.), (Westminster: Newman, 1952).

Ayres, L. & Jones, G. (eds.), *Christian Origins: Theology, Rhetoric and Community* (London: Routledge. 1998).

Badcock, G. D., *Light of Truth & Fire of Love. A Theology of Holy Spirit* (Grand Rapids: Eerdmans, 1997).

Balthasar, H. U. von., *The Glory of the Lord: A Theological Aesthetics*, J. Riches (ed.), 7 vols. (Edinburgh: T. & T. Clark, 1982-91).

Barth, K., *Church Dogmatics* I/1, G. W. Bromiley (ed.), (Edinburgh: T. & T. Clark, 1975).

Bettenson, H. (ed.), *The Later Christian Fathers* (Oxford: Oxford University Press, 1970).
Blastic, M.W., *Condilectio: Personal Mysticism and Speculative Theology in Works of Richard of Saint Victor* (Michigan: UMI, 1991).
Bloesch, D. G., *The Holy Spirit. Works & Gifts* (Illinois: InterVarsity, 2000).
Bobrinskoy, B., *The Mystery of the Trinity. Trinitarian Experience and Vision in the Biblical and Patristic Tradition*, A. P. Gythiel (tr.), (New York: St.Vladimir's Seminary Press, 1999).
Bok, N. den., *Communicating the Most High: Systematic Study of Person and Trinity in the Theology of Richard of St. Victor* (d. 1173), (Paris: Brepols, 1996).
Bonaventure., *Disputed Questions on the Mystery of the Trinity*, Z. Hayes (tr.), in G. Marcil (ed.), *Works of Saint Bonaventure*, vol. 3, (New York: The Franciscan Institute, 1979).
......, *Itinerarium Mentis in Deum*, P. Boehner (tr.), in G. Marcil (ed.), *Works of Saint Bonaventure*, vol. 2, (New York: Franciscan Institute, 1956).
......, *Itinerarium Mentis in Deum*, G. Boas (tr.), (Indianapolis: Bobbs-Merrill, 1953).
......, *The Soul's Journey to God, The Tree of Life, The Life of St. Francis*, in E. Cousins (ed.), *The Classics of Western Spirituality*, (New York: Paulist, 1978).
......, *What Manner of Man? Sermons on Christ by St. Bonaventure*, Z. Hayes (tr.), (Chicago: Franciscan Herald, 1989).
......, *The Works of St. Bonaventure*. 5 vols., J. de Vinck (tr.), (Paterson: St. Anthony Guild, 1960-1970).
Bonjoannis, B., *Compendium of the Summa Theologica of Thomas Aquinas*, W. Lescher (tr.), (London: Thomas Baker, 1906).
Bougerol, J. G. (ed.), *Sancta Bonaventura: 1274-1974*, 5 vols., (Rome: Grottaferatta, 1974).
Bray, G., *The Doctrine of God* (Illinois: InterVarsity, 1993).
......, *Creeds, Councils and Christ* (Illinois: InterVarsity, 1984).
Brennan, R. E., *The Trinity and the Unicity of the Intellect* (St. Louis: B. Herder, 1946).
Brown, D., *The Divine Trinity* (Illinois: Open Court, 1985).
Burgess, S. M., *The Holy Spirit: Eastern Christian Tradition* (Peabody: Hendrickson, 1989).
......, *The Holy Spirit: Medieval Roman Catholic and Reformation Traditions* (Peabody: Hendrickson, 1997).

Carpenter, C., *Theology as the Road to Holiness in St. Bonaventure* (New York: Paulist, 1999.)
Chase, S., *Angelic Wisdom and the Grace of Contemplation in Richard of St. Victor* (Notre Dame: University of Notre Dame Press, 1995).
......, *Contemplation and Compassion. The Victorine Tradition* (London: Darton.Longman+Todd, 2000).
Chenu, M.-D., Toward Understanding St. Thomas, A.-M. Landry & D. Hughes (tr.), (Chicago: Regnery, 1964).
Coffey, D., *Deus Trinitas: The Doctrine of the Trinity* (Oxford: Oxford University Press, 1999).
Collins, P. M., *Trinitarian Theology: West and East. Karl Barth, the Cappadocian Fathers, and John Zizioulas* (Oxford: Oxford University Press, 2001).
Congar, Y., *I Believe in the Holy Spirit*. 3 vols., D. Smith (tr.), (London: Geoffrey Chapman, 1983).
Copleston, F., *A History of Philosophy*. Vol. 2 (New York: Image, 1962).
Courcelle, P., *Late Latin Writers and their Greek Sources*, H. E. Wedeck (tr.), (Cambridge: Harvard University Press, 1969).
Cousins, E., *Bonaventure and the Coincidence of Opposites* (Chicago: Franciscan Herald, 1978).
Cowburn, J., *Love and the Person* (London: Geoffrey Chapman, 1967).
Cross, R., *Great Medieval Thinkers. Duns Scotus* (Oxford: Oxford University Press, 1999).
Cunningham, F. L. B., *The Indwelling of the Trinity. A Historico-Doctrinal Study of the Theory of St. Thomas Aquinas* (Dubuque: The Priory, 1955).
Damascus, J., *An Exact Exposition of the Orthodox Faith*, in *Writings, Fathers of the Church*, vol. 37, (Washington: Catholic University of America Press, 1958).
Davies, B., *The Thought of Thomas Aquinas* (Oxford: Clarendon, 1992).
Davis, S., Kendall, D. & O'Collins, G. (eds.), *The Trinity* (Oxford: Oxford University Press, 1999).
Del Colle, R., *Christ and the Spirit. Spirit-Christology in Trinitarian Perspective* (Oxford: Oxford University Press, 1994).
Delio, I., *Crucified Love: Bonaventure's Mystery of the Crucified Christ* (Quincy, Ill.: Franciscan, 1998).

......, *Simply Bonaventure: An Introduction to his Life, Thought, and Writings* (New York: New City, 2001).
Dodds, M., *The Unchanging God of Love* (Fribourg: Editions Universitaires Fribourg Suisse, 1985).
Emery, G., *Trinity in Aquinas* (Ypsilanti: Sapientia, 2003).
Erickson, J. H & Bird, T. E (eds.), *In the Image and Likeness of God* (Oxford: Mowbrays, 1974).
Evans, G. R., *Anselm and Talking about God* (Oxford: Clarendon, 1978).
......, *Anselm* (Wilton: Morehouse, 1989).
Evans, G. R. (ed.), *The Medieval Theologians. An Introduction to Theology in the Medieval Period* (Oxford: Blackwell, 2001).
Fairweather, E. R (ed.), *A Scholastic Miscellany: Anselm to Ockham* (New York: MacMillan, 1970).
Ferguson, S. B., *The Holy Spirit* (Illinois: InterVarsity, 1996).
Fiddes, P. S., *Participating in God. A Pastoral Doctrine of the Trinity* (London: Darton.Longman +Todd, 2000).
Forsyth, P. T., 'The Divine Self-emptying', in *God and the Father* (London: Independent, 1957).
......, *Marriage, Its Ethics and Religion* (London: Hodder & Stoughton, 1912).
Fortman, E. J., *The Triune God. A Historical Study of the Doctrine of the Trinity* (Philadelphia: Westminster, 1972).
Fortin, J. R (ed.), *Saint Anselm – His Origins and Influence* (Lewiston: Edwin Mellen, 2001).
Francis of Assisi, *Early Documents*, vol.1: *The Saints*, Armstrong, R. J., Hellmann, A. W. & Short, W. J. (trs.), (New York: New City, 1998).
Froget, B., *The Indwelling of the Holy Spirit in the Souls of the Just According to the Teachings of St. Thomas Aquinas*, S. A. Raemers (tr.), (Westminster: Newman, 1953).
Gardeil, A., *The Gifts of the Holy Ghost in the Dominican Saints*, A. M. Townsend (tr.), (Milwaukee: Bruce, 1937).
Gaybba, B., *The Spirit of Love* (London: Geoffrey Chapman, 1987).
Gilson, E., *The Philosophy of Bonaventure*, I. Trethowan and F. Sheed (tr.), (Paterson: St. Anthony Guild, 1978).
Gunton, C. E., *The Promise of Trinitarian Theology* (Edinburgh: T. & T. Clark, 1991).
......, *Theology Through the Theologians* (Edinburgh: T & T Clark, 1996).

Hall, C. A., *Learning Theology with the Church Fathers* (Illinois: InterVarsity, 2002).

Hall, D. C., *The Trinity: An Analysis of St. Thomas Aquinas' "Expositio" of the "De Trinitate" of Boethius* (Leiden: E. J. Brill, 1992).

Hankey, W., *God in Himself: Aquinas' Doctrine of God as Expounded in the Summa Theologia* (Oxford: Oxford University Press, 1987).

Haren, M., *Medieval Thought: The Western Intellectual Tradition from Antiquity to the Thirteenth Century* (London: Macmillan, 1992²).

Harnack, A., *History of Dogma*. 7 vols., N. Buchanan, *et al* (tr.), (London: Williams & Norgate, 1894-99).

Haugh, R., *Photius and the Carolingians. The Trinitarian Controversy* (Belmon: Norland, 1975).

Hayes, Z., *The Hidden Center: Spirituality and Speculative Christology in St. Bonaventure* (New York: Paulist, 1981).

......, *A Window to the Divine: A Study of Christian Creation Theology* (Quincy, Ill.: Franciscan, 1997).

......, *Bonaventure. Mystical Writings* (New York: Crossroad Book, 1999).

Haykin, M. A. G., *The Spirit of God. The Exegesis of 1 & 2 Corinthians in the Pneumatomachian Controversy of the Fourth Century* (Leiden: E. J. Brill, 1994).

Henry, P., *Saint Augustine on Personality* (New York: Macmillan, 1960).

Heron, A. I. C., *The Holy Spirit* (Philadelphia: Westminster, 1983).

Hill, W. J., *The Three-Personed God. The Trinity as a Mystery of Salvation* (Washington: Catholic University of America Press, 1982).

......, *Proper Relations to the Indwelling Divine Persons* (Washington: Thomist, 1955).

Hinze, B.E., & Dahney, D.L. (eds.), *Advents of the Spirit*, (Milwaukee: Marquette University Press, 2001)

Hodgson, L., *The Doctrine of the Trinity* (New York: Charles Scribner's Sons, 1944).

Hoogland, M-R., *God, Passion and Power. Thomas Aquinas on Christ and the Almightiness of God* (Leuven: Peters, 2003).

Hopkins, J. & Richardson, H (eds.), *Anselm of Canterbury*. 4 vols. (Toronto: Edwin Mellen, 1976).

Hopkins, J., *A Companion Study of St. Anselm*. Minneapolis: University of Minnesota Press, 1972.

......, *Anselm of Canterbury: Trinity, Incarnation, and Redemption. Theological Treatises* (New York: Harper Torchbooks, 1970).

Jenson, R. W., *The Triune Identity. God According to the Gospel* (Philadelphia: Fortress, 1982).

Jüngel, E., *God as the Mystery of the World*, D. L. Guder (tr.), (Grand Rapids: Eerdmans, 1983).

Jurgens, W. J., *The Faith of the Early Fathers*. Vols. I-III (Collegeville: Liturgical, 1970-1979).

Kärkkäinen, V., *Pneumatology. The Holy Spirit in Ecumenical, International, and Contextual Perspective* (Grand Rapids: Baker, 2002).

Kasper, W., *The God of Jesus Christ*, M. J. O'Connell (tr.), (New York: Crossroad, 1984).

Katz, S. T. (ed.), *Mysticism and Language* (New York: Oxford University Press, 1999).

Kenan, O. B. (ed.)., *The History of Franciscan Theology* (New York: The Franciscan Institute, 1994).

Kelly, A., *The Trinity of Love* (Wilmington, DE: Michael Glazier, 1989).

Kelly, J. N. D., *Early Christian Doctrines* (San Francisco: Harper & Row, 1978).

……, Early Christian Creeds (London: Longman, 1972³).

Knowles, D., *The Evolution of Medieval Thought* (New York: Vintage, 1962).

Küng, H. & Moltmann, J. (eds), *Conflicts about the Holy Spirit* (New York: Seabury, 1979).

Kuntz, M. L., & Kuntz, P. M. (eds.)., *Jacob's Ladder and the Tree of Life. Concepts of Hierarchy and the Great Chain of Being* (New York: Peter Lang, 1987).

LaCugna, C. M., *God for Us. The Trinity and Christian Life* (San Francisco: Harper, 1991).

Lampe, G. W. H., *God as Spirit* (Oxford: Clarendon Press, 1977).

Leff, G., *Medieval Thought: St. Augustine to Ockham* (Baltimore: Penguin, 1958).

Levering, M., *Scripture and Metaphysics. Aquinas and the Renewal of Trinitarian Theology* (Oxford: Blackwell, 2004).

Lonergan, B. J., *Verbum: Word and Idea in Aquinas* (Notre Dame: University of Notre Dame, 1967).

Louth, A., *The Origins of the Christian Mystical Tradition: From Plato to Denys* (Oxford: Clarendon, 1981).

Margerie, B. de., *The Christian Trinity in History*, E. J. Fortman (tr.), (Massachusetts: St. Bede's Publications, 1982).

Marsh, T., *The Triune God. A Biblical, Historical and Theological Study* (Connecticut: Twenty-Third Publications, 1994).
McGiffert, A. C., *A History of Christian Thought*. 2 vols., (New York: Charles Scribner's Sons, 1932-33).
McGinn, B., *The Foundation of Mysticism*. (new York: Crossroad, 1991).
......, *The Growth of Mysticism. Gregory the Great through the 12th Century* (New York: Crossroad, 1994).
McGrath, A. E., *Christian Theology. An Introduction*. (Oxford: Blackwell, 2001³).
McGrath, A. E. (ed), *The Christian Theology Reader* (Oxford: Blackwell, 2001³).
Meerson, M. A., *The Trinity of Love. Modern Russian Theology*(Quincy: Franciscan, 1998).
Meilach, M. D., *The Primacy of Christ: Life and Doctrine* (Chicago: Franciscan Herald, 1964).
Menu, M.-D., *Toward Understanding St. Thomas*, A.-M. Landry and D. Hughes (tr.), (Chicago: Regnery, 1964).
Merriell, D. J., *To the Image of the Trinity: A Study in the Development of Aquinas' Teaching* (Toronto: Pontifical Institute of Mediaeval Studies, 1960).
Meyendorff, J., *A study of Gregory of Palamas* (Alyesbury: Faith, 1966).
Migne, J. P. (ed.), *Patrologia Graeca*. 162 vols., (Paris: Vrin, 1878-90).
......, *Patrologia Latina*. 221 vols., (Paris: Vrin, 1844-64).
Moff, K. & Thompson, C. M. (eds.), *Resource Manual for the Study of Franciscan Christology* (Washington: Franciscan Federation, 1998).
Moltmann, J., *Trinity and the Kingdom of God*, M. Kohl (tr.), (London: SCM, 1981).
......, *The Crucified God*, Margaret Kohl (tr.), (San Francisco: Harper & Row, 1974).
......, *The Spirit of Life: A Universal Affirmation*, M. Kohl (tr.), (Minneapolis: Fortress, 1992).
......, *God in Creation: A New Theology of Creation and the Spirit of God*, M. Kohl (tr.), (Minneapolis: Fortress, 1993).
Mondin, B., *St. Thomas Aquinas's Philosophy in the Commentary on the Sentences* (The Hague: Martinus Nijhoff, 1975).
Ngien, D., *The Suffering of God According to Martin Luther's 'Theologia Crucis'* (Bern: Peter Lang, 1995).

Nichols, A., *Discovering Aquinas. An Introduction to His Life, Work, and Influence* (Grand Rapids: Eerdmans, 2003).
Nygren, A., *Agape and Eros*, P. S. Watson (tr.), (Philadelphia: Westminster, 1953).
Osborne, K. B. (ed.), *The History of Franciscan Theology* (New York: The Franciscan Institute, 1994).
Olson, R. E & Hall, C. A., *The Trinity* (Grand Rapids: Eerdmans, 2002).
Olson, R. E., *The Story of Christian Theology. Twenty Centuries of Tradition and Reform* (Illinois: InterVarsity, 1999).
......, *The Mosaic of Christian Belief* (Illinois: InterVarsity, 2002).
O' Carroll, M., *Trinitas. A Theological Encyclopedia of the Holy Trinity* (Wilmington: Michael Glazier, Inc., 1986).
......, *Veni Creator Spiritus: A Theological Encyclopedia of the Holy Spirit* (Collegeville: Liturgical, 1990).
O' Collins, G., *The Tripersonal God* (New York: Paulist, 1999).
O' Donnell, J., *The Mystery of the Triune God* (London: Shed & Ward, 1988).
O' Meara, T. F., *Thomas Aquinas, Theologian* (Notre Dame: University of Notre Dame, 1997).
Pannenberg, W., *Jesus - God and Man*, L. L. Wilkins & D. A. Priebe (tr.), (Philadelphia: Westminster, 1977).
Pegis, A. C., *Basic Writings of Saint Thomas Aquinas*. Vol. 1 (New York: Random House, 1945).
Pelikan, J., *The Christian Tradition. A History of the Development of Doctrine*. 3 vols., (New Haven: Yale University Press, 1971).
......, 'The Doctrine of the *Filioque* in Thomas Aquinas and its Patristic Antecedents. An Analysis of *Summa Theologica* Part I, q. 36', in *St. Thomas Aquinas (1274-1974). Comemorative Studies*. Forword by E. Gilson (Toronto: Pontifical Institute of Mediaeval Studies, 1974).
Peters, T., *God as Trinity: Relationality and Temporality in Divine Life* (Louisville: Westminster/John Knox, 1993).
......, *God - the World's Future. Systematic Theology for a Postmodern Era* (Minneapolis: Fortress, 1992).
Placher, W. C., *Narratives of a Vulnerable God. Christ, Theology and Scripture* (Kentucky: Westminster/John Knox, 1994).
Polkinghorne, J. (ed.), *The Work of Love: Creation as Kenosis* (Grand Rapids: Eerdmans, 2001).

Powell, S. M., *Participating in God. Creation and Trinity* (Minneapolis: Fortress, 2003).

Prentice, R., *The Concept of Love According to St. Bonaventure* (New York: Franciscan Institute, 1949).

Prestige, G. L., *God in Patristic Thought* (London: SPCK, 1952).

Prokes, M. T., *Mutuality: The Human Image of Trinitarian Love* (New York: Paulist, 1993).

Rahner, K., *The Trinity*, J. Donceel (tr.), (New York: Seabury, 1974).

Ribaillier, J. (ed.)., *De Trinitate: Texte critique avec introduction, notes et tables* (Paris: Vrin, 1958).

Richard, R. L., *The Problem of an Apologetical Perspective in the Trinitarian Theology of St. Thomas Aquinas* (Roma: Pontificae Universitas Gregoriana, 1963).

Richard, C. C., *The Doctrine of the Trinity* (New York: Abingdon, 1958).

Rout, P., *Francis and Bonaventure* (Ligouri: Triumph Books, 1996).

Schaff, P., *et al* (eds.), A Select Library of the Nicene and Post-Nicene Fathers of the Christian Church, series 1 and 2, 14 vols. (New York: Christian Literature, 1887-1894); (Reprint, Edinburgh: T. &. T. Clark; Grand Rapids: Eerdmans, 1952-1956; Peabody, Mass.: Hendrickson, 1994)

Schmitt, F. S., *Opera Omnia ad fidem condicum*. 6 vols. (Edinburgh: T. Nelson, 1946-61).

Schwöbel, C. & Gunton, C. (eds.), *Persons, Divine and Human* (Edinburgh: T. & T. Clark, 1991).

Sertillanges, A. D., *St. Thomas Aquinas and His Work* (London: Blackfriars, 1957).

Sherrard, P., *The Greek East and the Latin West: a Study of Christian Tradition* (London: Oxford University Press, 1959).

Smith, G. D. (ed.), *The Teaching of the Catholic Church. A Summary of Catholic Doctrine* (London: Burns & Oats, 1952).

Smith, T. L., *Thomas Aquinas' Trinitarian Theology: A Study in Theological Method* (Washington, D.C.: Catholic University of America Press, 2003).

Stump, E., *Aquinas* (London: Routledge, 2003).

Swete, B. H., *The Holy Spirit in the Ancient Church. A Study of Christian Teaching in the Age of the Fathers* (London: Macmillan, 1912).

......, *On the History of the Doctrine of the Procession of the Holy Spirit* (Cambridge: Beighton, Bell & Co., 1876).

Thompson, J., *Modern Trinitarian Perspectives* (Oxford: Oxford University Press, 1994).

Torrance, A. J., *Persons in Communion: Trinitarian Description and Human Participation* (Edinburgh: T. & T. Clark, 1996).

Torrance, T. F., *The Christian Doctrine of God: One Being Three Persons* (Edinburgh: T. & T. Clark, 1996).

......, *The Hermeneutics of John Calvin* (Edinburgh: T & T Clark, 1998).

Torrell, J-P., *Saint Thomas Aquinas*. Vol. 1: *The Person and His Work*, R. Royal (tr.), (Washington: Catholic University of America Press, 1996).

...... *Saint Thomas Aquinas.*, Vol. 2: *Spiritual Master*, R. Royal (tr.), (Washington: Catholic University of America Press, 1996).

Vanhoozer, K. J. (ed.), *Nothing Greater, Nothing Better. Theological Essays on the Love of God* (Grand Rapids: Eerdmans, 2001).

Viola, C. & Fleteren, F. V., *Saint Anselm – A Thinker for Yesterday and Today. Anselm's Thought Viewed by Our Contemporaries* (Lewiston: Edwin Mellen, 2002).

Victor, R., G. Zinn (tr.), (New York: Paulist, 1979).

Vischer, L. (ed.), *Spirit of God, Spirit of Christ. Ecumenical Reflections on the Filioque Controversy,* (London: SPCK, 1980).

Wadell, P. J., *Friends of God: Virtues and Gifts in Aquinas* (New York: Peter Lang, 1991).

Watkin-Jones, H., *The Holy Spirit in Mediaeval Church* (London: The Epworth, 1922).

Weinandy, T. G., *Does God Suffer?* (Notre Dame: University of Notre Dame, 2000).

Weisheipl, J. A., *Friar Thomas d'Aquino. His Life, Thought and Work* (New York: Doubleday, 1974).

Welch, C., *In This Name. The Doctrine of the Trinity in Contemporary Theology* (New York: Charles Scribner's Sons, 1952).

Wiles, M., *Faith and the Mystery of God* (London: SCM, 1982).

Williams, R., *On Christian Theology* (Oxford: Blackwell, 2001).

Yong, A., *Spirit-Word-Community. Theological Hermeneutics in Trinitarian Perspectives* (Hampshire: Ashgate, 2002).

Zizioulas, J. D., *Being As Communion: Studies in Personhood and the Church* (New York: St. Vladimir's, 1985).

Journal Articles

Ayres, L., 'Augustine on God as Love and Love as God', *Pro Ecclesia* 5 (1966): 470-87.
Becker, M. L., 'The Trinity in Johannes von Hofmann's Theology', *Pro Ecclesia* vol. XII (2003): 417-46.
Berry, D. L., '*Filioque* and the Church', *Journal of Ecumenical Studies* 5 (1968): 535-54.
Bligh, J., 'Richard of St. Victor's *De Trinitate*: Augustinian or Abelardian?', *Heythrop Journal* I (1960): 118-39.
Bracken, J., 'The Holy Trinity as a Community of Divine Persons', *Heythrop Journal* 15 (1974): 246-70.
Bray, C. B., 'Bonaventure's Proof of the Trinity', *American Catholic Philosophical Quarterly* 67 (1993): 201-17.
Bray, G., 'The *Filioque* Clause in History and Theology', *Tyndale Bulletin* 34 (1983): 91-144.
Burleigh, J. S., 'The Doctrine of the Holy Spirit in the Latin Fathers', *Scottish Journal of Theology* 7 (1954): 113-32.
Cavanaugh, W. T., 'A Joint Declaration? Justification as *Theosis* in Aquinas and Luther', *Heythrop Journal* 41 (2000): 265-80.
Cary, P., 'Historical Perspectives on Trinitarian Doctrine', *Religious and Theological Studies Fellowship Bulletin* (Nov.,-Dec., 1995): 2-9.
Charlton, W., 'McCabe on Aquinas on the Trinity', *New Blackfriars* 80 (1999): 491-501.
Clapsis, E., 'The *Filioque* Question', *Patristic and Byzantine Review* 1 (1982): 127-36.
Coffey, D., 'The Spirit as the Mutual Love of the Father and the Son', *Theological Studies* 51 (1990): 193-229.
......, 'A Proper Mission of the Holy Spirit', *Theological Studies* 47 (1986): 227-50.
Cousins, E., 'A Theology of Interpersonal Relations', *Thought: A Review of Culture and Idea* XLV (1970): 56-82.
......, 'Response to Zachary Hayes', *Journal of Religion* 58 (Supplememt, 1978): 97-104.
Cross, R., 'Two Models of the Trinity', *Heythrop Journal* XLIII (2002): 275-94.
Daley, B. E., 'Revisiting the "*Filioque*": Roots and Branches of An Old Debate, Part One', *Pro Ecclesia* X (2001): 31-62.
......, 'Revisiting the "*Filioque*": Part Two: Contemporary Catholic Approaches', *Pro Ecclesia* X (2001): 195-212.

Del Colle, R., '"Person" and "being" in John Zizioulas' Trinitarian Theology: Conversations with Thomas Torrance and Thomas Aquinas', *Scottish Journal of Theology* 54 (2001): 70-86.

Delio, I., 'Bonaventure's Metaphysics of the Good', *Theological Studies* 60 (1999): 228-46.

......, 'Revisiting the Franciscan Doctrine of Christ', *Theological Studies* 64 (2003): 3-23.

......, 'Does God "Act" in Creation? A Bonaventurian Response', *Heythrop Journal* 45 (2003): 328-44.

Dodds, M. J., 'Thomas Aquinas, Human Suffering, and the Unchanging God of Love', *Theological Studies* 52 (1991): 330-44.

Edwards, R. B., 'The Pagan Doctrine of the Absolute Unchangeableness of God', *Religious Studies* 14 (1978): 305-13.

Evans, G. R., 'St. Anselm's Images of the Trinity', *Journal of Theological Studies* XXVII (1976): 46-57.

Fatula, M. A., "The Holy Spirit and Human Actualization through Love: The Contribution of Aquinas', *Theology Digest* 32 (1985): 217-24.

Gresham, J. L., 'The Social Model of the Trinity and Its Critics', *Scottish Journal of Theology* 46 (1993): 325-43.

Hankey, W., 'The Place of the Psychological Image of the Trinity in the Arguments of Augustine's *De Trinitate*, Anselm's *Monologion*, and Aquinas' *Summa theologiae*', *Dionysius* III (Dec., 1979): 277-86.

Haight, R., 'The Case for Spirit Christology', *Theological Studies* 53 (1992): 257-87.

......, 'The Point of Trinitarian Theology', *Toronto Journal of Theology* 4 (1988): 191-204.

Hayes, Z., 'Christology and Metaphysics in the Thought of Bonaventure', *Journal of Religion* 58 (Supplement, 1978): 82-96.

......, 'The Meaning of *Convenientia* in the Metaphysics of St. Bonaventure', *Franciscan Studies* 34 (1974): 74-100.

......, 'Incarnation and Creation in St. Bonaventure', *Franciscan Studies* 34 (1974): 309-29.

Heron, A. I. C., '"Who Proceedeth From the Father and the Son"': The Problem of the *Filioque*', *Scottish Journal of Theology* 24 (1971): 149-66.

Keane, K. P., 'Why Creation? Bonaventure and Thomas Aquinas on God as Creative Good', *Downside Review* 93 (1975): 100-21.

Kelly, A., 'The Gifts of the Spirit: Aquinas and the Modern Context', *Thomist* 38 (1974): 193-231.

......, 'Trinity and Process: Relevance of the Basic Christian Confession of God', *Theological Studies* 31 (1970): 393-414.

......, 'God: How Near a Relation?', *Thomist* 14 (1970): 191-229.

Kiesling, C., 'On Relating to the Persons of the Trinity', *Theological Studies* 47 (1986): 599-616.

LaCugna, C., 'The Relational God: Aquinas and Beyond', *Theological Studies* 46 (1985): 647-63.

......, and McDonnell, K., 'Returning from "The far Country": Theses for a Contemporary Trinitarian Theology', *Scottish Journal of Theology* 41 (1988): 191-215.

Lienhard, J. T., 'The "Arian" Controversy: Some Categories Reconsidered', *Theological Studies* 48 (1987): 415-37.

Mackey, J. P., 'The Holy Spirit: Relativizing the Divergent Approaches of East and West', *Irish Theological Quarterly* 48 (1981): 256-67.

Mahoney, J., 'The Church of the Spirit in Aquinas', *Heythrop Journal* XV (1974): 18-36.

......, 'The Spirit and Moral Discernment in Aquinas', *Heythrop Journal* 13 (1972): 282-97.

Marshall, B. D., 'Action and Person: Do Palamas and Aquinas Agree About the Spirit?' *St. Vladimir's Theological Quarterly* 39(1995): 379-408.

Masiello, R. J., 'Reason and Faith in Richard of St. Victor and St. Thomas', *New Scholasticism* 48 (1974): 233-42.

McCabe, H., 'Aquinas on the Trinity', *New Blackfriars* 80 (1999): 268-83.

McDonnell, K., 'A Trinitarian Theology of the Holy Spirit?', *Theological Studies* 46 (1985): 191-227.

......, 'The Determinative Doctrine of the Holy Spirit', *Theology Today* 39 (1982): 142-59.

McIntyre, J., 'The Holy Spirit in Greek Patristic Thought', *Scottish Journal of Theology* 7 (1954): 353-75.

Oberman, H., 'Luther and the *Via Moderna*: The Philsophical Backdrop of the Reformation Breakthrough', *Journal of Ecclesiastical History* 54 (2003): 641-70.

O' Connor, T. R., '*Homoousios* and *Filioque*: An Ecumenical Analogy', *Downside Review* 83 (1965): 1-19.

Principe, W.H., 'Theology of the Holy Spirit in St. Bonaventure', *Cord* 24(1974): 235-56.

Quinn, J. F., 'The Role of the Holy Spirit in St. Bonaventure's Theology', *Franciscan Studies* 33 (1973): 273-84.

......, 'The *scientia sermoncinalis* of St. Bonaventure and His Use of Language Regarding the Mystery of the Trinity', *Miscellanea Mediaevalia* 13 (1981): 413-23.

Robb, F., 'The Fourth Lateran Council's Definition of Trinitarian Orthodoxy', *Journal of Ecclesiastical History* 48 (1997): 22-43.

Rosato, P. J., 'Spirit Christology: Ambiguity and Promise', *Theological Studies* 38 (1977): 423-49.

Stiegman, E., 'Charism and Institution in Aquinas', *Thomist* 38 (1974): 723-34.

Torre, M. D., 'St. John Damascene and St. Thomas Aquinas on the Eternal Procession of the Holy Spirit', *St. Vladimir's Theological Quarterly* 38 (1994): 303-27.

Watson, G., 'The *Filioque* – Opportunity For Debate?', *Scottish Journal of Theology* 41 (1988): 313-30.

Webster, J., 'The Identity of the Holy Spirit: a problem in trinitarian theology', *Themelios* 9 (1983):4-7.

Wells, C., 'Aquinas and Jenson on Thinking about the Trinity', *Anglican Theological Review* 84 (2002): 345-82.

www.ingramcontent.com/pod-product-compliance
Lightning Source LLC
Chambersburg PA
CBHW051737230426
43670CB00012B/2061